Walk to New York

Also by Charles Wilkins

Winnipeg 8 (editor and co-author)

Hockey: The Illustrated History

The Winnipeg Book

Paddle to the Amazon (co-author)

The Wolf's Eye (editor)

After the Applause

Old Mrs. Schmatterbung and Other Friends

Breakaway

Breakfast at the Hoito

The Circus at the Edge of the Earth

A Wilderness Called Home

Walk to New York

A JOURNEY OUT OF THE WILDS OF CANADA

Charles Wilkins

VIKING
CANADA

VIKING CANADA

Published by the Penguin Group

Penguin Group (Canada), 10 Alcorn Avenue, Toronto, Ontario, Canada M4V 3B2
(a division of Pearson Penguin Canada Inc.)

Penguin Group (USA) Inc., 375 Hudson Street, New York, New York 10014, U.S.A.
Penguin Books Ltd, 80 Strand, London WC2R 0RL, England
Penguin Ireland, 25 St Stephen's Green, Dublin 2, Ireland (a division of Penguin Books Ltd)
Penguin Group (Australia), 250 Camberwell Road, Camberwell, Victoria 3124, Australia
(a division of Pearson Australia Group Pty Ltd)
Penguin Books India Pvt Ltd, 11 Community Centre, Panchsheel Park, New Delhi – 110 017, India
Penguin Group (NZ), Cnr Airborne and Rosedale Roads, Albany, Auckland, New Zealand
(a division of Pearson New Zealand Ltd)
Penguin Books (South Africa) (Pty) Ltd, 24 Sturdee Avenue, Rosebank, Johannesburg 2196,
South Africa

Penguin Books Ltd, Registered Offices: 80 Strand, London WC2R 0RL, England

First published 2004

1 2 3 4 5 6 7 8 9 10   (FR)

Copyright © Charles Wilkins, 2004
Maps copyright © ArtPlus Limited—Sara Orr and Donna Guilfoyle

Author representation: Westwood Creative Artists
94 Harbord Street, Toronto, Ontario M5S 1G6

Excerpt from *Finding Mom at Eaton's* by permission of George Morrissette.
Excerpt on page 177 from "The Country North of Belleville" by Al Purdy.

Manufactured in Canada.

LIBRARY AND ARCHIVES CANADA CATALOGUING IN PUBLICATION

Wilkins, Charles
Walk to New York : a journey out of the wilds of Canada / Charles Wilkins.

ISBN 0-670-04450-4

1. Wilkins, Charles—Travel—Ontario. 2. Wilkins, Charles—Travel—New York (State)
3. Ontario—Description and travel. 4. New York (State)—Description and travel. I. Title.

FC76.W45 2004   917.1304'5   C2004-903485-5

Visit the Penguin Group (Canada) website at **www.penguin.ca**

For George Morrissette,
with gratitude and affection.

And for my children,
Matthew, Georgia and Eden,
with love.

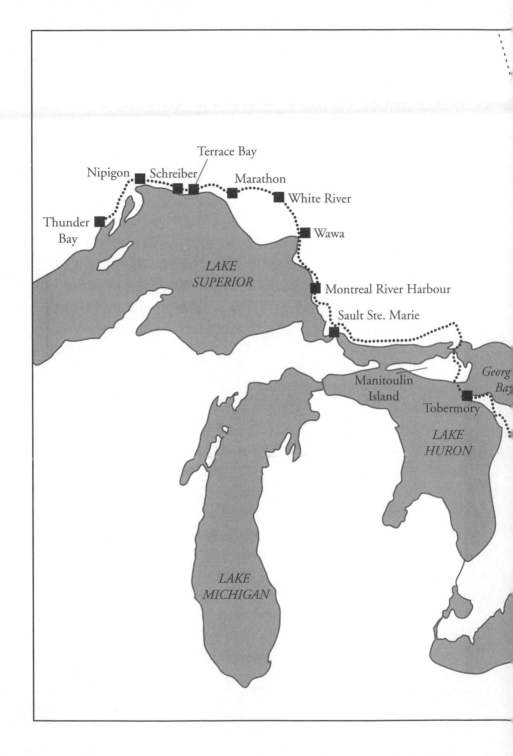

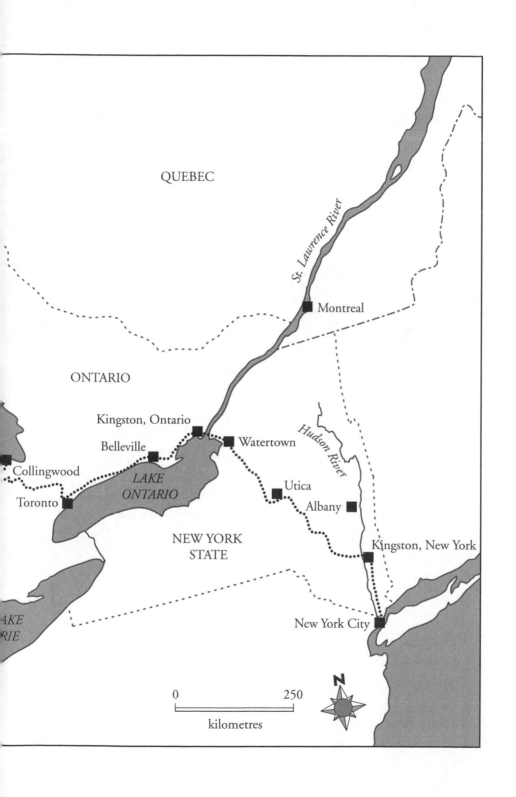

QUEBEC

St. Lawrence River

Montreal

ONTARIO

Kingston, Ontario

Belleville

Collingwood

Toronto

LAKE
ONTARIO

Watertown

Hudson River

Utica

Albany

Kingston, New York

NEW YORK
STATE

New York City

AKE
RIE

0   250

kilometres

N

Walk to New York

Unfit for the Road

It was an adventure that began amid snowstorms and gale-level winds on the north shore of the world's largest and wildest body of fresh water, and ended 2,200 kilometres away—two and a half million steps—in hundred-degree heat, among celebrating Hispanics and bare-breasted lesbians, the self-proclaimed Dykes of New York City.

Betweentimes, there were sixty-three nights on the road—nights that varied in comfort and circumstance from the fiery cold of a threadbare tent in a Lake Superior blizzard to the front seat of a rusted Dodge Caravan, from mosquito swamps, gravel pits, and wilderness mansions to the "Elvis Suite" of the toney old Warwick Hotel in Midtown Manhattan.

It was a journey in the most ancient sense of the word—on foot—and by the time I arrived in New York City I had walked farm roads, interstate highways, and ancient aboriginal trails, had walked past bears, bull moose, and pit bulls. I had walked two of the longest streets in the world: Yonge Street in Ontario, which extends 1,600 kilometres from downtown Toronto into northern Ontario, and the world-famous Broadway, which runs without a name change from Battery Park in

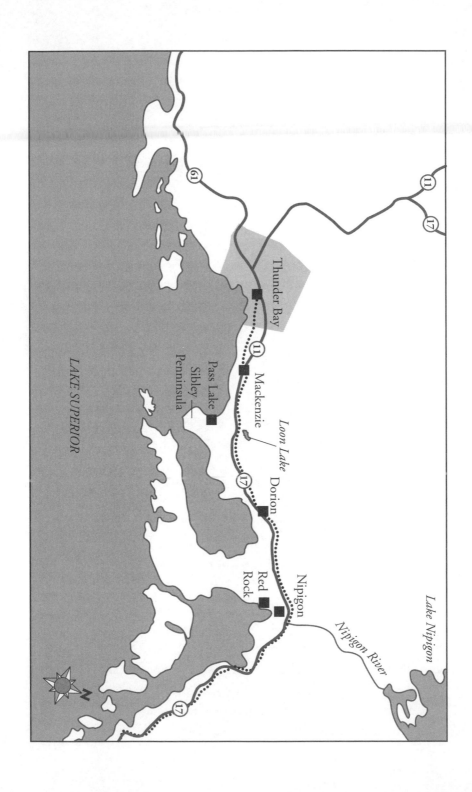

Lower Manhattan, north past the grim canyon where the twin towers once stood, into the theatre district, through Harlem and the Bronx, and then two hundred kilometres up the east side of the Hudson River.

I had seen my calves and knees expand by five centimetres in circumference; had sun-baked my skin to a scabby grey-brown; and grown a crop of hair on my legs and groin the likes of which I had not seen there in two decades. Despite consuming nearly half a million calories, I had dropped 25 pounds to a sinewy 145.

I had exchanged greetings, small talk, life stories with hillbillies, jazz musicians, and restaurateurs; with drug addicts and real-estate executives AWOL from the rat race.

I had balanced precariously above Lake Superior to view the rock tracings of tribesmen nearly a thousand years dead; and on a cold May morning west of Sault Ste. Marie, in the dense uninhabited bush, had turned to find myself being followed by a baronial black African, who during five hours beside me, spoke with mystic authority of his days as a foot messenger on the West African savannah and his year in the torture dungeons of one of the most satanic dictatorships on earth.

I had nursed a hundred blisters, lost four toenails, and dreamed wild, vivid dreams. In one of those dreams, I looked down to find that my shoes and feet had been entirely worn away and that I was walking on the nubs of my shins.

ON THE MORNING of my departure, I drove over to Lauri's Hardware in the Finnish quarter of my home city of Thunder Bay, Ontario, and bought a cooking pot and some enamalled tin plates and cups— and visited the supermarket and the bank. People had heard a pre-trip interview I had done a couple of days earlier on CBC Radio, so virtually everywhere I went, I met well-wishers, several of whom expressed surprise, even dismay, that I was still in town. Had I been delayed? Was something wrong? Was I nuts?

When I got home, my neighbours Gerry and Lila Siddall presented me with a "bug jacket," which I now believe I left hanging in a tree on a cliff in Bruce Peninsula National Park, where it may yet be enjoying the hundred-kilometre view of Georgian Bay. A few days earlier, Gerry had given me an immaculately finished diamond-willow walking stick that he had cut and polished, an *objet d'art* so lovingly turned out that I was reluctant to use it except on forest trails, riverbanks, and so on— preferring, anyway, to have my hands free on the gravel shoulders of the highway.

At about 1:00 P.M., I said goodbye to the kids as they headed off with friends for the afternoon. Half an hour later, my wife, Betty, left to help a friend with a catering gig. Our marriage was over—twice recently friends had reported to me that Betty had said I was "living in the house as if it were a hotel" and that it was time to "check out." However, she paused long enough in the front hall to give me a hearty hug and to wish me well. For both of us there were tears, which to our credit, took the moment somewhat beyond the standard hotel check-out.

And so it was that, on the afternoon of April 26, 2002, I laced on a pair of Columbia Johnny Rail hiking shoes, stuffed a bag of dried apricots into my pocket, and walked out the front door of my home on Prospect Avenue—as it turned out for the last time.

The temperature was barely above freezing, so I was bundled against the cold, and for the first few kilometres was elated to be on the road at last. I stepped briskly down the hill on River Avenue and turned east on Algoma Street, past the old General Hospital, where my daughters had been born. As I reached the Current River, it occurred to me that it was the first of perhaps a hundred rivers I would cross, the last of which would be the Hudson and its tiny spur, the Harlem, which separates the Bronx from Manhattan. As I walked along the dam that forms the south end of Boulevard Lake, I took a lingering look east to the spectacle of the grain elevators and shipyards, and across the tufted bay beyond to the mountainous Sibley Peninsula.

Unexpectedly hungry by the time I had walked three or four kilometres, I stopped at Robin's Donuts on Hodder Avenue, bought a coffee to go and inhaled a month's quota of trans-homicidal fats in the form of a chocolate and a maple-glazed doughnut. Then I headed out Lakeshore Drive, planning to follow Lake Superior directly for twenty kilometres, spend the night at a local backpackers' hostel, and hit the Trans-Canada Highway in the morning. My hope was to cover at least twenty-five kilometres for each of the first couple of days, and build my pace gradually to thirty and eventually forty kilometres a day.

And for the first ten kilometres I was a mule, a sled dog, a machine. Perhaps, I thought, it would be easier than I had anticipated. But all the bright hopes in the world made no difference after twelve kilometres or so, when the adrenalin subsided and I felt the first inkling of weariness. Then, as the runners say, I hit the wall.

An hour later, a flurry of snow twisted out of the north, and an east wind began to gust off the lake. In the fading light, I felt an intense sense of forlornness—of ignorance and ineptness and age. As an antidote, I pulled out my cellphone, which had the allure of a new toy— in fact, was a new toy—and called my friend George Morrissette, a Winnipeg poet whom I had persuaded to drive my van to New York, keeping close enough to me along the route that he could meet me at the end of each day. I told him I was about two-thirds of the way to the hostel and that in perhaps two hours, he might consider driving out there from Thunder Bay for the night. I further reported that my neck, back, and hip joints had begun to ache, that my nose was running blood-tinged mucus (the effect of a lingering bout of respiratory flu), and that my right knee was beginning to buckle under the pressure of the railway spike that some imaginary extremist seemed to be driving into its outer ligaments.

As each car passed, I would step off the edge of the pavement, where it was easiest to walk, and drift down the shoulder to where it met the grass, and then angle back up to the pavement. But as my exhaustion deepened, it took greater and greater effort to force myself to grind back up onto the road.

At perhaps the twenty-kilometre point, I began sporadically to misstep and once or twice wobbled and nearly turned an ankle. By this time, I was experiencing brief, intense sweats from which I would emerge shivering. I had soaked three handkerchiefs from blowing my nose and was slowly filling my pockets with used tissues, increasingly streaked with blood.

At a point where it was all I could do to will one foot in front of the other, a junkyard German shepherd, a four-legged terrorist, exploded out of a rural lane. Normally, my response to such creatures is a craven cartoon of panic—a lot of yelling and backing off as I scan my surroundings for the likes of a hockey stick (the national weapon of choice). But in this case, I did nothing. Because there was nothing I had the strength to do. Except keep walking. If the day's effort was destined to end in a puddle of blood on the roadside, so be it. Go ahead, eat me, I thought. End my misery. The inevitability of it all relaxed me, and the effect was magical. The dog simply didn't know what to do with someone who appeared to pay no attention to him. In no time his snarling dwindled to mere barking, and he did a big half-circle behind me and, I assume, disappeared up the lane.

As I REFINED MY CAPABILITIES for self-reliance, I became, like Blanche Dubois, more often than I might have liked, dependent on the kindness of strangers—or at least people I did not know well. It started the moment I staggered into the Longhouse Hostel, a one-time rural motel that since the mid-1970s has been run as a travellers' respite by Lloyd and Willa Jones. *The Lonely Planet Guide to Canada* refers to the Longhouse as "the best hostel" in the country, and Lloyd and Willa are undoubtedly among the country's most committed and hard-working hosts. They are thoroughly fine people who have helped bring to Canada some 1,500 political refugees—from Vietnam, from Ethiopia, from Sierra Leone—many of whom began their liberated lives at the Longhouse. A magazine story once characterized Willa as an earthly stand-in for the Madonna, a likeness immediately apparent in her determination that George and I be lovingly housed and fed, for which she and Lloyd would not take even the modest fee they normally charge.

Unfortunately, I was in a kind of stupor by the time I arrived and could do little more than sit pie-eyed on the couch while Willa made tea and then dinner. Except for a bout of scarlet fever when I was ten years old, it was perhaps the only time in my life that I was too weak either to move or to carry on a conversation. During my first hour there, I did not have the resolve so much as to remove my outdoor clothes—just sat sprawled on the couch, sipping at a can of cranberry pop that Willa brought to me with a smile. Even so, I felt rude simply lying there while other guests talked and laughed in the kitchen, from where I was plainly visible—especially since I had been introduced to them enthusiastically as a writer who was walking to New York (and, by implication, would have some ripping good yarns to tell). Willa, bless her heart, had gone so far as to pitch me as a kind of literary Ernest Shackleton.

At one point, a muscular young Australian in a gaucho hat wandered over and said, "So, mate, you're walking to New York— fabulous! How long you been on the road?"

"Six hours," I whispered.

"Great!" he enthused. "How's it going?"

"Worse," I told him.

Later, I sat in the bathroom, afraid to look at my feet. I thought, *I can't do it!* What am I going to do? In the bedroom, I settled into a drugged and fitful sleep and awakened stiff to the point where I had to lever my legs one at a time over the edge of the bed. Back in the bathroom, I leaned over the toilet and involuntarily expelled a mass of orange goop about as big as a golf ball. Whereas I had at first assumed stubbornly that I was merely out of shape, I had to admit at this point that I was sick, too sick for what I had set out do. However, four 222s, two flu tablets, and a slug of cough suppressant took the edge off my despondency, and after a hot shower, I slouched out to the kitchen, where Willa, who had been reading one of my books, volunteered a cheery good morning. She hastily poured me a cup of coffee and made me three or four pieces of toast, only one of which I could eat.

As I sat there contemplating my impending disgrace, Willa said, "Well, you've got a beautiful day for walking."

Till then, I had not thought to look out the window.

"Yes, I have," I said, and having excused myself, I shuffled back to my room determined that my walk would not end here in humiliation. Sitting on the edge of the bed, I packed Moleskin—thick, self-adhesive pads—around my blisters, pulled on my outdoor clothes, and having arranged with George to meet me later in the day, thanked Willa for her hospitality and confirmed that I would be returning to the hostel that night (*if I'm alive,* I might have added, although I did not want to alarm or distress Willa, who I would eventually learn was already well alarmed by my condition).

UNDERSTANDABLY, my gait that morning was a pathetic echo of what it had been out of Thunder Bay. In fact, for the first four or five kilometres, I might as well have been dragging a plow. But then, miraculously, I felt better, quite a bit better. And for the next four or five kilometres, my muscles and joints performed more or less normally.

I took it as a sign of recuperation that my appetite began to return, expressing itself in callithumpian rumbles from my lower abdomen. At a house that advertised smoked fish for sale, I found four old Finns playing cards in a basement shop area. "I'd like to buy my lunch," I said, at which a muscular older woman rose solemnly from her chair and led me into a refrigerated room where the shelves were stacked with hoary-looking black masses. As my eyes adjusted to the dim light, these came into focus as individual fish.

"Vawnt herring?" she said, and when I told her I preferred trout, she turned and, like a slugger pulling his bat from the rack, yanked forth an immense wizened laker and proceeded to chop off a portion of its tail. Out in the shop, she took a pair of scissors that might have been salvaged from a medieval ship's surgery, trimmed off the fin bits, and wrapped the meat in butcher paper. And charged me $2.50—which as it turned out was, by a significant margin, the best $2.50 I had spent in a long time.

But for now I did not want to stop to eat, preferring to get the most out of my timely energy.

A week would pass before I had the latitude to see anything much beyond the exigencies of hourly survival. But on that first day on the Trans-Canada Highway, with my privileged view of the ditches and right of way, I became aware for the first time of the extraordinary array of junk—the demonstrable anthropology of a culture—that hides in the long grass or in the ditches, invisible to motorists. Coffee cups, magazines, tires, hubcaps, burger wrappers, dishes, cigarette packs, pantyhose, hats, shoes, gloves, groceries, pop bottles, construction materials, used condoms, wrecked furniture, beer and liquor bottles. The ditches are, moreover, an open mausoleum for the carcasses and skeletons of deer, moose, foxes, wolves, porcupines— any animal that has been hit and has managed to drag itself from the road before collapsing, or has been knocked from the pavement by the force of a collision. At one point, as I approached the Pass Lake truck stop, I was startled to see below me in the gutter the full skeleton of a moose, dinosauric and forbidding, stripped clean of soft tissue and marred only by a row of shattered ribs where it had been struck.

By the time I had walked seven or eight kilometres, the pain in my knee, which during the previous day's walk had been occasional, was a lurid constant—so painful ultimately that I could only keep moving by turning around and walking backwards, which for some reason put less stress on my knee. Where medical conditions are concerned, I have enjoyed modest success at self-diagnosis and treatment (once having closed a cut in my foot by overlapping the skin and applying superglue). Eventually, on a brainwave, I sat on a rock, rolled up my pant leg, and wrapped my scarf twice around my knee, knotting it tightly behind. The improvement was immediate. The problem was that to keep the scarf in place, I had to tie it as tight as a tourniquet, so that it restricted circulation, forcing me to stop every few kilometres to untie it until my lower leg regained its colour.

Perhaps ten kilometres east of Loon Lake, unable to get full oxygen because of the accumulating gunk in my bronchial tubes, I scrambled into the spruce bush and sprawled on a slope of moss. As much as my feet screamed for attention, they were going to have to wait as I had no tolerance for tending to them in the cold. What I did have was my fish, which I devoured in thick oily flakes, pretty much solid protein, addictively tasty.

I had intended to walk another two or three kilometres, but as I attempted to rise, I realized I was finished for the day. Because I was out of cellphone range and could not call George, I limped back out to the highway and hitched a ride with a pair of spangle-faced teenagers, one of whom had a dozen or more ear, nose, and eyebrow rings and no front teeth.

My feet when I reached the hostel were in tatters. Blisters as big as dollar coins had broken, yielding flaps of loose skin and bright seeping flesh.

Again barely able to eat, I sat at the dinner table and listened to two feverish Dutchmen, each of whom ate a rhino's helping of unadorned macaroni. They were on a six-month tour of the universe, and had bought an '81 van in Sault Ste. Marie, which a day and a half later had blown its water pump and radiator. They asked me what I thought they should do, but I succeeded only in introducing them to the word *overheated,* which they latched on to and repeated like an incantation. Willa eventually ran them a double sink of dish and rinse water, and they proceeded to wash the dinner dishes by swirling them first in the rinse water, then dipping them briefly in the wash water before depositing them in the dish rack, covered with suds.

My blisters were so sensitive, even to bedsheets, that by morning I doubted I could walk at all that day. At the breakfast table, I was given courage and some good advice by a young French bush pilot, François, who was in the area looking for work and who had once walked the entire Appalachian Trail suffering "horribly not nice" blisters of his own.

"Let me seeing your feet," he demanded, and I dutifully took off a sock and crossed my bare foot over my knee.

"*Merde,*" he gasped, giving me hope that he would order me off the road. Instead, he told me that under no circumstances must I quit walking, even for an hour. "Eef you stop," he said gravely, "your feet has won." If I kept walking, he explained, my feet would adjust and eventually toughen. He recommended that I buy pantyhose, cut the feet off them, and wear the latter underneath my socks to protect the skin. Ever the economist, it occurred to me that I might have brought along some used ones (creating the potentially drastic irony of my tottering along the highway in Betty's spent nylons). He also suggested that I buy antibiotic cream and, at every opportunity, rub it aggressively into my feet.

Beyond his prescription, I desperately needed a knee brace that would flex with the joint and breathe. Unfortunately, I was still fifty kilometres from Nipigon and a drugstore, where I could be fitted for such an appliance.

AMONG THE QUESTIONS I am most often asked about my walk are, How long did it take? How many pairs of shoes did you go through? And, Did you cheat?

Since they are all questions that aim at something reducible about an essentially irreducible enterprise, they are easily answered.

Including eight days in New York City, I walked for ten weeks straight—and did not ruin even a single pair of shoes. The three pairs I wore were contemporary, slightly lumpish affairs that were space-age tough and broke down eventually not in the treads or vamps but on the insoles, which from the daily soaking and pressure began gradually to compact. By the time this happened, some 1,500 kilometres into my trip, I was so committed to my main pair, both emotionally and physically, I couldn't bear to stop wearing them. Instead, I stuffed in a pair of Dr. Scholl's cushioned insoles, walked until they were the thickness of a communion wafer, then stuffed in another pair, and kept walking.

As for cheating, I had no reason to. I did, I believe, cheat fate—particularly at the beginning, when by rights I should have quit and gone home, or lain down by the roadside, as I often wanted to, and awaited the arrival of the ravens.

More prevalently, I am asked why I went. Or sometimes, Why on earth? Or in heaven? And the simplest answer is perhaps the best.

Because I felt like it—which is not an answer people find easy to accept in this age of business plans, mission statements, five-point programs, and endless career or project objectives. I was fifty-three years old, had gotten myself into a rut and needed risk, excitement—needed a journey, the oldest and still perhaps the best way of resetting one's compass and reintroducing the possibility of surprise. I would not presume to say that in walking I expected to find answers in any absolute sense. I believed, however, that somewhere out along the road, I might, as Pico Iyer put it, locate "better questions."

There is, of course, at the bottom of such an adventure, an irrationality, a desire to do something based not on reason or utility but on faith and a sense of adventure. Which was as big a part of the attraction as anything else. In any event, walking to New York City seemed highly reasonable compared to what most of my contemporaries would be doing for the next seventy days, and the next seventy and the next: behind the desk, in front of the sales force, making cold calls, at the front of the classroom, on the shop floor, in the warehouse or chemical lab.

As to why I went on foot, the idea was not to move as slowly as possible but merely at the pace of a more observant chapter in human history—to slow things down to where noticing becomes not just possible but unavoidable.

Walking is such an inversion of the travelling norm these days that to go any distance at all on foot comprises something of a political statement—or at the very least a spit in the eye to the dehumanizing influences of media and technology, and to the shrinkage and "virtualization" of the planet. Whereas jets and the internet collapse the planet, walking expands it and returns to the walker a sense of its proportions and the intimacy of its appeal to the senses.

I went, too, because I was interested in walking's history and decline. Several times a year, my maternal great-grandfather, a Muskoka farmer, walked 160 kilometres, round-trip, between the central Ontario towns of Bracebridge and Orillia to mill a seventy-five-pound bag of grain, which he carried on his back. "Why didn't he take a horse?" I once asked my aunt, to which she responded, "He didn't have a horse—couldn't afford one."

For many people, walking was simply how distances on land got covered in those days. My dad walked up to seven or eight kilometres a day well into his eighties, and, like his forebears, viewed travel afoot as the most natural and obvious way to get somewhere. As a teenager, I did a fifty-mile walk with others at the instigation of President Kennedy, who urged young people to get out and experience the world. We walked from Cornwall, Ontario, south across the St. Lawrence River to Upstate New York, into the foothills of the Adirondacks, and back. I remember well the grinding spirit of accomplishment that came at the halfway point, and the grim optimism of thinking we had "just twenty-five miles" to go—feelings decidedly revisited on the way to New York as I walked eight hundred and then a thousand kilometres, thinking, at times rather soberly, that there were now just a thousand kilometres to go.

As for the timing, I was ready to go—ready, as the Hindus put it, to detach from what I was and knew, and to reconnect with a more basic version both of the planet and of myself.

If I needed additional motivation for going, I had, on top of everything, lost my job—as a husband. And while I was desperate to remain true and connected to my children—at the time aged seven, eight, and fourteen—I had also come to an opportune time to get away and re-evaluate.

What I could never have anticipated was that the most persistent question of all about my trip—the most skeptical question—would be from the beginning, Why New York City? Was it about the collapse of the World Trade Towers? Or for media attention? But neither had even the slightest bearing on my decision.

Months before 9/11, I had become fascinated by the idea of a marathon journey on foot. I had been hankering, simultaneously, for a good long visit to Manhattan, where I had not been for more than a twenty-four-hour stretch since I was fifteen years old. One night during June 2001, Betty said to me, "Why don't you just combine the two and walk to Manhattan?"

In the morning, on my desk, there was a note: "Walk to New York—copyright Betty Carpick."

The possibility took root—and with it a sense that in walking to the great city I would be exploring, a step at a time, the largely unexplored axis between rural culture and the more artful, articulated culture of big city civilization. Or, in this case, between the vast Precambrian wilderness (one of the most isolated and magnificent parts of the continent) and the centre of North American cultural and financial life.

Where history is concerned, the wilds north of Lake Superior are about as close as one gets these days to conditions that existed prior to European settlement in North America. New York, by contrast, is pretty much the edge of history's forward motion on the continent.

One thing I did *not* want the trip to become was overweening, overly cerebral in its ambitions, or overrationalized as a journey toward selfhood. I believed then (and still do) in a certain amount of rationalization—walk as therapy, meditation, personal challenge. At the same time, I agree with writer Ron Strickland's view that "voluntary walking is no mere rejection of technology but a reaffirmation of the pleasure of having two legs."

So, I COULD TALK THE TALK, as the hipsters used to say. The question was, could I walk the walk? Could a fifty-three-year-old guy battling incipient arthritis, stiffening arteries, and the atrophying muscles of middle age hope to hike across half a continent? And if so, at what cost? Let me be clear, I was not in good physical condition when I left in late April 2002. I had done nothing to get fit, largely because for weeks I had been battling a stubborn dose of bronchial flu. It never occurred to me that people's doubts about my prospects might be justified. When anyone asked what I'd been doing to get into shape, I'd joke that I was "intellectually" or "psychologically" prepared (which itself turned out to be false). Betty would look at me wheezing around in my dressing gown and say, "Charlie, you're not fit to walk across town, let alone to New York." But it made her no less persistent in her campaign to get me out of the house, out of her life, and on my way.

If I had any clear inkling of what was to come, I got it two or three nights before my departure, when I decided to test a pair of shoes by walking a kilometre or so downhill to a meeting. No problem on the downslope. However, the flu was so deep in my respiratory apparatus that, as I came back uphill, I had to stop every hundred metres or so to catch my breath, and arrived home enervated and somewhat less confident than I had been.

I might have waited a little longer to begin, except that I had by now concocted an elaborate itinerary, including a projected arrival time in New York with free use of a hotel room, organized all manner of support and beds along the way, and arranged to make regular road reports to CBC Radio, beginning the following Wednesday.

Plus, the pressure on me to vacate the Harmony Hotel was by now so intense that, when I mentioned to Betty on the day before my departure that I might need another day's rest before hitting the road, she immediately called her lawyer, who called my lawyer, advocating something along the lines of psychic disembowelment if my seventeen years of cohabitation with Betty extended to seventeen years and one day—all of which struck me as a trifle extreme, but did help keep me on schedule.

It didn't help matters that, as in the tragedies of Shakespeare, where wind and storms tend to echo the affairs of the characters, the weather through late April had been, and would remain, a scourge of wind, rain, hail, cold, and snow.

AND YET I REMAINED OPTIMISTIC—with at least sporadically good reason. During the weeks before my departure, I had, through a series of bold pleas to strangers and strategic requests of friends, pieced together a support plan whose seeds were planted the day I realized that three or four changes of decent outdoor wear and shoes were going to cost me perhaps fifteen hundred dollars. On a whim, I sought out Jeff Timmins, the Canadian sales manager for Columbia Clothing, an Oregon company that I knew manufactured most of the items I coveted. Jeff and I chatted enthusiastically, exchanged pertinent information, and a week before my departure, two enormous cartons arrived at the house, crammed with shoes, jackets, pants, fleece wear, rain gear, and so on.

Eden, my youngest, was home from school the day the shipment came, and together the two of us unpacked it all, elated, even gloating, over this indisputably fine windfall. When my son, Matt, got home, he was gleeful that his old man was now "sponsored," as his snow-boarding heroes are sponsored by clothing and gear manufacturers.

Buoyed by my good fortune, I contacted an old university friend at Rogers Communications and in no time had arranged to have both a cellphone and a car phone, with free calls anywhere for the ten weeks' duration of the trip.

When I inquired at the Warwick Hotel about accommodations for a visiting writer, the sales manager invited me, without hesitation, to make the hotel my home, gratis, for as long as I was in New York. A day later, the director of public relations with the Ontario Provincial Parks agreed to let me stay free in Ontario's parks.

However, my best bit of pre-trip planning was to persuade George to come along in a kind of shadow role, to haul supplies and to rendezvous with me at the end of each day, or at least every second day, so that I could walk unencumbered by a thirty-kilo pack.

George had lived in New York City with his wife and sons for a dozen years during the sixties and seventies, and had earned his M.A. in fine art at Lehman College. But he had eventually been chased out by high rents, the deterioration of his neighbourhood in the Bronx, and finally by the loss of his job at the Kennedy Fine Art Gallery on East Fifty-second Street. He had last made his living in New York driving gypsy cab in Harlem and the Bronx, all but masochistic work that had itself contributed to his fleeing the city. He had nonetheless developed a desire and taste for the life of Manhattan, which, at the time of our trip, had gone frustrated for the better part of three decades (decades marred by, among other occurrences, the suicide of his wife).

Now he was on his way back, his story in part paralleling my own, in that his relationship to the woman with whom he lived had become distorted to the point where he was more than ready to give himself up to the road.

As THE DAYS TO OUR DEPARTURE DWINDLED, I reinforced my fragile optimism by mapping a detailed itinerary that would take me east and south along the shore of Lake Superior to Sault Ste. Marie, on to Espanola, southeast to Toronto, then east along Lake Ontario to Kingston, where I would enter New York State and follow the western-most flank of the Adirondacks to Cooperstown and the Catskill Mountains. The last glorious days, as I imagined them, would take me straight down Highway 9, Broadway Avenue, along the east bank of the Hudson into New York City.

The route would, among other things, trace that of the earliest fur trade voyageurs, the first transcontinental railway, the Erie and New York Canal, and more personally, the path of a branch of my ancestry that made its way north into Canada in the wake of the Salem witch hunts.

I tightened my resolve during those last days of preparation by assembling my camping and survival gear, and building up a modest inventory of nonperishable foods. In all, I estimated we had about twice as much gear as we would need—this in the face of everybody else's estimates that we had about half as much.

2

The Gales of Superior

So as not to belabour the farce of those first few days, I shall report only that late on the afternoon of the twenty-ninth, after another two days of blundering through snow flurries, I shuffled into Nipigon, one of the oldest and grimmest mill towns on Superior's north shore. By this time I was consuming perhaps a dozen 222s a day, which did not help the stomach pains that would start after several hours of walking. As an antidote for those, I was popping Pepto-Bismol tablets every couple of hours and for the symptoms of my virus, four or five flu tablets a day, plus a wino's dose of cough syrup. I would eventually add vitamin C and echinacea to the regimen, but for now was determined only to get a knee brace and some pantyhose.

George picked me up on the motel strip along the Trans-Canada, and we drove down into the town proper to Foulds' Pharmacy, where at the request of a middle-aged clerk I rolled up my pant leg and removed the scarf from my knee so that she could measure me for a royal blue neoprene support. The scarf had been a trip-saver, but it had begun to tear the skin off the back of my knee. I bought antibiotic ointment, more Pepto-Bismol and cough medicine, and exited

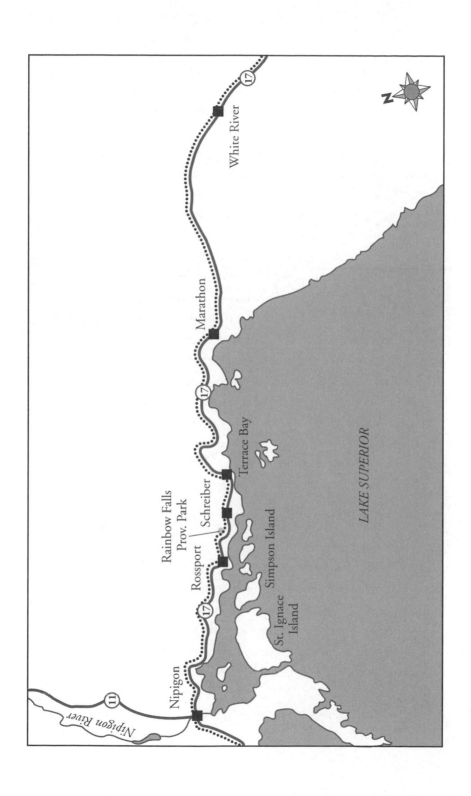

wearing my brace, which gave me an inkling of what athletes must feel after reconstructive knee surgery.

It had been snowing all day, and for the past couple of hours I had been longing for a bowl of chicken soup—in fact, began now on the street to discuss such soup with George: how it should contain rice or noodles, vegetables, chunks of chicken, and of course, be made from actual chicken stock, lightly spiced, a little fresh pepper, etc. With this fantasy in mind, we walked into what appeared to be a functioning restaurant, a place advertising a Chinese lunch special, but which turned out to be nothing more than a large dimly lit room featuring a Naugahyde bar, where a couple of lumpish bikers *manqués* sat fondling their beer bottles in front of a sallow-faced bartender.

I felt suddenly self-conscious, just a little too "outdoorsy" in my Columbia regalia. Meanwhile, George slouched behind me in his Greek sailor's hat, a copy of Homer's *Odyssey* under his arm.

"Hi!" I said enthusiastically and, turning to the bartender, "I was wondering if I could get a bowl of soup."

I have heard of words having a paralyzing effect but until that moment had not actually witnessed people struck speechless and motionless by my personal sentences. However, the three of them hunkered there like pig iron, refusing even to cast an eye my way.

"No food, huh?" I said after a few seconds and having failed on soup, thought it pointless, if not unwise, to inquire as to where I might be able to buy pantyhose.

At a clothing store down the street, I discovered, instead of nylons, extremely thin polypropelene undersocks specifically for hikers. This delicate hosiery had been reduced to about a third of its original price, calling forth in me a rare burst of profligacy as I scooped up the entire stock of four pairs (a seemingly small commitment that would significantly change the course of the next ten weeks).

GEORGE AND I SPENT THAT NIGHT and the next in the main lodge at Bungalow Camp, a grand old fishing resort at Lake Helen on the

Nipigon River, just north of Nipigon. The place was built by the Canadian Pacific Railway during the 1920s, when it could be reached only by Great Lakes steamship or rail and when the railway was encouraging passenger traffic by constructing sea-to-sea lodges and railway hotels.

My friend Kal Nikkila, a one-time Thunder Bay lumber dealer, bought the resort in a state of dilapidation during the mid-1990s and, with his sons and daughter, set about restoring it. And has now pretty much done the job—to magnificent effect. Like Lloyd and Willa, Kal is a provider on the order of Saint Anthony—he had, for example, six indoor fires burning when we arrived (a phenomenon likened by George to the mythic spectacles of *The Odyssey*). What's more, on that first evening, Kal prepared a five-course dinner that began innocuously enough with soup, crackers, cheese, and Kal's homemade Finnish coffee bread—and proceeded to salad, wine, spaghetti, pickerel fillets, more home baking, fresh fruit, and coffee.

The problem for me was that I was as sick as I had been at the Longhouse and sat down at the table barely able to force food into a stomach that by the end of each day, insisted stubbornly on protecting itself from even the modest work of digestion.

My protracted dining at least afforded me an opportunity to gaze out at the swollen river, on which floating pans of ice, acres of them, glowing a luminescent pink in the late-day sun, were drifting downstream to Lake Superior. The Nipigon is the largest river flowing into the Great Lakes. For millennia before the Europeans showed up, it provided a sustainable plenitude of trout, pickerel, and sturgeon to area aboriginals. However, sport fishermen from as far away as the southern U.S. and Europe eventually discovered it, and for half a century, from the 1860s on, the river was, according to a 1887 issue of *Field & Stream* magazine, "the finest trout stream in the world." Hungry poachers were said to throw dynamite into the Nipigon, take three or four fish for dinner, and leave three or four hundred floating downriver for the gulls and ravens.

The walls of Bungalow Camp are, understandably, a museum of bumper stuffed trout, as well as pickerel and bass, and of photos from the days when gentlemen anglers in fedoras, ties, and tweed jackets spent their days on the water with Native guides, and their evenings playing bridge and getting plastered on single malt scotch.

In 1884, an American writer named Henry Vail wrote that there wasn't "the slightest danger that the fishing in the Nipigon will be spoiled so long as the bites of mosquitoes, sand flies, and blackflies are painful to men." Like most optimistic forecasts for the ecology of the planet, this turned out to be nonsense. Within twenty years, fish stocks were severely depleted and by the mid-twentieth century had become so puny as to push sport fishermen north to Lake Nipigon or out onto Lake Superior, where the fishery was also in sharp decline.

Kal lost his wife to cancer during the late 1970s and told me at the table about the profound effect her death had had on him and on their children—about her acceptance of fate, her refusal to complain, and in particular their last trips together into the north, where they both loved to fish and canoe.

Kal is a risk taker who has enjoyed success in business and invariably offers enthusiastic moral support for the career endeavours of anyone with whom he comes into contact. For days afterwards, George would happily recollect Kal's asking him if things were "prosperous in the poetry business these days" (poetry being a notorious financial flatliner in which prosperity has, for a century or so, been measured not in dollars or even cents, but in the delicately nuanced currency of the psyche and senses).

As Kal and I talked, George sat at the table reading Homer and writing a sort of verse letter, more or less in the style of *The Odyssey*, about the first few days of our travels—an almost comically idealized document that he intended to send to an old girlfriend in Minnesota, together with a copy of his book *Michif Cantos,* as an inducement to have her join us at a point on our travels.

That night in our room, for the first time since leaving home, I, too, did a little reading, from Rebecca Solnit's wonderful book *Wanderlust: A History of Walking*—in particular from a chapter in which Solnit explains that it was neither reason nor imagination nor spirituality that set the earliest hominids on the road toward civilization, but plain old upright walking; in fact, that our species wouldn't exist had the early hominids, the smartest of the four-legged apes, not realized some 3.6 million years ago that they would be able to see farther and hunt better—if they stood and ventured forth on their hind legs.

I told George, who was across the room in a single bed, about the symbolic "humanizing" significance of what I was up to, and he began to laugh.

The science lesson goes as follows: the buttocks, relatively small in the primate, gradually became the largest muscles in the body. The spine straightened, and the head and neck grew more erect. Sexually, the "missionary" position became an alternative to whatever else primates had figured out beyond the basic mammalian rear entry.

By far the most important change, however, was that the new possibilities for liberated "arms" and "hands"—gathering food, building shelters, wielding tools or weapons—initiated an evolutionary preference for greater intelligence. In short, those with bigger brains had more successful lives. The brain and cranium expanded, a development that not only set early humanity apart from the apes but led to humankind's eventual domination of the planet.

It is surely one of the most glaring paradoxes of nature and evolution that in addition to expanding the intelligence of *Homo sapiens,* walking also restricted our intelligence, in that upright posture eventually led to a streamlining and narrowing of the pelvic structure and hence a narrowing of the birth canal, so that only a certain-sized skull (and brain) could be accommodated. Had it somehow been otherwise, human heads might now be the size of basketballs, able to do math with the efficiency of a computer. I saw all three of my children born and, like most other dads and moms, can attest to the fact that it is that big bony head that tends to jam in the birth canal, not the shoulders or torso, which once the head is out, emerge like fluid.

In short, walking made us what we are—and had done a good job of making me what I was that night, which is to say pained and poleaxed (but smart enough to read), and feeling an uncommon empathy for those thick-skulled hominids with their obstinate desire to step out.

ON THE MORNING we left Kal's, I did my first road broadcast with CBC Radio back home in Thunder Bay, a five- or six-minute exchange—for the most part a rave—that, among other things, touched on blisters, blizzards, bad dogs, roadside junk, and more positively, on the Longhouse Hostel and Bungalow Camp. I concluded my freewheeling rodomontade with a drastically condensed review of the 3.6 million years that had put me on the highway to Manhattan.

WHEN WE HAD SAID OUR GOODBYES to Kal, George drove me to where I had ended my walk the previous day, about fifteen kilometres east of Nipigon. I was in a kind of torpor from the long sleep at Bungalow Camp—perhaps equally so from Kal's teeming breakfast of oven pancakes, sausages, bacon, Finnish coffee bread, leftover pork chops, and of course, three or four cups of the national elixir of Finland, prescription-strength coffee.

Even so, for the first few kilometres, everything went swimmingly. The views of Superior along this stretch of the Trans-Canada are an elixir unto themselves, at times taking in several hundred square kilometres of sapphire-coloured water, plus an ever-shifting panoply of beaches, granite, spruce forest, and three-billion-year-old mountains, the oldest on the planet. But the hills are long and in some cases steep, and by noon I was beginning to think longingly of a soft place to stretch out.

I found that place somewhere east of Kama Bay on a little shelf of moss behind a rock cut, where I took a few slurps of Gatorade to wash back my 222s and, having nibbled at a pork chop, lay back and promptly fell asleep.

Perhaps stimulated by my medication, I had the sort of dream that I had had commonly as a teenager but otherwise had experienced just once or twice in perhaps twenty years—a vividly cinematic drama in which I could fly—along shorelines, across water, beneath hydro wires as people shouted warnings to me from below to come down, *now*, to end the foolishness and get on with reality.

When eventually I awoke, the sun had arched over the trees and was flooding my little grove. Despite the cool air, I was sweating and was racked by a stiffness that ran from my knees and hips right up into my shoulders and neck.

I had told George to give me seven hours of walking, till three o'clock. But now at one, as I pushed up the first long hill of the afternoon, I found myself thinking longingly of a reprieve, not to mention the six toasty fires we had left behind at Kal's.

I walked invariably on the left side of the two-lane highway, and where there were passing zones—in other words, a dotted centre line— I had already developed the habit of stepping off onto the shoulder when I heard a vehicle or vehicles approaching from behind. In this way, I protected myself from getting sideswiped by a car or truck overtaking another in "my" lane. At this point, however, I was so consumed by the effort of getting back into some sort of rhythm that I had wandered a metre or so out onto the pavement. Suddenly a station wagon blew in behind me in the passing lane and whisked past, horn blaring, close enough that I could have reached out and touched it.

It rattled me that my focus could be so spotty, and for the next few minutes I sat on the guardrail, contemplating not just my ineptitude but the violence of the highway and the relative negligence of drivers toward any living thing not protected by a ton and a half of steel armour. Already that day, in the ditch, I had seen two deer carcasses, a dead dog, and what I took to be a decomposed wolf, as black as a raven, grimacing up out of a trickle of rust-coloured water. I had passed a number of tiny roadside crosses marking the sites of crash fatalities and, as I did every day, had seen the scattering of ditched glass and car bits, and occasionally the scarred earth and rock where recent crashes had occurred. The most daunting sights since leaving Thunder Bay had been the two or three spots where a volume of animal blood had spilled onto the highway leaving a stain as big as a tablecloth.

Sickness and snowstorms aside, one of the oddest things about these early days was the unpredictability of my energy and moods. Now, at about two o'clock, as I crested a hill and headed down a two- or three-kilometre slope, I had a sudden feeling (despite blisters) that the day wouldn't be long enough to do the walking I had it in me to do. Part of this was, of course, that I was going downhill (literally now instead of figuratively). But it was also, I suspect, the inspiration of the view, which at this point took in a ten-kilometre fetch of Nipigon Bay and in the distance the basalt cliffs of St. Ignace and Simpson Islands. What's more, the sun now broke through, imparting the sensation that I had been lifted by a benevolent hand and lowered gently into a warm bath. I took off my toque, loosened my jacket, and whereas a half hour before I had been virtually praying that George would show up early, I now found myself hoping he would show up half a day late.

Excess was selling cheap, and I wasn't more than a third of the way down the hill when the radical thought occurred to me that just maybe we could try pitching the tent, particularly if we could get into the provincial park at Rainbow Falls, east of Rossport. However, it seemed unlikely that the gate would be open because a provincial civil servants' strike was keeping all parks closed.

And, sure enough, at the park entrance, we were met by a trio of solemn picketers and a sign informing would-be intruders that trespassing during the strike was "strictly and absolutely prohibited" (a superfluity of terms that George felt was itself a rather sobering trespass on public wilderness).

As we were about to move on, however, I noticed a narrow gravel road leading to the lake just east of the park boundary. We bumped and jounced down the hill, twice banging the undercarriage of the van off embedded boulders, to a small clearing within twenty metres of where sunlit rollers, barely rippled by a southwest breeze, surged onto the beach. The shoreline was a slope of stones, each so perfectly sculpted by centuries of tumbling that the smallest of them might have been mistaken for ostrich eggs, the largest for volleyballs or curling stones.

Thinking only of grabbing an hour or so of sleep, I hauled my Hudson's Bay blanket and sleeping bag fifty metres up the lakeshore to where a patch of dwarf spruce behind the beach offered an inviting little solarium. George brought a supply of food and then went back for the tent, which we spread like a throw rug amid the mosses, moose-berries, and dried leaves.

While George took a walk up the beach, I lay in a kind of daze, sniffling, listening to the waves, enjoying the slight cool of the breeze as it passed above me. Then I was in another country, sweating as I had during the morning, half dreaming, seeming to feel the poison being drawn from me into the soil and water, into some other time zone or tense, leaving me immune and asleep in a kind of cloudless, sky-like present.

For three hours, I barely moved. At times, George read aloud from his copy of *The Odyssey* about the beautiful young Nausicaa and her maidens who had come down to the sea to wash their clothes and play. There, on the shore, they had discovered the tattered and exhausted Odysseus ("and his driver, George," added George) who had been shipwrecked on the island of Phaeacia.

Odysseus said to them, "I am aware of the sorry state in which the world has left me." And with these words he took the oil Nausicaa had brought and went to the shore where he cleansed himself of the encrusted salt and sand. Meanwhile the maids, with many frightened sighs, said to Nausicaa, "Let's run away! Can't you see how ugly that man is?"

About an hour before dark, with the sun sinking and the temperature dropping, we got out the tent poles and figured out what went
where and how. Within fifteen minutes, we had the tattered old thing
gloriously erect, and our beds made—mine, for lack of a mattress, atop
the folded Hudson's Bay blanket, George's on an inch-thick (or more
accurately inch-thin) inflatable foam pad. George had insisted all
along that his sleeping bag, bought twenty-five years ago, was "fine,"
would be plenty warm; his son Vince had been using it and had
expressed no complaints. Unfortunately, since George had used it
years ago, it had been ripped and patched so many times that every
shred of insulation, every feather and fibre, had gradually escaped the
thin nylon compartments. What was left of the bag could have been
rolled into, say, a jacket pocket, and when I saw it I was less than optimistic about George's chances for the night.

By darkness, the temperature had dropped to the freezing point.
Mercifully, there was no wind, just the Odyssean roll of the waves. I
piled on half the contents of my duffle bag, including my CBC toque,
and as an extra measure of insulation from the ground, stuffed spruce
boughs underneath the floor of the tent. George looked like the mad
trapper in his rain jacket and an old muskrat hat (flaps down) that he
had salvaged from my things in Thunder Bay.

"For comfort," as he so optimistically phrased it, he slipped a
flannel sheet inside his bag, which was no longer a sleeping bag in any
conventional sense but a kind of sleeping condom—utmost sensitivity, virtually nothing between you and the world you love.

What followed was one of the most excruciating nights of my life—
easily matching a night during my early twenties when, to escape a
hard rain, I had "slept" without underpadding or covers on dusty
concrete beneath the loading ramp of a partly constructed hotel at the
tip of the Sinai Peninsula.

By the middle of the night on the hard ground, my hips were in all
but unendurable pain, which kept me rolling, fidgeting, flinging,
attempting anything I could to get one or the other of them a little

better protected. But when I lay on my back or front to give them a break, my spine was, in no time, in the same state of discomfort. Plus, of course, I was freezing and aching from the flu.

What George must have been going through, I can only wince at. "Thank God for literature," he had said to me rather plaintively before going to sleep, and he had proceeded to explain that *The Odyssey* had been essentially a holy book for the ancient Greeks— had for eight or nine hundred years been that culture's central educational and moral text. What most caught my attention, however, was his description of it as a kind of "courage manual," and we agreed that in a sense most great literature down through the ages somehow fitted that description.

More than anything in the world, I could have used such a manual, and the courage it brought, when, at perhaps 7:00 A.M., I wrenched myself off the ground and opened the tent flap to find yesterday's paradise buried in five inches of wet snow, snow that continued to fall in flakes the size of dimes.

George, whose mood was approximately that of the typhonic lake before us, was all for tearing the tent down pronto and heading back to Kal's or into Rossport or Schreiber. Or all the way back to the Longhouse. And undoubtedly he had the right idea. But we couldn't do it immediately, in that first I needed to get my feet ready and my shoes and socks in order.

"You're not walking today," he said.

The statement was inflected faintly as a question, but its overall effect was that of an unnegotiable directive.

It had occurred to me already to take the day off, not so much because of the snow, but because of my various aches and lesions. But I have never responded well to being told what to do. And in George's voice there was something a little too presumptuous for my state of mind.

"Actually, I am," I said as I pulled my fresh socks on. "It's only a little snow."

From outside the tent, where George had gone to take a leak, there came a burst of semi-indecipherable hollering, something about a blankety-blank blizzard. "If you walk in this weather," he said as he came back in, "I can't be responsible for you."

"You're not responsible for me now," I told him, and well wrapped against the day, I yanked the tent down and threw it wet into the van. On a breakfast that included antacid pills, decongestants, and 222s— the bacon and eggs of the pharmaceutical world—I headed up the embankment, already half-covered with snowflakes, and shambled off east down the highway.

WHILE I HAD LONG APPRECIATED how walking expands time and the proportions of the planet, what I had not anticipated, especially during these terribly difficult first days, was how in a quite extraordinary way it expanded my sense of connection to, and appreciation of, the past. At some point every day as I trudged along, I found myself peering with doleful fascination into the spruce forest or up a rock face or down a wilderness river—the Steel, the Cyprus, the Little Pic— thinking that barely beyond the traffic signs and bridge rails existed a world essentially unchanged since tribespeople draped in caribou skins and rabbit pelts made a life, undoubtedly a short and hard one, out of fish, game, berries, birch trees, and flint.

Where wildlife is concerned, it is a short flight of the imagination from the pile of bones by the creek's edge to a time when caribou roamed these watersheds by the thousands or when the implausible woolly mammoth—part elephant, part Pekingese—lumbered through the spruce forests grazing on blueberries, pickerelweed, and ferns. It is another short flight from the skeleton of a wrecked cedar strip in the banks of, say, the Gravel River to a flotilla of birchbark freighter canoes (just out of sight beyond the islands) slicing silently down-current on a silver- and copper-trading mission to the sea. Or to voyageurs plowing up-current from Montreal to Fort William, on the site of what is now Thunder Bay. There they rendezvoused with both

French and aboriginal trappers—and as the mythmakers tell it, drank, fought, and fornicated until, ten days later, they got in their canoes and headed east again, loaded with furs.

The illusion is in large part sensory; the suspension of the present comes easily amid the uninterrupted sounds of wind, ravens, and rushing water. It comes with added emphasis when one is moving at the pace of nature, of generations of land travellers who before the coming of the railway or roads, made their way across this wilderness in moccasins or on snowshoes. There is nothing like the interior of a minivan or Toyota, or the presence of a laptop or Discman, to insulate us from a past in which the height of technology was the bow and arrow or canoe paddle, or a bone and rawhide tool.

For a quick trip back to the present, I had only to pause to consider, say, whether George was on his way to meet me in the warmth of the vehicle or whether we had cellphone service on this or that stretch of highway. Or whether the thinner or the thicker polypropylene socks would be easier on my blisters (something the French fur trader Jean-Baptiste Lagimodière didn't have to worry about when he walked from what is now Manitoba to Montreal in the winter of 1815 to pick up the mail and deliver the news that the prairie Métis were on the verge of revolt).

As for more recent history, an afternoon didn't pass when I was not reminded of what utter folly and violence it must have seemed to construct a railway through these rocks and hills and marshes, particularly if you were a Chinese peasant brought to Canada by the Canadian Pacific Railway to make a new and better life in this glorious land of opportunity. The stretches of track along the north shore of Superior were the last to be completed in the transcontinental railway, and with good reason. They were the toughest to build. Even the Rockies are said to have been an easier challenge, and money saved unexpectedly in the blasting of tunnels and the building of rail bed through the formidable western mountains was quickly used up in attempting to breach the endless rock chasms, the marshes, rivers, and creeks north of Superior. In the end, 100 bridges and an average of 15 culverts a mile were constructed along the north shore (by 12,000 men on rations of 350,000 tons of food and 4 tons of tobacco a month). More than twice as much money was expended in masonry on the stretch of rail between Thunder Bay and Nipigon, a distance of 105 kilometres, as on the rest of the railway.

The job was completed in 1885 only because of CPR president Cornelius Van Horne's opportunism in seeing that he could lever money out of the government of Sir John A. Macdonald to continue work on the Lake Superior stretches so that government troops could more easily make their way west to put down the perceived challenge to Canadian nationhood that was being mounted on the prairies by the Métis leader Louis Riel. Van Horne said that with the completed railway he could get the troops from Toronto to Manitoba in ten days, and Macdonald went for it.

To make good on his promise, Van Horne's navvies laid hundreds of kilometres of track not on rail bed but directly onto frozen ground and snow. It was a temporary and slipshod job. And the soldiers, who were travelling in winter on open flatcars, were half dead by the time they got into the area east of Nipigon (where there were still gaps in the line, across which they had to march). Nevertheless, the tale is told of men, all but comatose from cold and exhaustion, raising their heads as they came close to Nipigon to take in the grandeur of the passing scene.

The builders themselves were not much better off. As construction money ran out, so did food supplies, with the result that labourers were often paid in whisky rather than money and were obliged to live exclusively on whatever fish could be bought from the local Natives. No fruit, vegetables, or flour. They lived in hastily built lean-tos or, in reported cases, in rock caves or in canvas-covered holes in the ground. Even the ever-present travelling brothels, some employing as many as fifty prostitutes, were constructed of logs, or at least decent canvas. In winter the temperatures went to –45°C, and in summer the black flies and mosquitoes bit with such ferocity that men were said to live for weeks with permanently suppurating sores on their necks, faces, and scalps. It is hardly surprising that some of them stayed drunk pretty much from dawn till bedtime.

If liquor had been available to the horses used to build this section, they, too, might have stayed drunk. Of the five thousand of them that worked the north shore, hundreds died of food shortage and exhaustion. Some are said to have been butchered and eaten where they fell.

Beyond all this, there was an ever-present danger from falling rocks, steam engines, and dynamite. The stone bridge towers that were to carry the railway across the Nipigon River and gorge, near Kal's Bungalow Camp, collapsed three times, each time with loss of life, before the bridge that stands today was safely in place. At Red Rock, just west of Nipigon, Van Horne tried to bypass rock cliffs by building a stonework embankment out into Lake Superior. But the lake bottom proved so unstable that when several tons of rails were unloaded onto the structure from a ship, the entire thing, representing weeks of work and the lives of several men killed during its construction, disintegrated and sank.

The dynamiting along Superior was so pervasive that rather than import dynamite from the United States, Van Horne set up three north shore factories to make the stuff at a cost of $7.5 million, approximately what it had cost to lay rail for a thousand kilometres across the prairies. Local Natives were hired to carry barrels of nitroglycerin to the blasting sites—and like so many others, regularly lost their lives when, in the words of historians John Kelso and James Demers, "explosions caused them to disappear in a pink mist."

BY COMPARISON, all I had to contend with were torn feet, a little snow and wind, and a worsening case of bronchial flu. But it was enough for me. And by the time I walked into Schreiber late on the afternoon of May 3, I was a bigger mess than I had been at any point so far. By the time George and I had checked into the TransCan

Motel, I was hardly able to walk—and within minutes of sitting down and removing my shoes, was hardly able to stand up. My muscles and resolve had quit.

I went straight to bed and slept for six uninterrupted hours. When I woke up at perhaps ten o'clock, George had been out walking in the snow and was in no mood to be trifled with. He was fed up with the weather; fed up with my sniffling and hacking; fed up with what he now considered a hare-brained agenda that was going to kill us both. He stood by the end of the bed, his pipe in his mouth, gestured futilely with his palms, and said, "I have no idea anymore whether you can keep going or if you're just gonna fall over and die on me out there on the road."

"Well, I'm not going to die," I predicted, "so you can relax." I said I suspected the fact that I was not yet dead was decidedly in my favour. Surely having survived this first two hundred kilometres augured well for the future.

George chose the moment to reveal that Kal had expressed dire reservations not just about my health but about the gruelling challenge ahead. Whether George was just tarnishing the already-well-tarnished lily here, I never discovered—I never asked Kal. But George was convinced that we should either drive back to the hostel outside Thunder Bay or to his home in Winnipeg to wait out the weather. Or drive to Duluth and head south until we reached a climate in, say, Missouri or Kentucky that would enable us to head east in comfort.

"I don't want to walk across Kentucky," I said. "I want to walk across Ontario and New York." I added that what I felt really had to change wasn't the route but George's attitude. However, with snow gusting in the open window—and the Weather Channel bleating its warnings of frosty catastrophe—it seemed a stretch to try to persuade him that he should alter his attitude based on reason, or that summer was about to blow in.

If there was a change for the better in my health as I sat there on the bed, it was that for the first time since leaving home, I was famished.

I would have settled for a big bowl of oatmeal with raisins, except that we had no way of cooking it in the room, and I had no energy to go out. So I persuaded George to go down the highway to Rosie and Josie's restaurant, where he had had a beer earlier, and bring me back a double order of chicken soup.

Having lapped that up, I committed what, in retrospect, was an unfortunate error, asking George if he would mind doing "one more thing" for me by going to the van to get my pillow, which was more comfortable than either of the sacks of cement posing as pillows on the bed. "I don't want to go out in the cold," I told him.

"Well, you're going to have to," he said without taking his eyes off the television, "because I've done all I'm going to do for you."

I pondered this for a moment, attempting to contain my frustration, and said, "Till when?"

"Till you stop demanding attention and start doing something for yourself."

It would be an understatement to call what ensued "an exchange of unpleasantries."

I told him, in harsher terms than I care to put in print, that it wasn't my fault I was sick. And he told me in his own poetic terms that it wasn't his fault I was an obstinate mule and that we were holed up in a snowstorm in a poky motel in the middle of nowhere.

I told him he was being, let us say, *unreasonable*. And what's more, to quit referring to us as "a couple of old men," because it was starting to get on my nerves. And he told me if I couldn't walk to the van to get a pillow, I couldn't walk to New York.

For twenty minutes or so, we sat in a pulsating silence.

Finally, I said, "George, I'm walking, you're driving. I'm sick, you're not. I need your support more than you need mine. So, give it to me."

"I'm giving you too much support already," he said. "It's wearing me out. You're getting dependent."

"Then go home," I said bluntly. "I'll buy you a bus ticket in the morning. I'll carry on by myself." While I might not have realized it at the time, this was a bluff and a stupid one, in that my best hope by far for what lay ahead was with George.

"You may be paying me," he said. "But I'm not an employee."

"I'm not paying you as an employee!" I fired back. "I'm paying you as a friend—for your help. And when I need it, I need it."

After a silence, he said, "I don't want to talk about it anymore."

"Well there's still a lot needs saying."

The truth of it was that whereas George might not have cared at this point, at least not enough to stay with the plan, I couldn't bear to fail at this thing I had set out to do. It was intended to be an antidote to failure—of which there had been plenty during the past year.

"Do you know what Betty told me before we left?" George said.

"No, and I don't care what she told you, although I have a feeling I'm about to find out."

"She said, 'George, I've had him for seventeen years. Now you've got him. Good luck.'"

"Is that all?"

"That's all," he said, and I told him it was one of the nicest things Betty had said about me in months. I said, "I thought you were going to tell me something hurtful."

I spent a restless night pondering the possibility of carrying on without George—waiting out the weather, buying a lighter tent, and taking to the road unaccompanied. Or would it be easier, I wondered, just to drive the van to Mexico and lie on a beach at Barra da Navidad more or less for the rest of my life?

WHEN I WOKE UP at 7:30, George was gone from the room, and I leapt out of bed to see if he had taken the van. But it was there, covered in snow. A minute later the door opened, and he stepped in with doughnuts and two cups of coffee. And a retooled attitude so chirpy and convincing that we had only to exchange an insult or two to reach a consensus on spending another night at the TransCan.

With my feet washed and disinfected—and enjoying some zesty new energy from the long sleep—I pulled on my socks and shoes, and turned my attention to a map of the Casque Isle Trail, which would take me fifteen kilometres along the lakeshore to Terrace Bay.

As I slipped into my jacket, George said brightly, "I think I'll go with you on the trail part, or I'll walk what I can of it and come back."

After the night of the long knives, I was more than pleased to wait fifteen or twenty minutes while he got himself ready.

We ate ham and eggs at Rosie and Josie's—including four or five cups of coffee with which I washed down my 222s and decongestants—and for the next four hours enjoyed a gloriously wind-free walk through spruce woods, along beaches, over headlands, all of it on paths that had been used for centuries by both people and woodland caribou. In these parts, the latter have tended to travel near the coast, where they have the advantage of being able to move quickly over the rugged and rocky shoreline, leaving the shorter-legged wolves behind. Or where, in a pinch, being excellent swimmers, they can take directly to the water and swim to islands as far as three or four kilometres offshore.

By a sheltered cove along the lake, under a granite overhang, I found the first wildflower of the season, a tiny five-petalled pink bell cupped open to the sky, a flower I have never been able to identify. George and I stooped over it like a couple of spooky-toothed priests, unsure whether to pick it or worship it.

By noon the last patches of wet snow had melted off the trail, and the pliant soil and old leaf beds were a decided luxury underfoot. We saw wolf and moose tracks on the pink sand beaches, heard a hawk screaming, and debated whether the drought of the past couple of years was sufficient to have caused the deaths of thousands of area birches.

At a small open-air registry, where hikers were encouraged to write their comments in a notebook, we sacked out on a smooth rock incline in the sun. The notebook contained mostly standard entries on the "beauty," the "solitude," the "wildness," etc., of the trail. But two or three praised its suitability as a lovemaking grounds. One in particular from "Lindsay, Amy, Jay, and Chris" noted, "School is out, exams are over, and we have come out on the Casque Isle Trail to have some fun." Below it was a small, precise pencil drawing of a pair of cartoon pigs "having some fun."

Before I left Thunder Bay, a reflexologist had explained to me that we receive the earth's energy and healing most directly and naturally through the soles of our feet, and had encouraged me to take my shoes and socks off as often as possible and get my feet into beach sand or water or onto grass or moss. But so far it had been just too cold to go barefoot, even briefly. And the thought of sticking my feet into the perishing ice bath that is Lake Superior was no thought at all. Besides, with my feet routinely torn up, I was reluctant to get sand and soil into the raw blisters and lesions. However, the light polypropylene socks from Nipigon had significantly improved the condition of my feet, and the Nipigon knee brace had worked wonders.

My flu bug was still my worst enemy—and yet here, too, I thought I sensed a slightly expanded efficiency in my lungs, as well as in the muscles in my legs and back.

What I really feared was pneumonia, and as I walked past McCausland Hospital in Terrace Bay, now on my own, I went in on a whim and, having explained to a receptionist what I was up to, asked if, by chance, I might be able to see a doctor.

No way. Absolutely not. Appointments took time. Everybody was busy.

In the meantime, a dark-haired young man in hospital fatigues was standing five or six metres away, examining files while he listened to my description of my walk (I had learned already that if I wanted to get people's attention, I needed only mention that I was walking to New York City).

As the receptionist was telling me that I might perhaps see someone tomorrow, the young man stepped forward, excused himself for eaves-dropping, and said, "I can see you right now. I'd be happy to." And Dr. Michael Lisi and I went off to an examining room, where he took five minutes or so to eyeball my throat, finger my glands, and listen to my chest from every angle.

"There's nothing in your lungs," he said finally, explaining that what I had was a virus and since no prescription would touch it, the best thing I could do for myself was keep walking. "Maybe walk faster," he joked—a plausible variation, I thought, on the old boot camp notion that whatever doesn't kill you is likely to make you stronger.

My DIARY JOTTINGS on the Trans-Canada Highway between Terrace Bay and Marathon are a hodgepodge of observations on, among other things, a hawk I had seen disappear over the treeline with a squirming rabbit in its talons, a pair of ravens pecking at the guts of a roadkill moose, a skinny red fox with a blood-matted raven in its mouth.

And on the predominant sounds of the road in these parts—in order, wind, vehicles, ravens, trains, and woodpeckers.

And how restless I seemed to be in the hours between stretches of walking—restless to get better, restless about the weather, restless to get moving.

And on my phone calls home, or best I say "home"—how they possessed a remoteness and melancholy of their own, and more often than not left me with a deeper sense of longing than what had prompted me to make them in the first place.

I noted how the Trans-Canada itself was and is a Promethean feat of engineering, almost comparable to the building of the railway. Rock cuts thirty metres deep are commonplace along this north shore stretch, long steep-walled canyons varying in sometimes spectacular colour from silvery schist to coal black granite to pinkish quartz and iron red sandstone. It is no less impressive that the rock that came out of these man-made canyons—gazillion-ton masses of it—went to fill up the valleys, forming in some cases thirty-metre-high dikes, a bed for the highway, running as far into the distance as you can see. It is said in these parts that the Finns worked the woods, the Italians the rock.

Like the railway, it all represents years on end of blasting and bull-dozing, not to mention boozing and busted bones and lives.

I noted the poignant little roadside shrines erected with meticulous care where people had died in highway accidents—two-by-four crosses, crucifixes, plastic flowers, dolls, teddy bears, baseball caps, sometimes encased in thick plastic sheeting or in glass jars of the sort in which institutions buy pickles and mayonnaise.

LATE ON THE AFTERNOON of my tenth day of walking, George and I checked into the Pic Motel, a modest reinterpretation of the architectural style of Frank Lloyd Wright. The place sits on the stone ridge above the town of Marathon, from where the view out over the lake—on this day, grey and foreboding—was an approximation of any of a number of elegant and impersonal landscapes by the eminent Canadian painter Lawren Harris.

The view a little farther to the east is practically an axiom for towns along the north shore, including as it does a monumental pulp mill, Baal among the Canaanites, as I have sometimes thought of such places with their formidable stacks and effusions, their chain-link fences, their pervasive agendas, and rotten-egg smell.

At other towns there is a sawmill. Or a mine. And at each of them a supermarket, a doughnut shop, a couple of schools, a vehicle dealership. There is a library, a hospital, and two or three churches. And a couple of decent motels—and generally a fleabag operated less in the interest of hostelry than in moving beer from the barrels beneath the bar into the bellies of the local mill workers.

And there is an ice arena, the *sine qua non* not just of winter recreation in these parts but of the cultural life of the community.

Such towns can be brooding places, sometimes surly, but they can be genial and accommodating, too. They have in common the lake, the rock, the spruce forest—a short, sweet summer, hunting in the autumn, and a snow-burdened winter that goes on and on. And an endless-seeming wind off the lake.

The following morning, I attempted to cheat that wind, which came edged with frost, by having George drive me some forty kilometres east of Marathon so I could walk the stretch in reverse, with the wind at my back. Given that the trip thus far had been an extended exemplification of Murphy's Law, it hardly came as a surprise when, within forty-five minutes of my setting out, the wind swung hard into the northwest, so that I was again grinding into its teeth.

As always, there were diversions, both internal and external. Even in hard wind or snow flurries, I would find myself—for twenty minutes, for an hour—poring over the periods and places of my life, the people and pressures and possibilities. I had recently lost my father and often found myself reviewing our ties and antipathies; or the intense connection I share with my children; or scenes from my lapsed marriage, including the extended Mexican standoff of its final days. The memories surfaced in fragments mixing with images of the day's walk into a kind of waking dream—of ravens, sunlight, trains; moose and moose bones; half-forgotten books, old friendships, the sum of life's messes and miracles.

Just at the point I was buried deepest within, a duck would whirr up out of the ditch or a raven would dive down in front of me and hop along the shoulder with his head cocked, checking me out.

Of the many creatures I met along the way, the ravens were by far the most sociable and would often accompany me for several kilometres, resting in the spruce trees as I caught up with them, then swooping around me and flying on ahead. That afternoon, east of the Pic River, one joined me with a squawk, and I squawked back, initiating an exchange that continued, off and on, for several kilometres, when to advance the conversation, I shouted, "Hey!"

The corvids are said to be the most intelligent of birds—to have a disproportionately large hyperstriatum, the equivalent of the human cerebral cortex—and I had known since I kept a crow in the early 1980s that both crows and ravens are capable of mimicry. But it took me by surprise when, apparently just to keep the conversation going, the raven above me shouted out a clearly discernible "Hey!"—and another when I did not respond immediately.

And so began a dialogue that contained the vocalizations *ya, yo, quack, eeek,* and *honk.*

I had no illusions. My friend was attracted to me not because he or she craved my inspired conversation, but because, like all human beings, I represented garbage. No other creature in nature has shown the raven's ingenuity for exploiting its association with humanity. In their obsessive scavenging, ravens have been known to keep watch on travelling fishermen or hunters for days over hundreds of kilometres, waiting for butchered or filleted carcasses. They cruise landfill sites, patrol the streets on garbage day, ransack Dumpsters, and monitor the highways for roadkill. Ravens are such inveterate survivors that during severe winters in the far north, when little food is available, they have been known to follow dog teams and fight over the dogs' steaming dung. They bustle around in blizzards and fifty-below temperatures searching out a stray french fry or two behind a McDonald's restaurant or digging into a snowbank to locate a garbage bag. Because of their toughness and their Harley-black uniforms, they are sometimes referred to as "the bikers of the bird world." But they are athletes, too, superlative flyers that have been filmed soaring for fifteen minutes on a single updraft, as well as performing somersaults in mid-air, or "barrel-rolling"—behaviour thought to be related to mating.

One thing nature did not give these amazing birds is the capability to cut through mammal hide with their beaks, so that with roadkill they must either hope for a tear in the skin or wait until another scavenger—a vulture or fox, for example—tears into the carcass. The raven's reputation for eating the eyes of young animals, or dead animals, was historically thought to be a function of the bird's morbid or occult nature, but is in fact nothing more than its inability, initially, to penetrate the animal elsewhere.

LATE IN THE AFTERNOON as I plowed toward the Pic, an unmarked Ontario Provincial Police cruiser came along the shoulder toward me (the woods, as Kerouac noted, are full of wardens).

"Hi," I said to a young woman in uniform—I believe a trainee—who rolled down the passenger-side window.

"Did you have a breakdown?" said the young man driving.

"Not a mechanical breakdown," I told him.

"Have you got a vehicle?"

"I'm walking."

"I see that."

After a long day of blisters and rain, and the occasional hard gut ache, I wasn't in the mood for whatever sort of dalliance was on the menu and demanded to know what I could do for the pair.

"You can tell us where you're coming from and where you're going."

"Coming from Thunder Bay. Going to New York City."

There was a cartoon silence while the two of them pondered this, and the young man said, "Did you know you're heading in the wrong direction?" I might have reminded him, as I had recently noted in my diary, that there is, as the Buddhists say, no "wrong" direction, only the long road and the longer one. But not anxious to stand any longer in the cold, or to annoy them, I settled for an explanation of what I was up to, about my support vehicle and about walking this stretch in reverse.

"So you aren't actually walking to New York," said the cop.

"No, actually I am," I said.

"Are you staying in Marathon?"

"At the Pic Motel."

"Is your driver there?"

"I have no idea."

"Well," the guy said finally, "we're sorry to bother you, but we get a lot of transients coming through, and you didn't look like a transient."

In retrospect, I took his comment as strange, in that I *was,* in fact, a transient—literally, for a change, instead of just philosophically or professionally. Indeed, for the first time in perhaps thirty years, I was genuinely of no fixed address. En passant. Nevertheless, it occurred to me to wonder what I did look like if not a transient, and what would have happened *had* I looked like one.

If there was small retribution in all this, it lay in the fact that throughout our conversation I had had to keep my head virtually inside the open window just to hear what they were saying above the wind and the sound of rain on the car roof. At the stooped angle, my sinuses had begun to run, and as I raised my head, a streamer of mercifully clear mucus fell free and splashed into the window slot in the cruiser door, well noted by the female cop—and noted again, with dismay, as she raised the window, painting a perceptible line of half-frozen snot down the middle of the glass.

THE WEATHER FORECASTS continued to feature tornadoes in Ohio, snow drifts in Marathon, gale-force winds in Thunder Bay. So it was almost a relief to be peering into nothing more than cold dense fog as I slogged toward White River the following morning.

And it was an unqualified grace note to see, mid-morning, a magnificent bull moose, with half his winter coat intact, clamber up out of the ditch perhaps a hundred metres in front of me, look my way, and lope across into the spruce forest on the far side of the highway.

The sight went a way to erasing the memory of four grisly moose legs sawn neatly off below the knee and discarded in the ditch about five kilometres east of my starting point—and a perfect little fox carcass a few kilometres farther up the road. And a dead porcupine, indistinguishable at five metres from the twisted head of an industrial push broom. And a scattering of green garbage bags—three or four dozen of them—that I suspect had been thrown off a pickup truck and pulled open by ravens or perhaps bears. Plus all the packaging and car parts and of course the "piss bottles" tossed out by the truckers, which on the Trans-Canada between Marathon and White River, are the most prevalent item of roadside contamination. They are out there by the hundreds—one litre, two litres—full of pale yellow urine or bright yellow or tea brown or rose-petal pink, giving me reason to wonder about the health of some truckers' bladders and kidneys. I was also moved to consider how the truckers, many of whom cannot see over their paunches, manage, at 120 kilometres per hour, in the dark, in their trembling cabs, to urinate into the one-inch neck of a plastic pop bottle. I know enough about male anatomy to understand that even the daintiest of truckers would be (quite literally) hard-pressed to fit his appliance into the constricted neck of such a bottle.

But it was not until late the next afternoon, in the parking lot of the White River Motel in White River as I was talking with an easygoing trucker named Gerry Ferrier that I thought to ask how he and his confreres got the yellow stuff into the bottle. Without hesitation, he threw open the door of his truck and produced from beneath the seat a sado-masochistic-looking contraption of half-centimetre rubber tubing, in appearance a sort of cross between a catheter and the tubing on a home distillery unit. A two-litre bottle (half full) was corked onto one end of it, while the other end bore a forbidding rubber funnel— yellowed, warped, undoubtedly a septic disaster zone—the purpose of which required no guesswork.

When the sun came out twenty minutes later, George and I, who were settled in the White River Motel, crossed the Trans-Canada, went down into the old part of town to the railway station, and on a whim walked east along the tracks into the forest. The mild air and sunshine were a sweet and drunken dream after the days of sleet and snow, and the railway quickly tucked in along the north bank of the White River (a body of iron-black water that in the annals of nomenclature must be among the all-time elite of oxymorons). Loons and ducks slipped purposefully over the half-frozen surface, and at one point near a high-water swamp, the knock of a pileated woodpecker came in atop frog voices in a symphony that might have been improvised from the avant-garde compositions of Stockhausen or Philip Glass. Moose and wolf tracks lay as neat as field-guide samples in the sand of the rail bed, and twice we saw brimming piles of bear scat seeming to contain at least a chomp or two of fresh grass and browse. Despite the total absence of either new grass or browse along the highway and in the woods, this was not quite the mystery it might sound. Most locally educated bears know an early spring meal awaits them on the strip of thawed ground that covers the Trans-Canada gas pipeline just north of the highway—a strip that because of the heat in the gas line, is free of snow by early March and green with life by early April. Naturally, this Canada-wide banquet also feeds winter-famished mice, rabbits, deer, and moose, which in turn become a feast for opportunistic owls, hawks, foxes, wolves, and ravens—a carnage that extends eventually down the food chain to flies and their revolting alter egos, maggots.

In Europe, what we were doing would have been called a "trespass walk"—that is to say a walk through territory where walking is against the law, as it certainly is along the CN and CP railways. And for good reason. You could do serious damage out there—could dislodge a rail or rail tie, or fiddle with a switching mechanism, with deadly results.

Or you could get yourself walloped by a train—as we nearly proved where the tracks cross the river on a narrow bridge about three kilo-metres east of White River. Rather than cross the bridge, I wandered down the embankment and was luxuriating in the sun as Curious George ambled slowly out along the rails. When he was about halfway across, I caught a glimpse of a great dark freight dieselling through the forest toward us, its rumble muffled by dense spruce and wind—and by frogs—as well as by the rush of water beneath the bridge. "George!" I called, "there's a train coming!" which brought from him such an insouciant glance that I knew he hadn't heard me.

"Get off the bridge!" I hollered. "There's a train coming!" At which point the engine exploded out into the clearing, and George, after glancing into the water (thinking to jump?), came crashing like a full-back toward me, his pipe a mini-Vesuvius, his feet gobbling up the rail ties more nimbly than I might have imagined. As in a scene out of some wretched old duster of a movie, he reached the end of the bridge and sprawled rolling onto the gravel embankment, pipe now in hand, as the big diesel clattered on through with its whistle blaring.

THE FOLLOWING MORNING, I was up with the alarm for the second of my chats with Lisa Lacko at CBC Radio in Thunder Bay. Having vented, with dismissive conviviality, my frustrations over the weather (as I spoke, snow was again driving past the window), I told her about George's near miss with the train, and then about coming into White River the previous day and checking out what had appeared to be a suitable dive of a motel outside town. I had pulled out my Visa card in the office, and handed it to the woman in charge who, in the process of running it through, asked casually if I was "with Hydro."

"No," I told her, "I'm with George."

"Is that a company?" she said solemnly.

"An individual," I told her. "My driver. I'm walking."

She paused and said primly, "You're walking?"

"To New York," I said, at which point, without missing a beat, she removed the Visa slip from the machine, ripped it in half, and said, "That'll be cash, sir."

Having no cash in my pocket, and being suddenly less captivated by the flophouse in question, I did a military 180 and took my much-cherished business over to the well-scrubbed, friendly (and equivalently priced) White River Motel, from where, even as I broadcasted, the parking lot was filling up with idling transports whose drivers were unwilling to risk the build-up of fresh ice on the Trans-Canada.

Not so I, of course.

Walk Man.

Dressed in thermal underwear, five or six layers of upper-body cotton, fleece, and nylon, plus toque, scarf, and hiking boots—and with a softball-sized lump of hankies and Kleenex in my jacket pocket—I got George to drive me perhaps thirty-five kilometres southeast of White River, from which point I would again attempt to cheat the elements by walking back into town with the wind.

Needless to say, you do not "cheat" a pestilence-level crosswind, driven ice pellets, and a wind chill that brought the temperature to perhaps –20°C.

Within minutes, ice had begun to settle on my eyelids, my fleece gloves were wet and then frozen solid, and my nose was draining a witch's brew that, by comparison, made the standard occult cauldron seem positively appealing. Moreover, the Moleskin pads that I had (against all advice) so carefully poulticed in around my blisters had slipped free and were bunching into the toes of my boots.

Had it not been so cold and the ache in my joints so profound, I might have taken it all for a joke, some pathetic Chaplinesque cartoon masquerading as a page out of my fifty-fourth year. But on that morning, more than most, a kind of pathos seemed to curl in around me, a despondency not just at being out there in the cold, but at being someone for whom it was even half-*plausible* to be out there, middle-aged, sick, walking from somewhere to somewhere, by choice, on such a day. Time and again, I had heard myself explain—to reporters, broadcasters, skeptics—that the walk would restore life rhythms lost or compromised by decades of technology and speed, would recall the pace of an earlier generation of travellers.

But after two weeks of tough sledding, the venture, with brief exceptions, had inspired little more than an inkling of the grimmest possibilities that must have confronted our forebears on their travels from farm to farm, town to town, or on their map-making and rail-building ventures. Or confronted early woodland aboriginals as they set out during a first thaw to find last year's rosehips or berries or, in a dire season, to beat the ravens to frozen deer or caribou carcasses. It is said that in times of malnutrition the early tribes' craving for edible vegetation was so great that late-winter or early-spring hunters would slit open the stomach of a fresh-killed caribou and devour a semi-digested slaw of lichens normally undigestible by human beings.

George reminded me daily that the locals—more precisely, a guy back in Schreiber—had said the weather wouldn't improve till the end of the month, maybe not at all this year. My response to which was, Sure it will! And if it doesn't, who cares? In a couple a' days, we'll be outta here, headed south.

As for my sense of the recuperative mantra of putting one foot in front of the other, of having nothing else to think about but walking, the reality was, so far, less an invocation to inner balance than a succession of endless sniffles and snot-clearings, of attempts to adjust my footfall so as not to tear up my slowly healing blisters—of uncontrollable shivers, viral sweats, gut aches, 222s, Pepto-Bismol, and dreams of hot baths, warm beds, hot soup, soft chairs, dry air.

"And women," George had told me the previous day. "Don't forget women."

A few days earlier, I had invented for George a fantasy woman, Gloxinia—poet, artist, model—who would be waiting for us, soft-lipped, open-armed, at the next motel or town, or would be coming along at any minute in her convertible T-bird with a picnic lunch, bringing sunshine and soul. Only occasionally, however, did we catch glimpses of her—in a car, in a house window, on the shoreline, as elusive as the sirens.

George, by the way, had packaged up his Odyssean letter to Ann Klefstadt in Minnesota and had sent it off with one of his artfully hand-bound books, urging Ann to join us as we made our way south.

In addition to whatever else was going on in my head, I had realized by this time that I had perhaps too lavishly spread the notion of the pleasure and value of doing something not because it is rational or explicable but because it is *ir*rational, unaligned, based not on utility but on faith. As it was, I had to keep reminding myself to *have* faith, to indulge adventure, to reject a sense of meaninglessness and despondency. The more faith I had, certainly, the more it occurred to me that the meaning of what I was doing lay in the thing itself, in the process and exploration, and not in some abstract overlay concocted for a world that seemed always to require a rationale.

EVEN WHEN EVERYTHING WAS MOST ABJECT, there were, of course, sustaining episodes, moments of inspiration and enlightenment—or, occasionally, intense excitement.

That morning, early, as I walked beside a three- or four-metre-high rock cut, I sensed the subtlest of movements above me, glanced up from under the peak of my cap, and saw looking down a predatorially wide-eyed lynx, long legs torqued to spring, head well extended over the rock ledge. I am, to say the least, uncomfortable around wild carnivores, particularly cats, and my first instinct was to vamoose. With no conscious thought, and with adrenalin exploding into my limbs and throat, I leapt sideways toward the asphalt, at which point the cat sprang up, half putting its brakes on, but not quickly enough to prevent itself vaulting down over the rock ledge onto the gravel, pausing for a moment, staring at me, front paws spread, before tearing off down the shoulder and disappearing into the spruce woods. The episode left my heart racing, even though reason told me that no lynx would ambush an animal as big as an adult human being. Months later, when I mentioned the encounter to a Native acquaintance from Nakina, he told me I was lucky, that a hungry lynx would certainly take on a human being, at least from an advantaged position, and that one had come down out of a tree onto a friend of his, an experienced woodsman, and had left deep claw scars in the friend's face and head.

Twenty minutes later, a red compact car, clearly a veteran of the pothole wars, pulled off the highway coming toward me, and stopped a few metres from where I was walking. A woman of perhaps forty stuck her head out and said, "I heard you on the radio, and thought I'd come out to say hello and wish you good luck." Her name was Sarah, and she lived in Thunder Bay, but was working in White River for a day or two and had expected to find me barely outside town walking east. I explained why I was where I was, and she said gaily, "I thought you were cheating!" And with a beep of the horn, she made a U-turn on the highway and was gone into the flying snow.

Under the circumstances, I felt genuinely touched that with nothing to gain, on such a miserable day, she had driven a round-trip distance of seventy or eighty kilometres to show me her goodwill. But in the weather and the compressed sentiment of the moment, I had found little more to say to her than "Thank you so much," and that I appreciated her thoughtfulness.

Despite our differences, George, too, provided inspiration—for example, in his recent description of our project as a "performance piece," a kind of cutting-edge work of abstract art. Which I liked, inasmuch as the walk was, indeed, an elaborate piece of staging, complex in its dimensions and (for me, at least) dreamlike in its protracted time and distance. George was particularly impressed by the preparation that had preceded the walk and had become integral to its enactment and documentation: the phones, the clothing, the gear, the maps, the radio reports, the accommodation, the endorsement of Penguin Canada, the hotel at the end of the line—and perhaps above all, the exaggerated assumption that it could be done.

The fact that a scrawny middle-aged man was actually out on the highway walking seemed at times the smallest part of it all. And yet it was the tenuous thread on which it all hung.

It is indicative of how esoteric a notion long-distance walking has become in this culture that it has been transfigured, quite literally, into performance art by the likes of Marina Abramovic and (the single-named) Ulay, Eastern Europeans who, during the early 1980s, did a number of what they called "performance walk pieces." The pair's masterpiece was perhaps their Great Wall Walk, for which they began at opposite ends of the 4,500-kilometre Great Wall of China and walked toward one another until they met in the middle some ninety days later. The irony of their walk was that by the time the artists met halfway, they had come to the realization that their relationship—the magnetic power of which was intended to be manifested by the performance—was over, and they went their separate ways.

Given the spousal strain George and I had both been embroiled in back home, it had seemed equally ironic when, a couple of nights earlier, George had proclaimed half-heartedly that our own version of the Great Wall Walk was "worse than a marriage," and he was now entangled in it to the point where he feared he was "going to have to start drinking," as he invariably did to help him cope in such relationships.

But he did not begin drinking. And he did cope. In fact, by the time we left White River, after two nights, we had achieved a modest truce—an understanding that the trip would happen as planned, that George was in for the long haul, and that we would do our best to stay out of one another's hair. We had shaken hands on it over dinner in the old Green Gables Restaurant, and solemnized it back at the motel with a slug of the rot-gut whisky that George had sequestered in his backpack for precisely such a joyful occasion.

3

Spring, the Sequel

Understandably, I did a fair bit of thinking about walking as I trudged along—about the fact, for example, that it is the most ancient, and still perhaps the foremost, way in which we measure our bodies against the earth. And in which our bodies measure and understand themselves. What's more, it has been essentially unimproved over millions of years. Beyond transportation, walking is history, politics, and culture. And metaphor and language: to walk in, to walk out, to walk on, to walk over, to walk away. A widow's walk, a sidewalk, a boardwalk, a catwalk, a cakewalk, a walkway, a walk-on, a streetwalker, a floorwalker, a walk in the park, the walking wounded, the walking dead—to walk the walk, to walk on air, to walk on water, to walk on eggshells, to walk the plank, to walk with God.

Betty's joke as I left Thunder Bay was that I had "walked out" on the marriage.

One morning near Obatanga Provincial Park, southeast of White River, I recorded on the back of a restaurant placemat not just the images listed above but the names of thirty-one song, book, or movie titles on the theme—among them, *A Walk in the Spring Rain, A Walk on the Wild Side,* "Walk in Jerusalem," "These Boots Are Made for

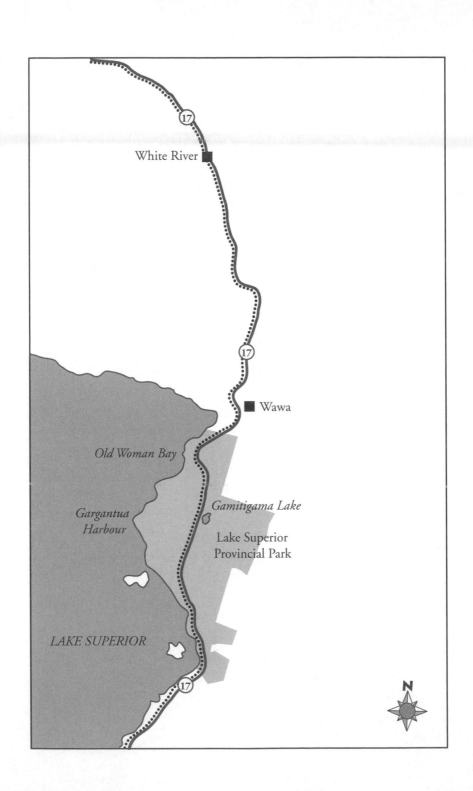

White River

17

17

Wawa

Old Woman Bay

Gamitigama Lake

Gargantua
Harbour

Lake Superior
Provincial Park

LAKE SUPERIOR

17

N

Walking," "Walking Blues," "Walkin' to New Orleans," "Just a Closer Walk," "You Gotta Walk That Lonesome Valley."

In the weeks leading up to my departure, I had read with fascination the books and essays of some two dozen writers or philosophers who had walked extensively and written about the meaning of movement on foot: Descartes, Rousseau, Wordsworth, De Quincey, Emerson, Thoreau, Dickens, Whitman, Gandhi, Frost, Steinbeck, Mao Tse-tung, Che Guevara, Jane Austen, George Sand, Virginia Woolf, as well as contemporaries such as Harry Crews, Edward Hoagland, Paul Theroux, Rebecca Solnit, and Annie Dillard.

Charles Dickens said, "If I couldn't walk fast and far, I would explode and perish." He is said, at times, to have walked all night, and once got up at 2:00 A.M. and walked fifty kilometres into the country before breakfast, at his customary pace of some six kilometres per hour.

The father of the Danish philosopher Søren Kierkegaard walked as many as a dozen kilometres a day *indoors,* pacing back and forth in a single room, imagining the outdoors and streets, and describing his "travels" to his infant son. The philosopher eventually took his father's passion into the streets of Copenhagen, where he was a familiar, benighted, sometimes scorned figure, who claimed to do all his writing on foot.

While Friedrich Nietzsche preferred what he called "the mental transport of long solitary walks," Virginia Woolf wrote of the release of stepping out after a day's work, "and becoming part of that vast republican army of trampers, whose society is so agreeable after the solitude of one's room."

Because for centuries writers have tended to be walkers, as well as the predominant reporters on their cultures and times—and because their work has tended to feature their own activities—we might be led to believe that the great walkers of history were mostly literary men or women. But this would ignore the countless farmers, soldiers, athletes, hikers, map-makers, mountaineers, lumbermen, hitchhikers, beachcombers, hunters, and tribesmen, most of whose prodigious walking has been left unreported, except perhaps orally or in local documents.

Howie Morenz, the most prolific professional hockey player of the 1920s and '30s—and a driven soul on the order of Dickens or Kierkegaard—often walked all night through the streets of New York or Chicago to deal with the stress of a lost game or season, or what he perceived to be deficiencies in his play. The avant-garde rock singer Patti Smith, who spoke of the "outlaw romanticism" of walking, once reported that to prepare for a concert she focused, went as deep as she could into her psyche and emotions, by walking sometimes for as much as four or five hours in whatever city she happened to be performing.

I found the inner experience of my own walk perhaps best summarized in the words of Jean-Jacques Rousseau, who in *Meditations of a Solitary Walker,* wrote, "Walking and the recounted walk encourage endless digression and association"—encourage, in other words, a freeing of the imagination.

The theme has been reiterated by Eric Nesterenko, a former NHL hockey player whom I once profiled, and who for a month every autumn hikes alone in the formidable mountains of the Wind River country of Wyoming. "When I'm out there, I have the most extraordinary dreams and flights of fancy," he told me one night as we walked through the streets of his hometown of Vail, Colorado.

The gist of Eric's thinking is that human beings need a lot of silence, and that we spend far too much time surrounded by electronic distractions—television, computers, recorded music, and the like. He calls these "a reality, but a very superficial one that demands little or no effort" and believes that, over time, they suppress the imagination. Walking, he says, reinvigorates it.

Nesterenko was also one of the first to realize that walking, as opposed to running or more strenuous exercise, can create a high level of cardiovascular fitness. "You get out there hiking thirty miles a day up and down slopes with a sixty-pound pack on your back, and it isn't long till the heart and lungs and muscles are working at pretty high efficiency."

WHILE AN ENDEAVOUR such as mine undoubtedly had an eccentric element, it is perhaps too easily forgotten that the history and pre-history of North America are themselves founded on walking. One school of thought suggests the tale began some ten thousand years ago with the passage of the earliest tribes across the frozen Bering Strait. Another speculates that prehistoric tribespeople arrived here by boat across the South Pacific. In either case, or both, what followed was an epic migration, on foot, to the farthest corners of both North and South America.

Because the migration probably spanned hundreds of generations, it might better be called an epoch than a journey, and there were undoubtedly mid-epoch tea breaks of two or three centuries or more.

Regardless of pace, for more than nine thousand years walking remained the tribes' sole means of transportation over land. Indeed it was the main transport for early generations of Europeans on this continent. Wheels and horses arrived in the sixteenth century with the Spaniards (it is a curious twist of historical fate that horses had existed in North America until just before the first tribes arrived, but for unex-plained reasons disappeared from the continent about 8,000 B.C.). However, many European settlers were, like my great-grandfather, too poor to own a horse or carriage. For the most part, the Natives, too, did without. The Inuit and northern Cree, for example, never had horses, and until perhaps the early twentieth century made little if any use of the wheel.

In Europe and the Middle East, a walk such as mine would, even as recently as 250 years ago, have been unthinkable. From perhaps 1,000 B.C. to the late 1700s, walking the countryside was simply too dangerous. During that time, thousands of men and women scrounged their livings by robbing, if not murdering, anyone naive enough to venture into the country on foot. Christ was by no means exaggerating the conditions of his day when he spoke of "a certain man who went down from Jerusalem to Jericho, and fell among thieves, which stripped him of his raiment, and wounded him, and departed, leaving him half dead."

It is hardly surprising that until nearly 1800, nature itself was seen not as an attraction or as a stimulus to renewal and meditation, as it is today, but as hostile and unknowable—a world to be tamed but by no means embraced.

As unlikely as it might seem, the primary agent of change in this attitude was neither sportsman nor explorer nor woodsman, but the English poet William Wordsworth, who during the early nineteenth century inspired his countrymen with vivid descriptions of his hikes through the English Lake Country. Rural walking, as he depicted it, was pleasurable, soulful, and redemptive—not an endurance but an embrace of nature.

Wordsworth is said to have walked a total of 400,000 kilometres. His friend Thomas De Quincey, whose book, *The Confessions of an Opium Eater,* might suggest a man less committed to the outdoors than to the recesses of the city, was an equally avid walker—is in fact credited with pioneering modern camping, having toured Wales on foot during the early 1800s, carrying a tent and bedding so that he could pitch camp in the fields or woods.

My route along the north shore of Lake Superior may well have been walked in its totality by prehistoric tribesmen, though the first recorded walk was Lagimodière's when he hoofed from Manitoba to Montreal to inform Lord Selkirk of brewing dissatisfaction among the Métis. However, at least one source records that he did part of the route on horseback, with a Native guide to show him the way and protect him.

If there were subsequent walkers over the north shore during the next century and a half, their names are lost to history. As extraordinary as it might seem, the next person to cover the route on foot was probably Terry Fox, who as every Canadian and millions of others know, skipped, hopped, and smiled his way from Newfoundland to Thunder Bay during the summer of 1981, raising money for cancer research. A few years ago, in a conversation with the late Dr. Cam Pearson, a former chief of surgery at Port Arthur General Hospital, I came upon a small but intriguing part of the Terry Fox story that had never been recorded. Dr. Pearson told me that in mid-July 1981, he was summoned to the hospital to have a look at a teenage boy who had been brought in with suspected pneumonia:

> They told me it was Terry Fox. But I'd been so terribly busy during the past few weeks, I'd been paying absolutely no attention to the media. So I didn't know who they were talking about. I was surprised when I got down there to find that this kid had an artificial leg, and *shocked* when he told me he was running across Canada. Meantime, everybody else was shocked that I didn't know who he was. They told me he'd lost the leg to cancer, and I looked at his chest X-ray and could see secondary lesions all over, and I thought, Oh, my, my, here he is with his lungs full of tumours, and he's running across Canada. I said to him, "You've got problems with your lungs; you've got to go into hospital." But he was very stubborn; he wouldn't let us check him in. He wanted to get back on the highway. I said, "At least stay overnight—we'll get some fluid off." And he agreed to do that. And the next day the cancer doctor here saw him, and we agreed he needed a biopsy. But we decided he should have it back home in British Columbia, where they could proceed with treatment. And that's how his run ended, in Thunder Bay.

UNLIKE NESTERENKO, I had of course abjured the sixty-pound pack for a load of about a kilo, in Gatorade, snacks, and medications. Even so, muscle was building in my calves and hips, and I was beginning to sense changes in my lungs and heart rate. I was also by this time ravenously hungry at all hours, the result, I assumed, of burning off increasing quantities of carbohydrates and converting ever more protein into muscle.

I set out for Wawa on the morning of May 12 knowing that my friends Dorothy and Peter Colby were driving from Thunder Bay to Grayling, Michigan, and would be coming along the Trans-Canada at some point that afternoon.

And sure enough, at about 2:30, they pulled up on the far side of the road, and I folded myself into their cozy GM Blazer, and we flew down the highway to a restaurant, where we ordered muffins and tea. My washroom visit a few minutes later was a kind of watershed, in that while I was blowing my nose, my sinuses produced an audible pop that resulted in a sudden change of pressure behind my nose and eyes. I will not linger on specifics, except to say that it was the as-yet-unrecognized beginning of a new phase of my freedom.

Dorothy is a fiction writer and newspaper columnist, her husband Peter an ichthyologist and world authority on pickerel populations— both are Michigan born. But on that day their enthusiasm was for how "really good" I looked (as far as I knew, I was still pretty sallow and emaciated) and how they wished I'd get an orange safety bib so that I could be seen better on the highway. They insisted in a nattery, parental way that in my charcoal-and-dark-blue rain gear, I was undif-ferentiable from the granite along the highway and that I had been almost invisible as they pulled up behind me. (I did eventually start wearing a loop of yellow crime-scene tape that I found by the highway near Montreal River Harbour.) Peter said that when he had jokingly told Betty he hoped they wouldn't run me down by accident in the fog, Betty had chirped, "Oh, let me drive!"—to which I responded in the spirit of her humour that with Betty at the wheel, I would undoubtedly be safer on the road than anywhere else.

In the car afterwards, Dorothy presented me with a dozen little bottles of brandy, Scotch, and liqueurs—prescription medicine to be taken as required at the first sign of shivers or a metaphysical sweat (or by George—by george—whenever he could think of a reason). I took my shoes off in the back seat, dried my feet, changed my socks, and felt briefly despondent as my friends pulled away, leaving me undifferentiable from my surroundings, on a cold afternoon under a sky the colour of old asphalt.

I stared for a while into the brimming Magpie River, just north of Wawa, and walked the last long uphill stretch to the turnoff that leads into town. While I had been walking, George spent several hours in the Wawa library, reading about local logging and mining and, for esoteric reasons not clear to me, boning up on the Russian Revolution. He reminded me during a quite splendid spaghetti-and-meatball dinner in the restaurant of the Wild Goose Motel that Lenin, Trotsky, and Marx had all been Jews, although the communist historians had never made much of it.

George was born to Ukrainian-Canadian parents, but was adopted at birth by a Métis couple from St. Boniface and has always considered himself Métis. My friendship with him was triggered by my review of his book of poems, *Finding Mom at Eaton's,* which among other things, details his adult search for his birth mother and his fleeting reunion with her by the bronze statue of Timothy Eaton in the old Winnipeg Eaton's store.

> Eaton's
>   place of sorrow!
>
> a short blond prim lady
> came up to me "… you must be George …"
>
> she was all I ever wanted her to be

George's interest in Judaism stems in part from his belief that Ukrainians and Jews are of distantly connected lineage. In fact, he attributes a degree of his own progress and (occasionally) preferred treatment in New York City during the early sixties to the fact that people assumed from his appearance and mannerisms that he was Jewish. It had been the key, for example, to his securing a first decent apartment for his wife, Winnie, himself, and their infant son, David, on Ninety-second Street. And to getting his job at the Kennedy Fine Art Gallery and gaining the confidence of the gallery's significantly Jewish clientele.

As we ate, he described to me his somewhat bold decision, in 1960, at the age of twenty-two, to move from Winnipeg to New York during Winnie's first pregnancy. At the time, George held a degree in fine art from the University of Manitoba, and in Manhattan he was happily, if anonymously, among painters, musicians, and writers. He attended jazz concerts, went to readings, enrolled at Lehman College, and of course worked at the gallery.

But for all his fascination with art, he never "fell hard," he said, for "the dominant aesthetic" of the era—for what he called "the huge sterile commentaries" and pop pieces of Roy Lichtenstein, Frank Stella, and Andy Warhol. Nor, because he had a wife and a child, did he, as he put it, "participate in the life of the flower children."

Even so, it had been a time of excitement and growth—very much the years before the fall, before the violence and relentlessness of New York got the better of him during the early seventies, before Winnie's breakdown, before he was beanballed by the realities of life as a middle-aged poet, artist, and musician.

Later that night in the motel room, where I lay half asleep, George lamented the passing of the New York he had known—a city of neighbourhoods, in which every little community had "a bar or two, a drugstore, a delicatessen, a shoe-repair shop, a coffee shop." Nostalgia of course isn't what it used to be, and we reminded ourselves that even during that easily idealized era when rents had been affordable, large parts of New York had been crime-ridden, garbage-strewn ghettoes.

"It was the energy that made it attractive," George said. "You could nourish yourself on it. You could walk miles in it. It was like theatre. In fact it *was* theatre."

I had last been in New York during the early 1990s on a writing assignment and was aware that the city was a vastly safer place than it had been thirty years ago. Yet part of my reason for choosing it as a destination now was that I knew its streets were as much as ever a stage for diversity, squalor, and grandeur—and of course, during the summer of 2002, for patriotic survivalism born of the losses of the previous September.

THE FOLLOWING DAY, it was warm enough that I set out for the first time wearing just a T-shirt and fleece pullover, although carrying a jacket. More important, it was warm enough that George and I were again ready to try tenting.

By mid-afternoon I had walked nearly forty kilometres south into Lake Superior Provincial Park, a vast boreal coastland covering several thousand square kilometres of mountains, forest, and beach.

When George picked me up near Lake Minjinimuntsung, we immediately began the search for a tenting spot—not as easy as it might sound in a park where the employees were on strike, meaning that the roads into its campsites and lakes were for the most part blocked by chained gates.

My preferred spot was at a place called Gargantua Harbour, fifteen kilometres west off the Trans-Canada along an ancient fish-camp road that winds and bumps over creeks and rock outcrops and through beaver swamps to one of the most remote and magnificent beaches on the north shore.

I had once stayed overnight at Gargantua with Betty and the kids as we travelled from southern Ontario to Thunder Bay, the five of us sleeping out on the beach by a bonfire under the stars on an uncharacteristically warm Labour Day weekend. I had returned alone for a few days a couple of years later, at a point when I needed both the risk and the reassurance of the wilds.

Unfortunately, when George and I got a hundred metres up the road, barely out of sight of the highway, we found that it, too, was gated and chained, spurring us into speculation, as we stood by the gate kicking gravel, as to whether or not the gate could be opened by force (the sort of activity on Crown land that two hundred years ago might have earned us a flogging, if not a year or two in jail). I was deeply exhausted from my walk, but finding a brisk second wind in the excitement of the peccadillo at hand, I took a hammer out of the tool box, walked over to the padlock and gave it two good whacks, the second of which deflected off the lock and gave my (good) knee a glancing but excruciatingly painful nick. "We need a bigger hammer," I complained. And as I hobbled around doing a passable simulation of the chicken dance, George smacked at the lock with the back side of our kindling hatchet.

What we needed, of course, was a bigger idea. Or at least a more intelligent strategy—and immediately, it seemed, we possessed one in the inspired notion that perhaps we could take one side of the double gate off at its unsecured hinges. This would require only a slight straightening of the gate post. Which would require just a few hundred heavy blows from the back of an axe and the modest excavation of perhaps a half-ton of gravel and a number of fifty-kilo stones from around the post. Which would be hardly any trouble at all, since we had wisely brought along a plastic slotted spoon for jobs just such as this.

That it all seemed a trifle tawdry was, in part, of course, because the Ontario Provincial Parks system, whose property we were attempting (unsuccessfully) to abuse, was one of the backers of my walk. While at this point, we had received no benefit from our association with the strike-bound parks, we would within days embark on a succession of free park visits during which we were treated with such generous goodwill as to make our current activities seem all the less savoury.

We were eventually rescued from ourselves by the appearance of a gear-packed SUV. The English driver, all jaw and derring-do, sprang out, took a look up the roadway, and intoned that he'd been going to "give Gargantua a shot," but that judging by the condition of the road, with its deadfall and potential washouts, "you'd have to be a blazing idiot" even to consider it.

Which was, of course, exactly what we'd thought, and within twenty minutes I found myself on my knees with a tire iron, levelling the gravel road into another lake, Gamitigama—a road ungated presumably because it led not just to the lake but up a mountain to one of the monumental telecommunications towers that you see in the Canadian wilderness.

We came quickly to a place on this new road where it was blocked with metre-high snowdrifts and, from there, carried the tent and supplies to a tidy little clearing on a wind-sheltered embankment within sight of an all-but-ice-free beaver pond.

Earlier in the trip, we had had, as noted, some difficulty finding a balance in the division of labour. At most times, I had not had the legs at the end of a day to carry anything in or out. Or to go fetch. And George, understandably, had resisted any pressure, imposed or imagined, to become the trip packhorse.

But today, in our pleasure at being back outdoors, we were intuitive in our divvying of the chores, pitched the tent without even the need to speak, and pursued our silent camaraderie into wood- and water-gathering, fire-lighting, the preparation of the camp and cooking sites.

Within the shadow of the hills, the sun disappeared precipitously, leaving our bivouac melancholy and dense with the smoke of wet spruce. In the cool evening air, we huddled by the fire, cobbling up a dinner of pork chops, rice, and reconstituted matsutake mushrooms.

In virtually every moment I spent on the site during the next day and a half, I was aware of a great blue heron, standing fishing in the shallows of the pond or from time to time rising—unfolding—like a great mechanized kite, to take fresh fish or frogs' legs to his brood. Woodpeckers and whisky-jacks fidgeted in the shadows, and at dusk a great grey owl swooped low over the campsite and perched on a nearby branch, where off and on well into the night, it crooned its spooky, prehistoric serenade. More exceptional, if less poetic, was the anachronistic sight of a few early mosquitoes flying dizzily across the remaining banks of snow.

For George, the night was a test not just of his tolerance for outdoor living in the cold but of the yet-uninitiated sleeping bag we had bought for him in Marathon—the magic carpet in which, cozily rolled, he anticipated soaring into dreamland. But not until he had first mummified himself in a flannel sheet and, further, in what was left of his threadbare old bag. Then, and only then, barely able to flex, did he shimmy into the well-padded womb of the Woods 452 Thermal and conk out.

It was a matter not so much of debate between us as of silent diplomatic grievance that George snores like a sawmill. On this night, however, I possessed a secret antidote, a natural anti-snoring prescription that would not have worked in any motel room, or for that matter outdoors, in most parts of the world.

You need to know that George had been much moved by the (movingly apocryphal) bear stories spun by the waitress back at the Wild Goose. Spring is a bad time for bears in northwestern Ontario. It is equally a bad time for any bug or beast that falls within the bear's dietary spectrum. Or builds flimsy-doored cabins or stores food or creates garbage, as does the oftentimes defenceless human being. For one thing, the bears are starved from the winter's hibernation. For another, there has not since the late 1990s been a legal spring bear hunt in these parts. So more hungry bears than ever were out there. If the waitress was to be believed, no one's children were safe. And no one's cabin or tent. Or peanut butter jar. Or dirty laundry. Or peace of mind.

As a measure of security, before bedtime, George had stowed our loose food in the cooler, and I had dutifully walked it to the van.

Now, in the tent in the dark, as his snoring ripped into—let us say collapsed—our modest mutual space, I said very quietly, "George, your snoring is going to attract the bear." This was, of course, not just any bear but The Bear, the mythic, nightmare, killer bear that swipes the walls out of tents, sets his locking dentation on an arm, leg, or skull, and draws his victim bawling and bleeding up the mountain— the bear that inflames the imaginations of waitresses and walkers.

The effect was magical.

The words were barely out of my mouth when George fell silent— and stayed that way for what must have been several hours.

And when he started up again, I had merely to re-administer the antidote to quiet him.

At one point, as I lay briefly awake, not snoring, he reached over, I believe in his sleep, touched me gently on the arm, and said, "Charlie, if you keep snoring you're going to attract the bear."

UP EARLY on the morning of May 14 and quick onto the road, I was almost immediately aware of a new vigour and energy. By ten o'clock I had not had to blow my nose once. The sun was warm, and at noon, atop a rock cut where I stopped for a rest and took my shoes off, I discovered, as usual, that the chafing inside my sock had peeled off an unholy-looking mess of skin. I carefully pulled it free and flicked it to the ground. However, instead of the customary pulpy pink beneath—a texture that, at its worst, had reminded me of watermelon flesh—I was elated to find a layer of dry, tender, almost normal-coloured skin.

I walked on through the afternoon, at one point removing my jacket and sweater, and treating my bare arms to a little sun. But it wasn't long before a cloud or two appeared, the wind off the lake grew cooler, and I had my fleece pullover and jacket back on and my hood up.

Even on the coolest days, I was often soaked within my gear—not from sweat, rain, or snow but, rather, from the condensation that developed when my body heat met the cold outside air across the membrane of my waterproof outerwear.

George eventually came out to meet me, and we drove back to Lake Gamitigama. By this time, my stomach was aching for food, and despite the relative warmth of the day, I was in a sensory funk from the long hours of wind. But when I had napped for half an hour, I felt sufficiently revived that I was able to accompany George on a grinding hike up the road behind the campsite to the mountaintop.

In a rip-snorting wind, we gazed westward over Lake Superior to Michipocoten Island perhaps sixty kilometres away, then snuggled into a wind-sheltered niche on the summit's southeast side. There, with the mountain falling directly beneath us, we sipped with civility at a pair of Dorothy and Pete's tiny bottles of French brandy and stared off toward New York City, across a landscape as soulful and intimidating as any I have ever seen.

On the way down we gathered armloads of loose birchbark, most of which we tucked pack-rat style into the van for eventual use as a fire starter.

How liberating it felt to be out of the motels! They'd been handy—in fact, had been our salvation. And they had been anything but expensive. I calculated loosely that the cost of nine or ten nights in motels along the north shore was, in total, about half the cost of a single night in the Warwick in New York. But the rooms were stuffy and dry—George and I had taken to keeping the windows open so wide that, at times, we might as well have been sleeping outside.

More important, the outdoors encourages bigger, more expansive thinking. Even the preparation of our meals, *cuisine brut,* felt freeing and rewarding after an enforced run of restaurants—as did sitting around jackpotting under the stars in the glow of the campfire. And compared to the dispiriting drone of the NHL playoffs on TV, it was as soothing as a lullaby to drift off to sleep listening to night creatures afoot in the forest, or a loon's call or a symphony of frogs. And was a treat nonpareil to awaken at dawn not to the nattering of the Weather Channel, with its endless forecasts of doom, but to the twittering of finches and warblers, and the sight of the spruce and mountain ash that, with the rocks, birches, and white pines, have for nearly fifty years been my sensory and ecological sustenance in the Precambrian wilderness.

ON THE MORNING of the fifteenth, I walked south from Gamitigama in a sporadic thunderstorm that, at a point during the late morning, was so intense it sent me scurrying under a rock ledge for fear that on the high ground of the highway I would be hit by lightning. For twenty minutes, I sat under several tons of granite on a damp slope of gravel, feeling forlorn and expendable, wondering whether if the plateau above me collapased I would be granted a narrow escape route, or would be trapped or simply crushed. The thought sent me back onto the road as soon as the lightning had moved far enough off that it posed less of a threat than the possibility of falling rock.

The hills of Algoma make for long steep ascents—sometimes of three or four kilometres—and as I laboured to the summits, I was obliged to accept that I was not over my flu. I will say for my muscles at this stage that they were doing more for me than I had expected. My calves were wood-hard and, in just sixteen days, were almost laughably bigger than they had been for the past twenty years. My rear end, a decades-long victim of gravity and sedentary work, and normally the consistency of blancmange, had added muscle in such a way that it was quite literally perched an inch or so higher on my thigh bones and pelvis than it had been when I started. This inspired the narcissistic habit of running my hands over my upper buttocks in appreciation of what was undeniably, again, a respectable ass. Moreover, my neoprene knee support had become notably tighter. At first I attributed this to its nightly washing. However, when I mentioned the shrinkage to a cyclist who had stopped on the highway to chat and who happened to be wearing an identical contraption, he laughed as if at a true duffer and said, "The support isn't getting smaller, man—your knee's getting bigger!" And he told me his own knees were twice the size they had been when he'd left Edmonton, heading east, at about the time I left Thunder Bay.

Sure enough, when I took a measurement that evening using a piece of string that I calibrated against an old carpenter's square in the toolbox, I found my knee had increased in circumference by more than two centimetres since I measured it on that dismal day in Nipigon.

All of this, I admit, was deeply satisfying, though not merely as a point of vanity at having achieved an infinitesimally better body (conspicuous flaws remained). What excited me was that my muscles and organs clearly still had the reserves to respond to a gruelling physical challenge. Like the old guy in the joke who has no complaints about his impotency, only about having no way to test it, I would have had no way to test the depth of my physical inadequacy or potential had I not set out on such a preposterous undertaking.

As a workout for my upper body, I occasionally did arm circles as I walked. Or if I saw a piece of steel at the roadside—an axle or shock absorber or brake drum—I would pick it up and swing it a hundred times and heave it back into the ditch. Or I would pick up an old tire, shake the water out of it, and simply carry it for ten minutes, sometimes above my head, to the delight, or dismay, of passing motorists.

That my anatomical clock was gradually cranking itself backwards was revealed to me most mysteriously by the fact that curly hair of a thickness that I had not seen on my body since I was in my twenties was sprouting wantonly on my calves and thighs and on my "groin," to use that genteel term from the sporting world. At first I took this as an illusion. If it was not, I reasoned, the hair must be proliferating as insulation or to prevent chafing. It was not until months later, when I mentioned it to a doctor, that I was told the intensity of my physical activity would have increased my testosterone production and thereby the hair, a secondary sexual characteristic, on my lower body. The theory also went a long way to explaining the persistently erotic, sometimes lurid, dreams I was having, some of them about girlfriends so far in the past that I did not even remember their names, or about women who had no names. In one of the strangest of those dreams, I was the lone man in a game of Red Rover, the battle line for which was formed entirely of bikini-clad women from the Mormon Tabernacle Choir, which I had watched briefly on television a few nights back.

When I quit each day, I would sit Indian-style by the fire with my Hudson's Bay blanket around me, covering head and all to trap the warm air, as I scarfed down a can of tuna or a half-pound of cheese, often with twenty or thirty soda biscuits and a litre or more of tea.

The food box was, by this time, a deli unto itself—stocked with sauces and condiments, exotic canned vegetables and fruits. And my five-gallon plastic cooler (refrigerated by a snap-lid container of snow, or by chunks of lake or river ice) held a fluctuating inventory of bread and fruit and dairy products. However, the buying of fresh food had become a low-glow flashpoint between George and me, in that we possessed such radically different tastes and dietary requirements. George eats like a Bedouin—a few gulps of air, a little tea, a beetle or two, a red ant for piquancy, a bit of camel's milk, a whiff of lemon (or in actual terms, an occasional sandwich or piece of fruit, a chunk of cheese, an egg, as well as tea and coffee or a beer or two). And he shops accordingly. There were days when he assumed quite innocently that I could get along on a few diced vegetables, a serving of rice, and a cup of tea. The gluttonous truth was that I needed five thousand calories a day to fuel my walking alone, plus vitamins and minerals, and a kilo or so of protein to maintain and build muscle. At Gamitigama, I developed the irredeemably piggy habit of opening a can of condensed milk at breakfast, putting half of it on a bowl of oatmeal porridge, with a handful of raisins, and glug-glugging the other half out of the can.

The one physical affliction that showed no sign of abating was the paralyzing leg and foot cramps that would hit me as I lay in my sleeping bag, usually when I was about to go to sleep. They were routinely so intense that I would have to leap to my feet—easier said than done in the dark in a sleeping bag with a paralyzed leg, in the confinement of half a tent—and put weight on the afflicted leg or foot until the cramping passed. Cramps are said to be a result of dehydration or loss of salts. But there were days when slopping back even six litres of water and Gatorade didn't result in a crucial restoration of the tissues.

LATE ON THE AFTERNOON OF THE FIFTEENTH, as I walked toward Katherine's Cove, a lumpish late-model black pickup—perhaps a

$40,000 vehicle, conspicuously over-engineered—lurched to a stop without pulling off the highway, and a young Native woman hollered out the passenger-side window, "Are you lost?"

"No, I'm fine, thanks," I said, to which the driver, a woman of perhaps forty, the oldest of three women in the front seat, responded, "Where you going?"

"New York City," I said.

There was a longish—let us say a pregnant—pause, then the younger passenger said with no hint of irony, "What year is it?"

"Nineteen fifty-seven," I said confidently.

Another pause, and more solemnly, "What province are you in?"

"Rupert's Land," I told them.

There was yet another pause, and quite suddenly they were laughing, seeming to allow that if I was crazy it was all right with them.

But the gaiety was short-lived, because at that moment an eighteen-wheeler came dieselling around the bend, horn blaring, and pulled out around them at such a speed that if a vehicle had been coming in the opposite direction, there would have been a terrible collision. "Get off the road!" I ordered the women, and the driver, who had never ceased smiling, eased two wheels onto the shoulder.

"How come you're walking to New York?" she asked.

"For my head," I said, and during the ensuing conversation, I mentioned that I intended to write a book about it.

It turned out they were sisters and a daughter, the Trouts, from Frenchman's Head, in extreme northwestern Ontario. The older sister, the mother, was an addiction counsellor, who had been to a seminar about fetal alcohol syndrome in Sault Ste. Marie, or the "Soo" as it is generally called.

They pulled away, and I had walked another hundred metres when I heard behind me an otherworldly whine, and turned to see the black pickup snaking down the highway in reverse, at perhaps eighty kilometres an hour, on the edge of control. When it jerked to a halt, the daughter poked her head out and shouted, "About that book! Put us

in it, will ya? It's T-r-o-u-t!" And away they went, squealing rubber like
I hadn't seen or heard since I was sixteen and used to floor my dad's
Oldsmobile at Fifth Street and York, in Cornwall, and deposit a stripe
that extended pretty much all the way to Sixth Street.

I caught up with George at about 6:00 P.M. at Sinclair Cove, where
you can follow a zigzag trail over the boulders and through a narrow
granite chasm down to Lake Superior. Unlike much of the wilderness
and rock in the area, this natural architecture hints at life that might
have passed this way hundreds if not thousands of years ago. The high
perpendicular walls, with their mossy patina, suggest tombs and
temples and mystic practice. Which is by no means out of sync with
the history of the place. The trail leads eventually to where the Lake
Superior surf thunders in ten metres below you, and signs point the
way along a treacherously sloped rock face that must be crossed if you
want to see the Ojibway pictographs that are thought to have been
painted onto the cliff face overhead as long ago as 900 or 1000 A.D.

On this particular afternoon, the waves were throwing up an intimidating roar, as well as ten-metre lashings of spray. George did not
want to risk the twenty-metre trip along the rock, which would have
been, at best, the equivalent of crossing a steep slate roof on an icy day
with nothing to hold on to but a few rusted bolt heads. If you slipped,
you were in the drink—being hammered onto granite boulders. Signs
in both official languages—neither of which, incidentally, addressed
the people who had painted the pictographs and had been here for
some 8,000 years before the official inhabitants showed up—warned
that visitors had died here by slipping into the water. But I was too
curious not to wriggle out along the rock slope, doing my best not to
glance down.

Eventually, clinging like a suction toy, I reached a series of small,
slightly faded images that, judging by appearance, might have been
painted with automotive base coat or rustproofing—a horse and rider,
a pair of snakes, a canoe bearing what appeared to be four beachballs
but were probably suns or moons. The most inspired figure was a

chimerical animal with a dog's head and spiky protrusions, like sturgeon fins, along its backbone. The paint is thought to be pulverized hematite mixed with animal fat or, as the poet Al Purdy speculated, with fish eggs and bear grease—"Imagine pitting fish eggs and bear grease against eternity." The story told by the images has been interpreted as that of a triumphal Ojibway war or hunting party, but it is impossible that anyone knows for sure. Purdy's satisfaction, like my own, lay in the fact that while the endeavours of the warriors and hunters are lost to the centuries, the work of the artist survives.

THE EXIGENCIES OF THE PAST couple of weeks had all but denied me the immense stimulation, and the endless small epiphanies, that typically accrue to me during time spent along the shores of Lake Superior. But the force had begun to come back, the stab to the heart that comes as you crest a hill and see the lake spread before you—the wildness of its shoreline; its vast and icy self-sufficiency; and its tendency, like the ocean's, to dwarf and bring perspective to human endeavour.

When the sun is out, the light over Superior is as hard and bright as the ice cap. The light *beneath* the waves, however—the half-light—is as dusky a medium as one is likely to encounter among the earth's bodies of fresh water. For sailors, Superior is a mythology unto itself, incorporating thousand-year secrets, the ghosts of old ships and drowned seamen, and the gales and cataclysms that put them where they are. Superior is the eeriest of the Great Lakes, inasmuch as the remains of those who drown in it are generally never found. The reason for this is that the gases created when a drowned body begins to decompose—gases that eventually bring the body to the surface— do not form in Superior. The water is simply too cold to support the necessary bacteria. The Michigan novelist Jim Harrison has speculated on the possibility that aboriginals who drowned in the lake centuries ago may still be down there, in effect cryogenically preserved.

Divers who during the mid-nineties explored the wreck of the *Edmund Fitzgerald,* which sits about twenty kilometres offshore from

Sinclair Cove, are said to have reported discreetly that those on board looked much as they must have on the night they went down.

Ships are down there by the hundreds, and because shipping routes on the Great Lakes tend to be relatively narrow, sailors are constantly passing directly over the spectres and wreckage of the past. Superior holds as much water as the other Great Lakes combined, and yet even here on the so-called Inland Sea, the connection between the surface and the depths is anything but remote. In fact, there is just one small area of Superior—a four-hundred-metre-deep trench near the Michigan shore—where the distance between boats afloat and the ghost hulks and corpses on the bottom is greater than the two-hundred-metre length of the average modern freighter. Toward the west end of Lake Superior, off the Minnesota shore, there is said to be a wreck that sits on end in some two hundred metres of water, so that its stern rises to within a few metres of the surface. When I heard I could not help considering what it might be like to cruise over it unawares in a small boat on a summer day and suddenly see its monstrous deathly presence beneath the waves.

FOR ALL LAKE SUPERIOR has meant to both its sailors and its shore dwellers over the centuries, its reputation today is most prevalently that of the world's largest single supply of fresh water, about a twentieth of the fresh water available to humanity. We are reminded regularly that drinkable water will be the "oil of the twenty-first century," or "blue gold," as Maude Barlow called it—although to call it either seems almost to curse it, to associate its debut as a global commodity with the sort of greed, violence, and ecological devastation that have typically accompanied the extraction of fossil fuels and precious metals from the earth. With per capita supplies of fresh water shrinking relative to surging populations and industry, and in an era of globally threatening climatic changes, Canada is in an almost inconceivably privileged position. Of the world's total supply of water, just 2.6 percent is fresh. But more than half of that is locked up in ice caps and icebergs, leaving just over 1 percent of the world's water available for human use. Canada controls—or controls jointly with the United States—more than 20 percent of what's available, a good part of it within view of where George and I were standing at Sinclair Cove. Yet our population is less than a half of 1 percent of the world's total. It is the sort of vastly inequitable distribution of wealth that has been known to trigger wars, and may yet threaten Canadian sovereignty as the need for fresh water gets more desperate, particularly among the water-desperate rich of Los Angeles, Arizona, and Silicon Valley.

The question is, Will the American and Canadian joint commission that currently protects Superior allow this greatest of natural resources to be "privatized" and consumed by the parched cities and corporations of the south (both NAFTA and the World Trade Organization advance the notion of water as a global commodity to be bought and sold subject to market forces)? Or will it resist the demands of affluent golf-course and swimming-pool owners, and use its influence democratically to help ensure that people everywhere have access to good water, that ecosystems are not fatally weakened or destroyed in what may become a kind of gold rush to make wealth out of water?

Goodbye Superior

It had long been part of my plan to spend a night or two at Montreal River Harbour, where my old friend Shaun Parent runs his Lake Superior Climbing school in a renovated antique lodge, once called the Trail's End Inn but now the Mad Moose. Shaun is a renowned international climber (Andes, Alps, Rockies, Himalayas) who is pretty much acknowledged to be the founder and patriarch of ice climbing in northwestern Ontario and the north-central United States. His round face is a perpetual study in curiosity, and his somewhat eccentric personality is what might be expected of a man who has devoted his life to scaling cliff faces and frozen waterfalls. His C.V. reads like a script treatment for half a dozen episodes of *Mission Impossible*. He has twice been caught in gun battles between Peruvian police and members of the Shining Path Maoist guerrillas, spends part of each year leading pack mules into the remote Andes on hazardous geological assessment missions, and has done stunt work on the Batman films.

When George and I walked into the lodge a few hours after visiting the pictographs, Shaun was sitting studiously behind the computer at the main desk, wearing his customary bright garments, making plans

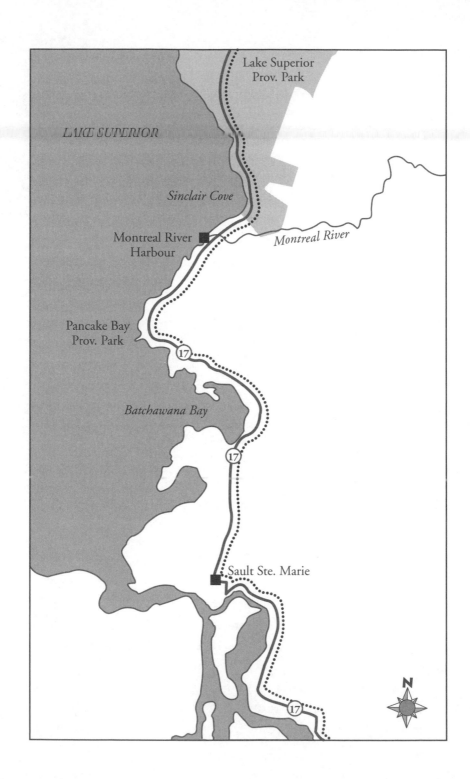

Lake Superior
Prov. Park

LAKE SUPERIOR

Sinclair Cove

Montreal River
Harbour

Montreal River

Pancake Bay
Prov. Park

(17)

Batchawana Bay

(17)

Sault Ste. Marie

(17)

N

for the arrival of a couple of dozen rock climbers expected the following weekend. He established his business at the lodge in 1999 as a tenant under previous ownership. But since early 2002, he has had an owner's stake with a trio of sedulously sporting Americans in their early forties, who, fed up with what life had become for them in Toledo and Columbus, Ohio, cast their lot with the Canadian wilderness. Since then, they have quite cheerfully been running themselves ragged—painting, plumbing, wiring, drywalling, landscaping, not to mention melting credit cards and writing thick heaps of cheques in order to transform the old resort.

We had no sooner said our hellos to Shaun when another of the owners, Jim Smallridge, emerged from the kitchen with the words "You guys must be hungry!" (correct). Jim's appearance suggested a compact hybrid of Henry Winkler and James Dean, and within minutes we were tucking into bowls of his fiery Cajun gumbo, a dish so *mucho de mucho gusto* that after a third bowl, I found myself thinking solemnly about a fourth.

The other two owners, Denny Thomas and Darlene Sikora, had been out all day transplanting fifty waist-high evergreens from the forest into the area around the Mad Moose's half-dozen cabins. But at 11:00 P.M. or so, they ghosted in and, when introductions had been made, we all sat down to what for George and me was our second unreconstructed belly-packer in a little over two hours. This second sitting featured Jim's mighty monster meat loaf, which *en forme* bore a passing resemblance to a rugger ball and which he served in inch-thick crosscuts with french fries, tossed salad, and baked beans.

While each of the owners had specific and preferred responsibilities, the appearance of the place was unquestionably the domain of Darlene Sikora, a sandy-haired former nurse, attentive and charitable in her ministrations but with a discernible layer of chain link beneath her unflappable surface. She had painted sky and clouds onto the dining room ceiling and a kind of fieldstone pattern onto the staircase leading to the main-lodge bedrooms—had brought in tree branches, driftwood, moose bones, rocks, feathers, all of it more or less in keeping with what the decorating mags might call "wilderness charm." Darlene had been a working medic when she met Denny during the early 1990s. To come north, she had given up her home, her social life, and her beloved herb, flower, and fruit garden—all of it now a memory measured against the satisfactions of living beneath forty-metre pines, waking up in the little cabin she and Denny occupied, and looking out at the lake or at an occasional moose or wolf that might have wandered out of the wilderness. Or watching the daily spectacle of the setting sun, visible fifty kilometres wide from the front windows of the lodge.

Nowhere on the north shore is Lake Superior more spectacular or nuanced than it is here at Montreal River Harbour. Nowhere is it more paradoxical in its embodiment both of a safe harbour and of a perilous navigational hitch. The river, whose mouth is visible from the lodge's front deck, spills out of the Algoma hills with such bullying weight that it throws up wild tufts of spray and metre-high standing waves where it hits the incoming wash of Superior as much as forty metres offshore. Beyond sunsets, one of the most stirring features of the view from the lodge's deck is the stygian black streak, perhaps twenty metres wide, that the iron-rich river paints as far as the eye can see out into Superior. The turbulence is so great at the river's mouth that during each of the resort's six previous ownerships, drownings have occurred when boats were unable to ride out the chaos.

Which pretty much characterizes Superior—grandiloquent in its beauty but capable in an instant of humbling, if not destroying, both the amateur canoeist and the experienced ship's captain and their craft (a hundred or more ships, including the *Edmund Fitzgerald,* have gone down over the years within sight of where the lodge stands).

The harbour, which can accommodate boats as long as thirteen metres, is one of just a half-dozen secure havens on a thousand kilometres of Superior's north coast. Its entrance lies entirely within Mad Moose property but, by federal law, it must be made accessible to any boat requiring shelter in bad weather—or for that matter, any weather.

On account of a hydroelectric dam just upriver, it is unlikely that lake trout or salmon any longer use the Montreal River to spawn. However, they assuredly did during the early nineteenth century, when according to a Thunder Bay biologist, trout were so abundant in Superior that they comprised as much as half of the lake's entire faunal mass. But with the opening of the Welland Canal during the mid-1800s, lamprey eels moved inland past Niagara Falls, and by the mid-twentieth century had wiped out Superior's lake trout, destroying not only a multi-million-dollar commercial fishery but a harmonious ecology that had existed in the lake for close to ten thousand years. Today, lake trout exist in Superior only because "lampricides" are used persistently around the mouths of the rivers where trout go to spawn. Thanks to such nifty chemical intervention—and as photos at the lodge attest—thirty-pound lakers can still be caught in the local waters, apparently untainted by chemicals.

WHEN THE DINNER DISHES had been cleared away, Denny, Darlene, and occasionally Jim sat with George and me at the long table by the windows swapping hard slants on topics ranging from the desecration of the American wilderness to the War on Terrorism to what it had meant to them to uproot in mid-career and, as Darlene put it, "pursue a dream."

Despite their abhorrence of the Trade Tower attack, the Ohio natives had nothing but contempt for American foreign policy under George W. Bush, whom Denny referred to as "worse than an embarrassment." They did not believe in what Darlene called "bombing the shit out of Afghanistan" or in arming the world and then disarming it with cruise missiles. Denny was appalled by the relative absence of political dissent, particularly on U.S. campuses, where in his day (and in my own) such expression had been a fundamental political and social rite of passage.

George, who had at first been somewhat skeptical about these three American expatriates for having "colonized" yet another chunk of Canada, was by now quite enamoured of them and would refer to them later as "ecological refugees" seeking a form of asylum north of the border.

At one point, Denny rhapsodized eloquently—and I thought ideal-istically—about Canada's "pristine environment" and the country's attitude toward its wilderness. He said that if the nearby pictographs were in the United States, "there'd be a paved trail to them or a souvenir stand, or they'd be behind glass or would be out of bounds altogether." I reminded him that the cultures that had created such art had been mauled just as badly on this side of the border as the other, and that of all state and provincial jurisdictions in North America, Ontario was the fourth worst polluter—as flagrant in the towns of northwestern Ontario as anywhere.

BEFORE HEADING SOUTH the next morning, I walked east along an old logging road to where Shaun was preparing climbing sites on a high diabase palisade. He had come to Montreal River Harbour knowing there were at least two climbs in the vicinity, had since discovered 250 more, and made "first ascents" on all of them. At one point, I caught a glimpse of him across the treetops, dangling from a rope high on a cliff, as tiny as a Playskool figure, and heard the chink of his hammer blows echoing down the chasm like a wind chime.

For reasons impossible to fathom, mossy sections of old-growth white pine nearly a metre and a half in diameter were strewn around the bush near the climbing site, left to rot perhaps half a century ago. I counted more than three hundred rings on one of them, meaning that the trees had emerged from the soil at a time when Newton's Law of Gravity had barely gained acceptance. They had been thirty metres high and had contained a thousand board feet of lumber by the time of the French Revolution.

Two hundred years ago, trees such as these were the billionth part of the endless white pine forests that shaded ridges and valleys from Maine and Newfoundland in the east to Minnesota and Manitoba in the west, and from as far south as present-day Georgia to the shores of Lake Nipigon in northern Ontario. I was once told by Will Carmean, an emeritus professor of forestry at Lakehead University, that in the early 1800s, it would have been possible to travel from Maine and New Brunswick all the way to the centre of the continent and virtually never be out of the shade of three-hundred-year-old white pines.

However, as early as 1810, agents of the British Crown were scouring the eastern forests, marking the tallest and straightest of the pines for use as masts, booms, and spars on thousands of British naval and merchant ships (Napoleon had recently cut the British off from their longstanding supply in Russia).

As Canadian immigration and construction blossomed in the mid-1800s—and as ships turned increasingly to steam power—emphasis shifted to domestic use of the white pine. Looking back from the high-tech mesa of the early twenty-first century, it is difficult to comprehend the pervasive significance of the white pine to the nineteenth-century inhabitants of eastern North America. For farmers, it was a formidable obstacle that had to be removed from the land (and usually burned) before crops could be sown. But for thousands, it meant jobs in the bush camps, sawmills, and finishing factories. And for millions, it was a utilitarian treasure that affected them from (pine) cradle to (pine) coffin. It was framing and lumber for their homes, churches, barns, and public buildings. Even brick and stone buildings were generally erected around pine frames. Inside those homes, pine was beds, tables, chairs, cupboards, and dressers. What's more, it was the principal material of transportation, essential in the making of bridges, boats, wagons, rail cars, and rail ties. It was mine timbers and wooden sidewalks.

In this part of Canada, at the forefront of the pine industry, there were hundreds of rowdy logging camps in which the languages were many, the comforts and amenities few.

The logging of white pine is personal for me in that my maternal grandfather, Walter Scholey, was for a decade during the late 1800s a timber cruiser whose job was to travel through the northern forests, by canoe, marking only the best pines for the lumberjacks who followed (subsequent timbermen marked the second, third, and fourth best trees).

A generation later, during the Depression, my father worked with Frontier College teaching English to immigrant loggers in the lumber camps around Longlac, north of Lake Superior. When I was a child, one of my favourite of his stories was how at Christmas, 1932, he persuaded Eaton's department store in Toronto to send up decorations, candies, and so on, plus a gift for every man in camp, at twenty-five cents a head. The drinking started early on Christmas Day, so that when it came time for the gifts, the loggers were well crocked, including Santa in a red suit that had come unexpectedly in the Eaton's box. The opening of the gifts had barely begun when one of the men insulted St. Nick who, before the brawl ended, had had his beard and suit ripped off, as well as bits and pieces of his skin, and had dealt black eyes and bloody noses to half a dozen of those with whom he was celebrating the birth of the Prince of Peace.

The survival of the white pine was no more a concern in such camps than it was among the lumber barons, who were entirely unburdened by questions about the future of the forests or wildlife. The more trees they could cut, the better it was for everyone—at least everyone they cared about. So they cleaned off a hundred thousand square miles, leaving only the isolated stands that remain today in remote areas or provincial and state parks, where the terrain made it too difficult to cut and haul out the trees.

As I DESCENDED the first long hill south of the Mad Moose, a slim cyclist, a tenacious cartoon of humanity, fought his way uphill toward me into a wind so discouraging that he was slowed almost to a walker's speed.

"Where ya headed?" I called out as he passed.

He stopped, and while at first noncommittal, he eventually revealed that he had pedalled from the Toronto suburb of Brampton to Sault Ste. Marie in seven days and was now on his way to Thunder Bay.

It is perhaps typical of people in challenging circumstances (even of their own making) to seek encouragement in the fortitude of others. Certainly that was my first reaction to Walter Bond, a rugged and implausible cowboy, who said that even in sub-zero weather he wore no gloves. The result was that his cracked and calloused hands looked less like a work of nature than of an incompetent mortician or taxidermist. His lips and eyebrows had been all but skinned bloody by the elements.

Walter's bike and gear were more or less representative of what serious cyclists own—high-end frame, shoes, helmet—but his black Levis and his Player's Light cigarettes revealed a hint of non-compliance, and his eyes, a saturated Superior blue, were as wild and disturbing as a wolf's.

For sustenance, he carried water and crackers, and for "shelter," a light nylon groundsheet under which he slept.

In particular, he made himself memorable by telling me that every time he saw a nail or piece of metal on the highway, he stopped and picked it up. Had done so for years, including two or three hundred times between Brampton and here. Over the years, he had been hit by spikes, breaking glass, wire, exploding tires, bolts, screws, and muffler parts. "Anything a truck tire can throw up, I've been hit by," he said, and he described being "blown off a bridge into a creek" when a transport tire exploded within a metre of him at high speed on a Quebec highway. He said, "I've had industrial wire go right through my lip and break my teeth." He now figured every piece of metal he picked up "was one more piece that wasn't going to end up embedded in some cyclist's windpipe or eye."

I was so impressed by his commitment that from that point on I, too, began picking up nails and pieces of stray metal and throwing them into the ditch.

Walter had cycled back and forth across the continent half a dozen times over the years—to Vancouver, to Florida, to Alaska. When I asked him what motivated him, he reflected for a moment, looked at me with his crazy blue eyes, and said, "Sadness."

For six years, he said, he had tried to talk to his ex-wife about their two sons—"just to talk about our lives"—but her attitude toward him was "so relentlessly hostile" and disheartening that the only response he felt he could make, the one that kept him sane, was, as he put it, "to get out on the highway and pedal."

I told him I was walking to New York City and why, and that the first few weeks had made me wonder at times if I had what it would take.

"Don't worry," he smiled, extending his hand. "You've got what it takes. How old are you?"

"Fifty-three."

"It's a nice age," he said, and as he pulled out into the wind, he called over his shoulder (foretelling the future more accurately than either of us could have known), "By the time you get there, you're gonna be browner and scabbier than me!"

WHILE MY THOUGHTS were still on Walter Bond, a carload of young men from Michigan pulled over, and one of the passengers called amicably out the window, "I thought we should tell ya since you're walking—there's a bear up ahead on the road."

It is apparent to me, in retrospect, why the Gospel writers produced such vigorously varied accounts of the complex life of Christ. Because, even with respect to the simple appearance of a bear a minute or two earlier, my questions "How big a bear?" and "How far up the road?" inspired responses so radically varied as to make me wonder whether the witnesses had seen the same animal. It was "quite a big bear," was "a cub," was "a medium-sized bear"—was "a mile back," was "two miles back," was "about five or six hundred yards back."

I was too polite, too Canadian, to ask whether the young men were sure it was a bear at all.

When I had walked fifty metres, another car stopped, this one carrying an aging and excited New Zealand couple.

She (breathlessly): "There's a bear up the road! We saw it! We really did! Just now!"

He: "It's a young one, I think. About two kilometres back."

She: "No, dear! The same song's still on the radio!"

He: "A kilometre."

She: "We thought we should tell you."

He: "I'm thinking maybe we'll go back for another look. Do you want us to drive you past it?"

"No, thanks," I said, "I'll figure it out."

It occurred to me that discretion might be my best move here and that I should perhaps just walk back to Montreal River Harbour and bide my time. On the other hand, the thought of a little risk was seductive, and in no time I had convinced myself that it was a privilege of sorts to meet a bear, an animal that in more than one branch of tribal belief is considered an embodiment of the spirit of healing. However, not so by the Thunder Bay friends who had advised me to carry a can of pepper spray for occasions such as this—or for bad dogs or bad people. My own perspective was that if I were being attacked by an angry bear or a weapon-wielding psychotic, it would be of small advantage to further rile my assailant by spraying pepper up his or her nose. So I didn't bring any (ironically, George brought a container, which he carried in the vehicle).

I was by no means cavalier, however, and because on the Trans-Canada one is never at a loss for junk, I was, within seconds, carrying a primitive equalizer in the form of a three-foot length of drive shaft that in the right hands (perhaps not my own) would have knocked out a mule.

I walked for fifteen minutes—no bear—and was beginning to feel a trifle over-armed, especially considering the bear's status as an expression of the spirit of healing. Then again, bears don't know they are expressions of the spirit of healing. Or if they do know, they consider chewing up the occasional human being to be within their redemptive mandate (which, in a broad sense, is fairly sound ecology).

As I walked, I scanned the woods and, to my surprise and excitement, eventually realized that, perhaps fifty metres back, a spirited black cub, an overgrown pompom, was tiptoeing gingerly along the shoulder toward me, sniffing the air. I stopped and turned, and he kept coming, stepping, sniffing—at one point even lifting his front feet in a kind of romp. I banged the drive shaft and shooed at him with it, and he stopped.

I turned and took a few more steps.

He took a few.

One of the ambiguities that exists between people and bears is that we misread them, thinking them dozy and cumbersome and a little numbskulled because of their lumpish look and gait. But it is a gross misunderstanding. Judging by its size, the little bear behind me would have recently come out of his second season of hibernation with his mother and have had a full year and a half of intimate hourly education as he grew—an education and nurturing that puts him among the smartest creatures in the animal world. At birth, in January, in the hibernation den, a black bear cub weighs just a quarter of a kilo, considerably less than, say, a porcupine's birth weight, and truly incongruous when measured against the animal's mature weight, which in males can rise to some 250 kilos, or 600 pounds. The reason for the minuscule birth weight is that it allows the hibernating mother, who is not eating at this point, freedom from the demands of heavy suckling. The newborn, on the other hand, gets the benefit of the months-long intimate care that everywhere in the animal kingdom converts directly into intelligence.

That intelligence, however, has not registered favourably with modern humanity. Bears enjoyed inordinate respect from the early tribes. Around Lake Superior today, however, they are the only animal hunted for the sake of the hunting (they are of little or no value as food, and there is no market for their fur). Outside hunting season, they are the only large mammals in Canada that are routinely shot merely because they constitute "a nuisance" to humanity (cougars and wolves, for example, are shot not as nuisances but as predators). While bears occasionally attack a human being, they are no longer even primarily predatorial. They will occasionally take down a moose calf or clean up a dead deer, and they enjoy fishing and eating grubs, but the heart of their diet comes from berries and vegetation, and from scavenging, particularly in dumps. One of my all-time favourite *New Yorker* cartoons shows a bear sitting at the linen-covered table of a fancy Manhattan restaurant, studying the menu, while a snooty, formally dressed waiter takes his order. "I shouldn't," says the bear, wearing a self-conscious grin, "but I'll have the garbage."

Hunters rationalize that if bears are not shot, there will eventually be a plague of them (although no one applies the principle to, say, skunks or porcupines). The irony here is that if male bears are killed (males are the hunter's primary trophy), the population actually increases, because mature males are one of the prime predators of bear cubs (though not their own). The public relations representative of a large American hunting organization told me recently that bears are "a big problem" in New Jersey, that there are far too many of them—to which I responded on instinct that it was perhaps not bears that were too plentiful in New Jersey and would eventually bring the state to its knees, but people.

At a certain point, I turned and hustled briefly toward my stalker, and he retreated. But when I turned to walk again, he followed—lighter on his front feet now, as if in a circus routine.

Needless to say, it felt somewhat aberrational to be out on the Trans-Canada at the beginning of the May long weekend with trucks and motor homes exploding past and with a bear that I could not get rid of following me down the road. "Go on!" I shouted at him (there being a limited number of things you can say to a bear in such a circumstance). "Get outta here!"

My concern, I might add, was less for myself at this point than for the cub, which I felt might be hit by a car. Admittedly, I had not seen (and would not see) a single dead bear on the highway, which attests significantly, I should think, to the species' high intelligence.

Finally, during a break in the traffic, I dropped the length of drive shaft, picked up a handful of small stones, took a few rapid steps toward the cub, and pitched them. Only then, with the gravel raining around him, did he turn and strike off into the woods, looking back at me as if to suggest that since I had chosen to be so rude, he might next time just dispense with his version of goodwill and bring his buddies along and eat my porridge, as he had famously done to Goldilocks.

As MUCH AS RAIN or snow or fatigue, wind had been my nemesis during these first few weeks, and by early afternoon, the west wind that had nearly halted Walter Bond had swung around and was gusting up the embankment off the shoreline as hard into my face as any I had bucked. I sloped into it like a factor in a physics equation— sometimes so far forward as to meet it with the top of my head. Even a tailwind, a stiff one, obliged an angling of the body—backwards— which, over time, tended to wear on the back muscles and spine. To vary the effects of the wind tunnels that existed between the rock cuts or between the edges of the forest on either side of the highway, I would occasionally cross the pavement and walk briefly with the traffic. But after more than six hundred kilometres, the muscles in my hips had adjusted to, and preferred, the left slope of the highway. Walking on the right, with its opposite camber, altered my gait in such a way that it made my hips ache, and I was forced to switch back to what I was accustomed to.

I MET GEORGE LATE in the afternoon a few kilometres west of Pancake Bay Provincial Park, where attendants were busily sawing up deadfall. It was our first awareness that the civil-service strike was over, and to test our letter of free passage, we drove in and I explained our privileged, though so-far hypothetical, arrangement to the first person we saw. "We were wondering if we could pitch a tent," I said and were told summarily that it wasn't possible "for safety reasons." I asked where the superintendent might be, and drove across the highway to the park office, where a big bewhiskered cigar chomper named Chris Caldwell said he knew who I was, that a memo had gone out to every park in the province to be on the lookout for me, and that he was "damned proud" that Pancake Bay was the first park that could offer me its facilities. "Take any site you want," he said. "In fact, take three or four! And use the firewood. There's lots of it."

And we did—tossing one block of spruce after another onto a reckless blaze that by mid-evening was so high and hot we could barely get close enough to it to add another ten-kilo chunk. After a dinner consisting largely of boiled potatoes and fried kielbasa, we pitched the old Woods nine-by-nine at the top of the beach, speculating as we did so on whether this dutiful canvas antiquity would withstand the gale that by this time was whistling off the lake. Figuring that it was less likely to go AWOL if we were in it, weighing it down, we filled a thermos with lemon tea, slumped inside, and with toques pulled over our ears, lay sipping tea and listening to the smashing of the surf.

Even tent weights have feelings of course, and as cheerful as we were to be at last in the tender care of the parks system, it was a dispiriting sight during the third week in May to see our breath sublimating in the frigid air above our pillows. And more dispiriting yet to realize, at 2:00 A.M., that the combination of cold air and hot fluid would necessitate a visit to the great outdoors—and another two hours later. At six or so, when George rose as blue as Lazarus to get a fire going, he reported that he had been out four times in the night—which I thought, by comparison, spoke well for my bladder and prostate. My self-satisfaction, however, was quickly laid waste by George's sobering announcement that if this kept up he was going to have to get himself "a piss bottle."

"Just make sure you don't use my Gatorade bottle," I muttered from within the recesses of my bag—his response to which (lots of *ph* and *ck* sounds) I shall leave unrecorded on the off chance these pages end up before the eyes of anyone's children.

I crawled from the tent at about 7:00 A.M., but was so cowed by the wind and frost that rather than make breakfast, I walked a mile or so up the road to the Bluewater Restaurant. There, before beginning my walk proper, I ate two Lumberman's Specials, each consisting of toast, hash browns, ham, eggs, and coffee. And unaware of the calamity that awaited me, I went more or less happily to work.

DURING THE SIXTY-THREE DAYS on the road between Thunder Bay and New York City, I twice suffered what snowboarders and skateboarders call "face plants"—both of them quite spectacular. One occurred without even a fall, on a serene rural road south of Watertown, New York, when preoccupied with taking notes on a slip of paper, I walked face-first, hard, into a sign that protruded a metre out over the shoulder at precisely the height of my head.

The first "plant" occurred a couple of hours after breakfast at the Bluewater as I walked south along the Batchawana Bay shoreline, where I had taken to the beach because for ten or twelve kilometres it ran parallel to the highway and offered welcome variety. Lake Superior's drainage basin takes in hundreds, if not thousands, of creeks and streams, several of which flowed across the beach where I was walking. The first I came to had cut a half-metre-deep gully, perhaps two metres wide, from the top of the beach down to the surf, and I decided that rather than return to the highway to ford it, I would simply back up a little, take a run, and jump over it.

However, my take-off foot had no sooner hit the sandy edge of the stream bed when I realized I had made a mistake. The creek's edge had none of the solidity of the beach proper, so that instead of rising, spring propelled, into a graceful running arc, I was more suddenly than I could have imagined knee-deep in something like quicksand. With my lead foot deeply entrenched, my trailing foot landed mid-stream, sank like the *Lusitania,* and I was, instantaneously, on my face in ten or twelve centimetres of flowing water, my mouth and nostrils full of sand.

The stream was so perishingly cold that I was upright before the water had properly penetrated my rain gear, so my pelvis and trunk were spared the dousing. But by the time I had extracted myself from the stream, my shoes were full of ice-temperature water and fine brown beach sand.

In the bitter wind and cold, I was not in the best of shape to walk another twenty kilometres. But I was already sixteen or seventeen kilometres from where I had started, had no phone, and had nothing to gain by returning to camp, where I was unlikely to find George. I had even less to gain by standing in the cold feeling sorry for myself.

I considered rinsing my shoes and socks in the lake, but the surf was two metres high, making it extremely difficult to get into position. Instead, I sat on a picnic table, cleared as much sand as possible from my shoes, and pulled my saturated socks, each the equivalent of a piece of fifty-grade sandpaper, back onto my feet.

And walked on.

George picked me up four hours later, by which time the toes of my left foot had gone numb. Back at Pancake Bay, I sat like Sam McGee in mid-cremation, sparks flying past me, just happy to be within scorching distance of a fire. I knew that I should tend to my feet, but still racked by shivers, I couldn't bear at this point to remove my shoes. George, to his credit, bustled around like Florence Nightingale, building up the fire, preparing soup from an envelope, and eventually dishing up a satisfying *pot-au-feu* that combined tomatoes, beef, ginger, garlic, green pepper, celery, the lot of it dumped over rice and served with a long shot of rum.

The wind by this time was so fierce off the lake that the tent, down by the beach, threatened constantly to rise with the gusts, inflating with a snap, tearing aggressively at its pegs and guy ropes, then deflating suddenly, and again snapping outward.

When he had cleaned up the dishes, George heated me a pan of water, containing a little Sunlight dish soap and a few ounces of hydrogen peroxide. Having removed my shoes, I soaked my feet without removing my socks (recalling the old joke about the use of a condom being tantamount to washing one's feet with one's socks on) and began meticulously to separate the socks from my flesh. In places, the skin was scored with a thousand tiny lacerations, each seeming to contain a molecule or two of sand or a few fibres of blue sock. I rinsed my feet as best I could, rubbed antiseptic cream into every part, rolled on a clean pair of socks, and slipped into dry shoes.

And stood up, my legs doing a convincing impersonation of a pair of boiled spaghetti strands.

At dusk, I took the three-wick emergency candle out of the van and, when we had battened ourselves into the tent, lit it between us where it cast a skittish yellow glow onto our faces and the tent walls. As the storm tore at the canvas around us, George—lubriciously cranked on rum—delivered an inspired eulogy to one of his art teachers at Lehman College, a man named Sachi Furuta, a gentle Japanese mystic who had worked part-time in advertising, part-time teaching, and part-time translating ancient Japanese poetry into English. George had loved the guy, loved his spirit, loved his gentleness and, wondering now if he was alive, made a mental note to find out when we got to New York City.

As we lay muffled in our bags, fully dressed and wearing toques, I asked George if he believed the candle was doing anything to warm the tent. He thought for a few seconds and said, "No. But it makes things a little more mellow"—a word I would never have thought to apply on such a frosty night in what was now an incipient blizzard.

THE EXTRAORDINARY EVENTS of the next day have in a sense transformed themselves into legend—or a dramatic two-hander that during the days and weeks to come I would find myself reliving in detail as I walked. But they began as fact, when in the dense forest north of Sault Ste. Marie, without a restaurant, house, or road sign in sight, I was aware quite suddenly of a presence behind me on the highway. I turned to find myself being followed within speaking distance by a striking-looking black man, perhaps thirty years old, in a black leather car coat and black jeans. His bearing, his teeth, his dreadlocks, the pinkish "whites" of his eyes suggested immediately that he was African.

Mauritanian, as it turned out.

Moslem.

Named Osama, of all things—although, out of prudence, in the slipstream of 9/11, he referred to himself as Ousmain, or *Ossman* as he pronounced it, a variation of the name of one of the four principal disciples of Mohammed.

"Who are you?" I said to him as we stood facing one another in the wind.

"Who are you?" he asked, laughing nervously.

And so began a five-hour walk, an exchange—a period of grace and enlightenment (mostly mine) and great conversational intimacy— with a man who, some thirty months prior, had been a political prisoner, barely alive, amidst rats and filth, held with eighteen others in a tiny cell in one of the most notoriously brutal prisons in the one-time French colony of Mauritania, on the northwest coast of Africa.

Understandably, his life had not always been so vile. And as we stepped along under a cold northern sky, Ousmain explained, with a minimum of prompting, that as a boy of eight during the early 1980s, he had been sent by his father, a local administrator for British Petroleum, from Mauritania's capital city, Nouakchott, to live with extended family in the country's rural savannah on the northern fringe of the Sahara Desert. There, in keeping with tribal tradition, he had become a child messenger—a *walker,* of all things—whose daily responsibility within the tribe was to walk from one primitive village to another, distances of up to eighteen kilometres, transporting messages, food, spices, tools, fuel, supplies of any sort.

"As we got older," Ousmain said, "the distances we were expected to walk got greater." A young man was expected to walk up to sixty kilometres a day.

It was a world, he explained, in which a family considered itself well off to have a donkey, a garden, and a fruit tree—a world without cars or even bicycles. Or plumbing or electricity or telephones. "Oh, it was grand," Ousmain said, and he described walking along river trails accompanied by "the sounds of five hundred birds"; and how he had fashioned bows and arrows out of saplings to hunt rabbits, gazelles, and wild pigs; had seen lions and zebras in their natural habitat; and had kept an eye out for the fabled black mamba, the most deadly snake on the savannah.

When I intruded on his tale, perhaps somewhat impatiently, to ask how he came to be where he was, he paused, addressed me calmly by name, and—being nothing if not thorough—told me that if I hoped to understand what he was doing out there on the Trans-Canada, I had first to understand that France had colonized Mauritania in 1880 and had taken control of its considerable natural resources, including its abundant fish stocks and iron-ore reserves.

I had further to understand that in 1960 France had given the country its independence and that in 1984, after a period of relatively sane government, Mauritania had fallen under the control of a murderous Arab dictator by the name of Maaouya Ould Sid' Ahmed Taya, a man every bit as brutal as Saddam Hussein. The result was "military-controlled terror"—a regime that, among other things, eliminated opposition, nationalized industry, and silenced its citizens with its secret police and torture chambers.

Ousmain said many of his friends had joined the army, hoping to effect a revolution from within. "But they disappeared. They were all executed. People just vanished."

For Ousmain's family, the shift in government had meant the loss of his father's position with British Petroleum and the loss of the family home. Nevertheless, Ousmain returned to the capital to attend high school and at the age of nineteen left the country to study international law at the École Nationale Administration Publique in Rabat, Morocco.

What he called "the pivot point" in his life came during the final year of his master's program. When it came time to choose a topic for his thesis, his adviser issued him a challenge. At its core was the fact that not one of the university's 1,300 Mauritanian graduates had ever had the guts to write about, or draw attention to, human rights abuses in his home country, which were, and are, among the world's worst. Because of Ousmain's intelligence and democratic politics, his adviser believed he was the person for the job.

"I knew that if I did it," Ousmain said, "it would probably get me killed." But, like his adviser, he knew it should be done. So for the next year he pored over U.N. documents on his homeland that revealed depths of depravity he had never imagined. "In the capital alone," he told me, "more than two hundred homes of wealthy people had been tunnelled out underneath to use as torture chambers. Thousands upon thousands of people disappeared."

Having written his thesis and graduated, Ousmain slipped back into Mauritania, unaware that government officials had been following his progress and already had a copy of the thesis. "One afternoon," he said, "a couple of policemen came to my parents' home, and that was that. They took me away. My parents believed they wouldn't see me again."

Like others I have met who have been touched by terror, Ousmain spoke softly, philosophically, of his time as a political prisoner—of hearing, daily, the screams of tortured men and women "down the hall"; of watching those in his cell being dragged away, paralyzed by fear and brought back with their teeth and bones smashed; of being fed a gruel of scummy rice mixed with occasional chunks of unidentifiable grey meat ("maybe donkey or horse, or bad fish"); and of having to urinate and deficate in a single tin can shared by eighteen others in the cell.

Every day for a year, Ousmain had expected to be taken to the torture room. But of all those in the cell, he was the only one spared.

"The authorities didn't really understand who I was. They were more concerned with immediate threats to their power—armed revolutionaries, expatriates plotting against them—but not thesis writers." Moreover, local prison guards, who had no particular axe to grind with the prisoners, tended to sympathize with Ousmain's assessment of ongoing human rights violations. "Some of them," he said, "were actually behind me."

Ahmed Taya had come to power on December 12, 1984. "Every year on that date," Ousmain said, "there were big celebrations, and people in jail for minor offences were released."

Ousmain considered it something of a miracle—and quite possibly a mistake—when on the morning of December 12, 1999, his name, too, was called with those who were about to be given amnesty. "I just shut up and prayed that it was for real," he told me. "When they let me out of the cell, I put my head down and headed for the outside gate. And never looked back."

He described his arrival at his parents' front door as "like something out of a movie. It was as if they'd seen a ghost." He said the only thing that mattered at that point was that he get out of Mauritania. And in no time, backed by an affluent French uncle, he had obtained a U.S. student visa and was on his way to Washington, D.C.

For the next year, Ousmain lived in a $1,400-a-month apartment, within blocks of the White House, and paid $1,300 a month for English lessons. "But I didn't make a good American," he said. "I didn't fit in socially with the white people, and because I was African, I wasn't really accepted by the blacks."

With his student visa running out and in mortal dread of returning to Mauritania, he decided to head for the territories: Canada.

The story of his "escape" from the United States might have been plotted by John le Carré. "From studying international law," he told me, "I knew that if I could get over the border into Canada, even without papers, I could claim refugee status—that they wouldn't send me back without a hearing."

With that in mind, he boarded a Greyhound bound for Montreal. "Someone should have checked my papers when I got on," he said, "but because I looked like any other American black guy, they didn't bother."

Ousmain's next concern was whether or not the driver would take the bus over the border before Canadian Immigration officials came aboard. "If he didn't, and I was caught, I'd have been kept in the U.S."

To help matters along, as the vehicle approached Canadian immigration, Ousmain moved quietly to a front seat. And as the bus slowed down, he prayed. Effectively, as it turned out. Because before the bus stopped for inspection, it cruised just over the line. "As soon as the authorities came aboard, I jumped up and said, 'My name is Ousmain Sy, and I wish to claim political sanctuary in Canada!' And they took me straight off the bus into the building."

Ousmain lived in Montreal on welfare for a year, attending a variety of meetings with immigration officials and awaiting a final meeting with the tribunal that would decide his fate. "My application was in doubt because, technically, I should have applied for refugee status in the U.S. So there was a possibility they'd send me back to Washington."

Ousmain's case for sanctuary in the United States was even shakier than his case in Canada (and, given that he is an African Moslem named Osama, would have gotten shakier yet after 9/11). He was convinced that a return to Washington would mean an enforced return to Mauritania, where, having left without proper clearance and unsuccessfully sought asylum in another country, he was, as he put it, "a dead man."

Out of curiosity about my own country's bureaucracy, I asked Ousmain how he had been treated by Canadian officials. He said, "Charlie, I could tell you anything to flatter you as a Canadian. But I'll tell you the truth. I was treated with great consideration and kindness."

Meanwhile in Montreal, Ousmain, who is six-foot-three and powerfully built, was attracting consideration of a different sort. "I'd go out to a bar once in a while," he said. "And I found Montreal women very friendly; they always seemed interested. But I usually felt it was just physical; they were curious about this big African guy, particularly my physique, and didn't really care what I thought or said."

One winter night Ousmain was introduced by a friend to a young Ojibway woman named Christine Chisel from Sault Ste. Marie, who was most certainly interested in what he had to say. And the feeling was mutual. Christine had a degree in psychology from Laurentian University and was working in addiction counselling in the Soo. "We met and we just kept talking," said Ousmain.

Within days, the two had fallen in love, and within weeks were married. "People wonder whether or not it was a marriage of convenience," he said, "and I wouldn't have been ashamed to get married for the 'convenience' of saving my life. But it wasn't. Nobody faked anything."

By the time Ousmain's immigration hearing came up, his refugee status was a moot point—he was the husband of a Canadian citizen. By the time I met him, he was the father of a Canadian child and was well on his way to citizenship.

Ousmain spoke five languages: French, Spanish, English, Poular, and Wolof. But his main means of communication were French and Poular. He was at work on his English, which was poetic in the way of those who are not yet burdened by the slipshod practices that can squeeze the music out of a language. In his attempts to converse as broadly as possible, he made occasional, sometimes humorous, gaffes; for example, once blurting out "moose" when he saw a Canada goose. Later, in describing the vast abundance of fish off the Mauritanian coast, he attributed such wealth to the "good weather under the sea."

As we walked, I could not help noticing that rather than use the edge of the pavement or the firm gravel, where I liked to walk, Ousmain preferred the sand at the lower edge of the shoulder—a throwback, he said, to his years on the savannah.

One of the more remarkable things about Ousmain was that he saw himself not as a victim, or even a survivor, but as a man of faith and good fortune with a message for the world. "My main goal in life right now," he told me, "is to let people know how it is in Mauritania. And what they can do about it." He quoted a United Nations projection that Mauritania will, within twenty years, "be the planet's worst violator of human rights." In the meantime, he said, the government's cruel politics are tacitly supported by France, with whom Mauritania maintains "sweetheart" contracts to supply endless tonnages of fish and iron ore. "It's beyond criminal," he said, explaining that the two countries have, for example, a twenty-year contract whereby France gets all the Mauritanian fish it wants—fish estimated to be worth $150 million a year—at a yearly cost of $1 million.

As for Africa at large, Ousmain was adamant that what the continent needs is not "care packages" but help in claiming control of its oil, metals, and gems from the hands of "a relatively few vicious dictatorships and corporate pirates."

His comments brought to mind the American writer James Ellroy's remark that "behind every great colonial power is a great crime" and had a local resonance for me in that I had recently been reading about how the early French colonists around Sault Ste. Marie had forcibly claimed land and resources and spread terror among seventeenth-century aboriginals. One of the first colonists to reach the area, Pierre Esprit Radisson, wrote in his diaries that he had arrived at the east end of Lake Superior with a dozen heads of murdered Iroquois rolling around in his canoe as a warning to others. He was also transporting four living Iroquois whom he intended to roast alive for entertainment.

A subclause of Ousmain's message was that al-Qaeda's terrorism was not based on Islam, but ran counter to the most basic teachings of the Koran and of Mohammed. "To a devout Muslim," he told me, "all killing is wrong," and suicide in particular "is unforgivable." He referred to the World Trade Center terrorists as "robots—ignorant young men acting not on faith but under the influence of extremist politics."

Ousmain described his life thus far in Canada as "a kind of dream, sometimes a very strange one" and told me that our time together was the first opportunity he'd had since escaping Mauritania to tell his story to someone in a position to spread it to a larger audience. "I don't expect it," he said, "but I believe in destiny, in a plan, and believe we're out here walking together for a reason." Later, he said, "What are the chances that two guys from opposite sides of the world would meet where we did on foot and walk thirty kilometres through the forest together?" I felt, as he did, that they were slim.

As for his presence on this remote stretch of the Trans-Canada north of Sault Ste. Marie, he explained that, early that morning he had driven with his wife and their baby to his father-in-law's cabin and decided to walk home—and that he had been surprised and curious to see another walker go by as he stepped along the side-road toward the highway.

We spoke of the differences between Christianity and Islam. And of Ousmain's grandfather, whose three wives produced thirty sons and daughters. And of the African custom of placing a person's family name before their given name. "At home," he said, "I'm Sy Ousmain. My family name indicates a tribal affiliation. So, when people hear it, they understand right away my lineage—who I am and where I come from."

Where a creek passed under the highway, we lurched down the embankment and sat in the sunlight out of the wind while Ousmain smoked a cigarette. When a blue jay darted overhead, he looked up and made a well-practised squawk that brought the jay immediately to a perch in a nearby spruce.

He was curious about wild animals and wondered why I wasn't nervous about being out around moose, bears, and wolves. I wondered, in turn, that as a child he hadn't been nervous about walking in a land of lions and black mambas. He looked at me as if I were daft and said, "But I *was* nervous. You're not."

As we walked into the Soo, we passed an enormous car dealership, Ousmain's first Canadian employer, where on a fiercely cold Saturday afternoon in early spring he had shown up for his inaugural day of work. His assignment had been to paint yellow parking lines onto a vast stretch of asphalt, which had been cleared of cars for the occasion. But first he and two others were instructed to sweep the lot clean. All night, and well into the next day, the men had swept in futility, as a swirling north wind blew the dust this way and that across the lot. After eighteen hours straight, in despair and half frozen, Ousmain phoned the boss and said he was going home, and that he should not be expected back.

He had recently been hired by a Soo-based agent for an American company that sold an obscure brand of cut-rate all-terrain vehicles. Because he spoke French, his job was to phone dealerships that sold similar products in Quebec and persuade them to carry the company's machines. During his first week, he had put three new dealerships under contract, qualifying him as something of a superstar in the field.

We stopped for coffee at a Tim Hortons, then trudged south across the city—Ousmain toward the apartment where he lived with his wife, Christine, and son, Aja, I to the decidedly unalluring Byways Motel, where I knew from a phone chat with George that he had installed us in a kitchenette suite more or less large enough to hold every other motel room we had slept in so far.

Whereas I was dressed for the Arctic, Ousmain had done the entire walk without hat, gloves, or socks. If we were cold, however, we were nonetheless reluctant to give up the day's camaraderie. So we delayed our goodbyes for sixteen hours, with an arrangement to meet briefly in the morning for tea at Ousmain's apartment.

Meanwhile, the coffee had put Ousmain desperately in need of a leak. Unfortunately, by this time, we were in the heart of residential Sault Ste. Marie, and by the time we reached a railway spur, where he could slip behind some brush, he was all but hopping from the pressure.

A minute later, at Highway 17, I held out my hand to him to thank him for the day. But he would not take it, Islamic custom dictating that after urinating, a man does not touch the hand of another until he has washed his own. The custom undoubtedly has practical roots in the hot-weather cultures of antiquity but, today, is observed equally in the avoidance of implied insult. Instead, Ousmain, in good humour, held out his forearm to me and said, "Thank you for the walk, my friend." I thanked him in return—and turned briefly to watch as, in his loping savannah gait, he coasted off down the road.

THAT NIGHT, late, I took George into the rough southeast innards of Sault Ste. Marie, into the shadow of the steel mill, where for years my kids and I have eaten at the Peking Palace restaurant, our all-time favourite chop suey joint. The proprietor, Betty, is a garrulous and hospitable Chinese-Canadian—a champion, chain-smoking neurotic—whose social tour de force is her breakneck free-ranging patter on everything that's fit to think or say. On this night, her commentary ranged from Washington prostitutes to her qualms over whether she had been too strict a parent to the Buddhist custom of honouring forebears one day a year by feasting atop their graves and burning play money—"heaven money"—as a symbolic sharing of wealth.

Betty is forthright about her Buddhism and, as we tucked into a platter of sesame chicken, was determined to make it clear to us that while Christianity stresses forgiveness of one's past, Buddhism stresses "making you live with your past"—enduring it. "You guys are lucky," she said. "I gotta suffer!"

When Betty, who is fifty-two, heard I was walking to New York, she immediately blurted out, "I'm going with you! I'll be the cook!" And for a split second I was speechless at the thought. "No, I can't," she grinned. "I got too much work here." But I felt certain that had she gotten it in her head to go along, no force short of her own steel-trap will would have prevented her from doing so.

The conversational highlight of the meal was Betty's description of how as she had climbed the narrow spiral staircase inside the Statue of Liberty several years ago, a fat man in front of her had somehow gotten wedged in the narrow fretwork and been stuck there until the fire department arrived from Staten Island to get him out.

George, who was a little overwhelmed by Betty and had pretty much dozed off, was suddenly alert and gleeful over the wonderfully ironic image of a fat American imprisoned in the great symbol of U.S. freedom.

THE BYWAYS made for a cozy night after the storms of Superior. However, I thought the place clung a little too strenuously to its advertised promise of "budget accommodation," with the implied repudiation of elegance. The television, for example, didn't get any channels, and only one of the room's three lamps had a bulb. The towels, moreover, had been laundered to the translucency of cheesecloth.

However, you could cook in the Byways, and in the morning, after a memorably fragrant breakfast of smoked whitefish and "cheese dreams" (broiled Roquefort on toast), we dropped over to Ousmain's spacious apartment on the ground floor of an old brick house in the south end of town. He was waiting sockless to greet us, affording us a look at the impressively large and well-calloused feet that, unencumbered by shoes, had walked perhaps twenty thousand kilometres of Mauritanian savannah. His hands were an equivalent marvel—big bony racquets with light-coloured palms and fingers the size of Cuban cigars. I had taken the opportunity to study his hands the previous day and, curiously, now, could not look at them without imagining them smashed by brutes—as the hands of his cellmates had been destroyed.

George and Ousmain rattled away in French, and presently Christine—a tall, pretty woman with cedar-coloured skin—emerged from the bedroom with baby Aja, as attractive a combination of races as you might care to imagine.

Christine made "English" tea, and when we had finished it and glanced at Ousmain's near-fatal thesis (in French), we said the goodbyes we had avoided the day before, and I was off down the road.

5

Heading South

By the time I was four or five kilometres east of the Soo, I was on the Garden River Indian Reserve, and having ducked behind some roadside spruce for the usual reason, I found myself quite unexpectedly in a mysterious, ill-kept little cemetery, with inscribed wooden crosses atop the pebbled outlines of graves. Like everyone else, I am aware of the sometimes disastrous social conditions, particularly for young people, on Canada's reserves. But these Garden River graves told a story far harsher and more depressing than anything I might have wanted to contemplate: Jacques Pierre 1988–1999; Buddy Tique 1985–1999; Jodi Carson 1982–1997; Sasha Spooner 1984–1998 ("Loved by Everyone").

However, as I passed a grave marked only with the name Cocoa and another marked Tuffy, I began to wonder what sort of parents would name their kid Tuffy. And then it dawned on me that the graves were not those of people at all, and I laughed out loud—and a minute later was back on the highway, feeling infinitely more hopeful for the Garden River Ojibway.

Which is not to say the reserve itself evidenced any strong reasons to feel positive. I passed several grim-faced young men who said

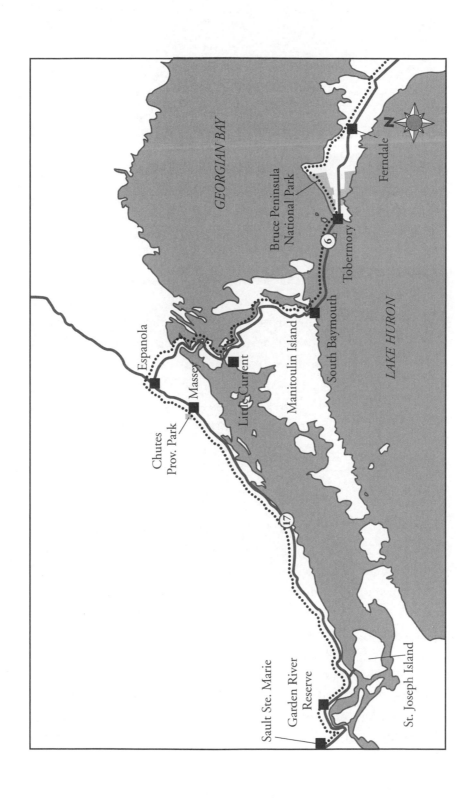

nothing when I greeted them, and saw a dozen or more houses that would hardly have been considered livable in the broader community. The owners of one wretched little shack surrounded by derelict cars had put out a four-by-eight sheet of plywood painstakingly painted with the colours and symbol of the Montreal Canadiens. But the shack itself had no paint. There were better buildings—a big log police station and band administrative centre, and houses constructed to such a standard that if you squinted a little you could imagine yourself amid the most conformist ticky-tacky on earth. And there was a golf course somewhere off in the woods. I am told by a Cree friend that golf is extremely popular in Native communities these days—in part because of the five-hundred-channel universe, which, like the Cockroach that ate Cincinnati, has devoured the aboriginal population as thoroughly and insidiously as the English and French chewed them up and reinvented them 250 years ago.

The steel railway bridge across the Garden River is emblazoned with the words "THIS IS INDIAN LAND"—intended, one might assume, as a show of contentious autonomy. But to my mind it was little more than a somewhat pathetic reminder of how piddling a piece of this massive and wealthy continent is still the domain of the once self-sufficient First Nations.

THE WIND AND COLD were a little less oppressive as I got farther from Sault Ste. Marie, reminding me of what I occasionally forget about the north shore of Lake Superior: that no matter how fervent or wishful you are, you cannot outwalk, outfox, or out-think it; you are at the mercy of its weather almost as much as sailors are at the mercy of the big lake's waves and water.

Maybe twenty kilometres southeast of the Soo, I came onto the first stretch of divided four-lane highway that I had walked since leaving Thunder Bay. A ditch down the middle of the grassy median was clogged with an oily iron-coloured sludge. But it didn't seem to bother the starlings and red-winged blackbirds that darted around amid the usual assortment of car parts, cigarette packages, and Tim Hortons cups.

I had intended all along to stop at St. Joseph's Island and stay a night with my friend Mike Jones, a former naturalist with the Ontario Ministry of Natural Resources in Thunder Bay. However, when I spoke to Mike's wife, Stephanie, that morning by phone (I had never met her), she told me Mike was away doing contract work for Ontario Parks, but that she had just baked a bear's helping of rhubarb crisp and that if I knew what was good for me I would get my blistered feet out onto the island a.s.a.p. and claim my share.

St. Joseph's is an old-world patchwork of cedar-rail farms and mixed forest and, according to local promo, is the second biggest freshwater island in the world (the biggest is Manitoulin, a little farther east in Lake Huron's North Channel). It is also the site of Fort St. Joseph, built by the British in 1796 as a fur trading post and garrison against the other rampaging claimants to the territory, the French. More peaceably, the island boasts the largest maple syrup works in Ontario.

Like the gang at the Mad Moose, Mike and Stephanie are ecological refugees who, sick of city life—even the modest depredations of Thunder Bay—arrived on the island in 2001 and established themselves in a nineteenth-century farmhouse, where Stephanie keeps a pair of beloved horses and Mike freelances his considerable knowledge of the outdoors to whoever might need the service.

George and I had barely arrived in their front yard, with its profuse gardens, old apple trees, goldfinches, and cardinals, when Stephanie, a part-time registered nurse, announced that we were all going for dinner at the home of another pair of Thunder Bay escapees, Janet McLeod and Steve Roedde, who in 1997 tossed over their medical practices in the city and realized an old dream of Steve's by buying a functional maple sugar bush along the north shore of the island. So seductive was Steve's dream in its unrealized phase that he had once tapped the birch trees in the couple's yard in Thunder Bay, boiling

down sap, as the Natives did a thousand years ago, at a ratio of eighty
to one, to get a litre or two of the rare but apparently exquisite birch
syrup.

Today, Steve and Janet's yard includes hayfields and a thirty-acre
forest, where the paying citizens, the maples, are all gartered up in blue
plastic tubing and, in effect, resemble an avant-garde art installation
(Cristo laces up the woods). In March the network of plastic tubes
transports some 40,000 litres of rising sap to the boiling shed, where
the sap is reduced, forty-to-one, above a hardwood fire that burns non-
stop for two weeks. From the boiling shed, the syrup is transferred into
plastic or glass vessels—many of them hand-decorated by Janet—in
which it is transported to the pancakes and cake holes of the world.

Janet is the doctor at the island's tiny hospital at Richard's Landing.
Steve does her on-call work and reluctantly spends two days a month
in the emergency ward of the general hospital in the Soo. But these
days, even twenty-four shifts a year in a city hospital expose him to
more heart attacks and car-accident victims than he wants to deal with
now that his true avocational concerns are cord wood, maple xylem,
and reduction ratios.

On the way to dinner, Stephanie had urged George and me to be
on the lookout for sandhill cranes, which migrate across the island and
in some cases nest on it, to the great pleasure of nature lovers, but
much to the disgust of the local farmers whose cultivated land can be
downgraded from seeded corn or oats to blown flyspeck when two
hundred or more of these living Rube-Goldberg machines go to work
on it for two or three hours on a spring afternoon. The cranes have
light greyish plumage with rust-coloured foreheads and beaks like
iron railway spikes. They stand over a metre tall and, at a distance,
resemble a gently inflated bagpipe delicately propped atop a couple of
jointed broomsticks. Their wing span is a preposterous two metres,
and unlike herons, which in flight fold their necks into an S-shape,
they fly straight out, playing Concorde to the B-52s that are their
cousins.

We had barely left the farm when, across a field at perhaps sixty metres' distance, we spotted the first sandhill crane I had ever seen and, as it turned out, the last. The species is nervous about the presence of human beings, and no sooner had we spotted the bird and stopped the van, than it took to the air, a sort of avian Icarus, pressed upwards and away, a centimetre of elevation at a time, by the almost slow-motion downstroke of its wings.

GEORGE AND I shared a well-quilted double bed next to Stephanie's sewing room—or at least did so until three or four in the morning when, rattled by snoring and the verbal semblances of George's nightmares, I took to the floor, leaping up on several occasions to get rid of leg cramps.

At breakfast Stephanie made the blue-plate suggestion that we stay on the island for another day. On her part, it was a simple kindness, but, after seven hundred kilometres of snow, rain, and wind, George and I interpreted it as the strictest of medical prescriptions.

So for the first time since leaving Thunder Bay, I took a "recreation" day, though by no means a day off, satisfying both my curiosity and my deepening addiction to endorphins with a hike of twenty-five kilometres around an island where there is still no such thing as a paved parking lot or stoplight. The postcard I bought at the Kentvale General Store showed an "Alutone" photo of the establishment with its green and orange awning, and with a '56 Ford and '57 DeSoto parked out front.

All of which is not to say that the dewiness and innocence of decades past is unmarred by the degenerate and nasty old present. At about 2:00 P.M., when I stopped on the Tenth Sideroad for a chat with an island veteran named Harold Kent—a man after whose ancestors Kentvale was named—I heard what I suspect were some of the more pressing of the island's ongoing concerns, among them that "the Ministry of Natural Resources doesn't know bugger all," and that "the deer hunting season should be two weeks, not one."

According to Harold, deer were so populous on the island that they had practically overrun the place. I told him I had seen a group of nine of them standing in a field, and he said, "People can't even keep gardens anymore." He pointed out where deer had cleared the lower browse off a robust forty-foot cedar tree and said that so many deer were being hit on the roads, the car insurance companies were beginning to ask questions.

At dinner the previous night, Steve Roedde had told me that when called to the local hospital to tend to drivers with injuries after collisions with deer, he always asked them what condition the deer was in. "If it's suffering," he said, "you want to go out there and deal with it." He had recently come across a deer whose rear legs had been snapped by the impact of a car. "It had to be shot," he said. However, before that could happen, Steve had to get a hunter who was willing to do the job, and get the permission of the Ministry of Natural Resources to shoot a deer out of season. "It was pretty horrendous," he said. "When we got there, the poor thing tried to walk away from us on its stumps."

Harold Kent told me the ministry should never have taken the bounty off wolves. "They kill sheep and calves," he said, "and there are fewer people farming because of it."

As for islanders giving up gardening because of the deer, it seemed to me that nearly every house I passed had a substantial garden. And if people had quit farming, it wasn't apparent. There were farms practically everywhere you looked. I asked Harold if placing a bounty on wolves and thereby decreasing the wolf population wouldn't allow deer to become more numerous than ever. He said, "That's how those guys think! What you have to do is shoot the wolves *and* shoot the deer."

"That's a lot of shooting," I said, and he told me some people thought the cranes should be shot, too.

Despite our differences of opinion, I was happy to have met Harold Kent, both for the unself-conscious savagery of his views and because he so shamelessly evoked a time before political and ecological correctness (not to mention penicillin, painless dentistry, and moral ambiguity)—a time all too readily "tidied up" in our sometimes idealized perspective on the past.

TWO NIGHTS LATER, during the early evening, George and I entered Chutes Provincial Park at Massey and, because no attendant was on duty, simply pitched our tent on the choicest campsite we could find. But within half an hour, as we cooked dinner, a sturdy little Punchinello, who introduced himself as Buttons or perhaps Button, pulled up to our picnic table in a park truck to check our credentials and collect our fee. I showed him our pass letter, and after taking it to his truck and studying its ten-line message for three or four minutes, he got out and announced with regimental gravity, "Well, men, it looks like you can stay free." Fires were allowed, he told us, eyeing with skepticism the smoky conflagration on which George had a piece of butt steak sizzling. However, the burning of even a pine needle or twig gathered on park property was "strictly" prohibited. Flouting the rule could fetch "a maximum penalty of three years in prison," as stated on a board at the park gate.

Given that our heap of gathered twigs sat a half-metre high by the fire pit (representing perhaps three or four life sentences) we were hardly in a position to deny wrongdoing. So like grovelling ten-year-olds, we promised never to do it again, beyond which I explained to Button that I understood, on principle, why the likes of ourselves couldn't just sashay around burning off the excess combustibles of a public park.

On the other hand, the presumed causality between the act of burning a few dead twigs and that of, say, felling three-ton old growth or busting up the park office to keep the fire going seemed about as remote as the presumption that burning a few sheets of newspaper in the living-room hearth was but a prelude to taking an axe to the piano or chesterfield. It seemed ironic, moreover, that in a surrounding wilderness of a zillion trees—in a part of the world where the same government ministry that runs the parks routinely licenses logging corporations to bulldoze and skid out megatons of living trees (toward the questionable necessity of printing another ten million Wal-Mart flyers)—we were prohibited from gathering up a few dead sticks and pine needles.

"What do we do for wood?" George asked.

"Well, we sell it," said Button, who promptly departed, rematerializing five minutes later with eight or nine bone-dry faggots in a net bag (made in China), for which he fleeced me five dollars. I declined to tell him that this level of crime, too, is punishable, but in the Court of Last Judgments. And the moment he had gone, George and I jumped in the van, left the park, and cut ourselves a load of deadfall spruce out along the highway—and spirited it back to the campsite.

IN THE MORNING, George drove me forty kilometres back west to where I had quit the previous day. It was windy, and the Trans-Canada in these parts is narrow, with narrow-sloped shoulders, making me more vulnerable than usual to the traffic. At times the explosion of air off an eighteen-wheeler passing at close range would straighten me up motionless for a second or two, as if I had slammed into a sheet of plywood. At one point, amid a blast of dust, my hat was pried loose and flew three or four metres into the air behind me and then off down the highway in the truck's slipstream as I went chasing after it.

It was exhausting, and during the early afternoon, traumatized by an overly close brush with a van, I took to the railway tracks for six or seven kilometres. For the most part, the tracks are just twenty or thirty metres from the highway on this stretch, but they are a decidedly different world. Their detritus is rail spikes, bits of diesel machinery, coupling pins, rail plates, great gobs of grease. There are fewer carcasses of small animals than on the highway, but there are more dead deer, perhaps because of the mesmerizing effect of the bright single headlamp.

Whereas during my childhood steel rail was manufactured and laid down in ten-metre lengths (the joins of which cause the endless clickety of the wheels), it is now made by extrusion moulding in lengths of two hundred metres that are transported to the site on eight or ten consecutive flatcars. But my response to these New Age rails, and to the coming of a train at about 3:00 P.M., was as intuitive and childlike as it had been during the 1950s. At the first distant rumble, I reached into my pocket, pulled out a penny, nickel, and quarter, and having wet them so they wouldn't shimmy off, set them overlapped on the tracks as my dad taught me to do. I then disappeared into the spruce woods to be well back from the blast and a minute later picked up the coins, gleaming and as big as poker chips, and welded together in the shape of a snowman.

The problem with the tracks is that cinders in the rail bed—some of them the size of potatoes—make the footing almost impossible. You can escape them by stepping on the ties, but to do so one at a time, as a child might, is too restrictive to the adult gait. And to take them in twos exaggerates the gait to where you are virtually leaping instead of walking. Besides, you have to stare constantly at your feet to avoid twisting an ankle. To walk the rail itself, as I did for a couple of hundred metres, takes entirely too much focus and, of course, also requires that you stare at your feet.

As I stepped precariously along the rail, however, a mysterious thing happened, a quite wonderful thing, in that I found myself briefly able to abstract my surroundings and to transport myself fairly effortlessly to a kind of fantasy version of the high wire. I have written about wire walkers, and once attempted to walk a practice wire a few feet off the ground—and had a sense there, too, of what it must be like to be eighty feet above the crowd.

For a few seconds, I was so absorbed in the hallucination of being high up, balanced against gravity, that when my focus wavered and I stepped from the rail, I could, in the split second before my foot touched ground, feel myself descending, like Alice, through space.

It was neither the first nor the last time that I experienced such convincing daydreams as I walked. I have wondered in retrospect if the implied mantra of endlessly putting one foot in front of the other—combined perhaps with a surfeit of endorphins or with being a trifle punch-drunk from the wind—occasionally eased me into a shallow hypnotic trance or waking sleep. Certainly there were times when, say, the honk of a car horn twenty metres away startled me into a vastly disproportionate response and left me with the feeling that I had been jarred out of sleep.

If it all seemed faintly familiar, it was perhaps because as a child I had been a sleepwalker, a very capable one, and at times woke up, for instance, with my hockey equipment and skates on by the back door of our house in Deep River, or drifted past my parents' bedroom with the explanation that I was going out to play football or build a snow fort. As a result, I am acutely aware that the border between our waking and sleeping lives is more delicate and permeable than we might assume.

DURING THE LATE AFTERNOON, the wind went down, and the day was quickly quite hot. However, as I settled to this brief but cherished respite, I was almost immediately surrounded by blackflies—at first just a few, but in no time clouds of them coming out of the swamp in the absence of the breeze. I had brought along the bug jacket lent to me by my neighbours Lila and Gerry. But of course I didn't have it with me—in part because Button had assured me the previous evening that "the good thing" about the blackflies, the few gazillion that were around, was that they weren't biting yet. Apparently, they had not yet entered the sadistic phase of their sexual cycle. Unfortunately, the blackflies had not received the memo on this, or had not read it, and (like the rest of us, at times) hadn't a clue what phase of their sex lives they were supposed to be in.

At any rate, within half an hour, they had bitten at least fifty craterous holes in my eyelids, forehead, and temples—anywhere they were able to smell the blood running close to the surface. I jogged the last kilometre into Massey, waving a blue bandana around my head, went straight to the hardware store, and bought a bottle of satanic-smelling insect repellent. By this time I looked like a kid with a heavy dose of chickenpox, and that night in the tent, as George tended the fire, I rubbed antibiotic ointment onto both ends of my anatomy, as much on my head as on my feet.

I WOULD HAVE BEEN GLEEFUL if the blackflies had become an infestation, or even a curse. It would have meant, above all, that the weather had stayed warm enough to hatch and sustain them. But by the next day, the wind was again twisting out of the north, and my first steps onto Manitoulin Island a day after that were accompanied by the now-customary scattering of snowflakes.

Manitoulin and its northern neighbour, La Cloche Island, are a borderland between Ontario's northern and southern worlds. Fittingly, they are part forest and part farmland, part Shield granite and part limestone of the sort on which much of central North America is founded.

Manitoulin is shaped like a tomahawk head, and is some two thousand square kilometres in area. But it was the island's dramatic and spectral geography, not its size, that centuries ago inspired its reputation as the dwelling place of the great spirit Manitou, the Almighty Voice of the Ojibway and Algonquin Indians.

One of the more interesting things I heard during my days on the island was that at a point during the nineteenth century Manitoulin was largely abandoned by the First Nations who, believing evil spirits had supplanted the good, were said to have set fire to as much of the island as possible and to have taken off in their canoes.

But little is made of it these days. Unquestionably, the First Nations are back—and, judging by appearances, are doing relatively well, at least on a material level. In fact, the Great Spirit of the culture is now the centrepiece of Native-run tourism on the island—a flourishing contortion of reality, one of the slogans for which is "Catch the Spirit" (as one can do, for instance, by taking the Great Spirit Circle Tour of the local highways or shacking up in a government-approved fireproof teepee or buying Tee Pee Takeout at the Wigwam Gift Shoppe and Motel). Certainly, there is an antic incongruity to seeing the Ojibway word *wigwam* partnered with the supposed old English of the word *shoppe,* and in a broader sense seeing the hard-won advances of the local Natives sublimated to a hucksterism that not only tolerates but romances the summer influx of honkies.

George took this subordination of his roots in stride. But he suffered the incipient transition from northern into southern culture with considerably greater discomfort—in fact reverted to what I recognized as a lingering, perhaps valid, prairie apprehension about the true and shadowy nature of Ontario.

That night in Little Current, where we had checked into the Bridgewater Motel, George carried his quietly burgeoning paranoia about Ontario greed, arrogance, and so on to the bar of an old downtown hotel. There, it so happened, one of the more public members of the Upper Canada establishment, Art Eggleton, a one-time mayor of Toronto and at the time federal minister of defence, was being feted in the hotel dining room. As if this were not offence enough to my Métis travelling companion (offence by proximity), Eggleton was pilloried in the press the next day and subsequently demoted from the federal cabinet for slipping a government contract onto the desk of his girlfriend (thereby, of course, confirming all suspicions about the dastardly leisure classes of southern Ontario).

When George came in at around 1:30 A.M., he was in a horse froth. To cap everything, he had met a man named Peter who had come to Manitoulin to escape the horrors of Etobicoke and had filled George's head with suppurating images of what awaited us down the line— impossible traffic and pollution, institutionalized avarice, indescribable corporate ill will. Ontario, George told me in thirty-eight ways, was an unlivable tyranny.

What bothered me more than his diatribe, however, was that while making it he left the door to the room wide open, allowing snow flurries to drift in.

"Would ya shut the door?" I said.

"It's too hot in here!"

"It was the right temperature until you arrived." I got out of bed, where I had been making notes, and pushed the door shut.

But as soon as I returned to bed, George opened it again and proceeded to tell me that he didn't know if he could stand going farther into this damnable province.

I said, "George, you don't know anything about Ontario. You've never even lived here." Much to his disgust, I then told him that I had met more (and more egregious) right-wing snobs and idealogues in Winnipeg than I ever had in Hamilton or Toronto.

"The rents are crushing people," he said.

"Crushing who?"

"Peter. The guy's exhausted with it."

It turned out Peter was on a disability pension, was having troubles with his ex-wife, and had decided "the Big Smoke," as Steve Roedde had called it, was to blame.

"So what are you telling me?" I said. "That you're going home?"

George shook his head, turned mournfully to the food box, and began making himself a peanut butter sandwich.

"You *want* to suffer," I said. "You're worse than Mrs. Gummage."

"Ah, shut up," he said softly. And when he had eaten his sandwich, he stood in the open doorway for a minute, then lit his pipe and, without speaking, headed out to the parking lot to smoke.

He returned ten minutes later, subdued if not relaxed, and lay silently on his bed.

Eventually he said, "I dunno what's the matter with me."

"I do," I said. "You're stressed out. Nothing's going to happen to us in southern Ontario."

I assured him, in fact, that what lay ahead was going to be paradise after the blizzards and stresses of Lake Superior. "Plus," I said, "you'll be able to get your fiddle out and do some busking."

"I miss playing," he said.

"Well, play! Go get your violin." And two minutes later, he had his fiddle under his chin—his one true sedative—and was slowly pacing the room playing quiet variations on a few old jigs and blues tunes.

When I had nearly drifted off, he reached into his jacket pocket and produced a rolled plastic bag. As if tossing a bone to a dog, he threw it on the bed beside me. I peeked in and discovered a substantial chunk of cooked trout. His pal Peter had sent it over, part of a nine-pound laker he had caught that afternoon in the channel between Manitoulin and St. Cloche Islands.

"Is it for me?" I said somewhat apologetically.

"It's for you," said George, and I jumped up, put the fish on a plate, and doused it in lemon juice and salt.

"Who exactly is this guy?" I said between bites, feeling suddenly more kindly toward the man responsible for the past half-hour's antipathies.

MY ROUTE THE NEXT MORNING took me south on Highway 6 over contours of dazzling amber limestone; through beaver bogs, meadows, and poplar woods. It is not difficult to understand why the early Natives named the island as they did. In places from the highway, you can see across miles of trees and rock to the open water of Manitowaning Bay and beyond that to Georgian Bay, oceanic in the morning sun.

My instructions to George were to pick me up after seven hours, and sure enough as I walked into Manitowaning, there he was, alight with the news that if we hustled back to Little Current, Peter would take us up to Swift Current, to the Narrows, for a little trout fishing. I told George I thought I needed a rest. But by the time we got back, I was feeling somewhat revived. After a quick shower at the motel, I slipped into the back seat of Peter's '78 Eldorado—the vehicular equivalent of the Norse longboat—and we cruised off up the highway. Peter was a slim, somewhat childlike bundle of nerves, a sporadic practitioner of meditation who, George told me, more consistently regulated his psyche with concurrent doses of Prozac and marijuana. He was in love with fishing and, for reasons that were beyond me, felt compelled to tell us en route that he had not actually caught the nine-pound lake trout that he had so generously shared with us the night before—"I lied about that," he said placidly—but had "scored it from some Americans" who had handed it over as an act of goodwill when he himself had caught nothing.

"Oh," said George, nodding gently as he squinted into the pipe smoke before him (penny for your thoughts, old boy?).

It was not difficult to see why Peter was down on his luck as a fisherman. When we got to the Narrows, he revealed that he had neglected to bring bait.

To compensate for the debacle, he embarked on a brisk hunt for crayfish, eventually announcing that the crayfish were "still hibernating." Instead, he loaded his hook with a dead beetle he had found. The Narrows is a fast-flowing channel of green water between the northern reaches of Lake Huron and the upper extreme of Georgian Bay. It is surrounded by mile after mile of shoreline alvar—flat yellow limestone crowded with ring-shaped or fibrous-looking fossils and by bands of iron-red ore so intricately laid down as to suggest the touch of a stone mason. As I hiked around, examining the rock and the shallows, Peter cast his dead beetle and then a treble-hooked spoon, with almost preternatural inefficiency. The water in the channel is so clear that from time to time we could see trophy-sized trout drifting in the current. But they wouldn't bite. And there were no benevolent Americans to save the day.

It had begun to rain, but I was so curious about the shoreline that instead of riding back into town with Peter and George, I walked up Cloche Island, across the alvar, through a strewn archive of old ship's chains, antique boat and engine parts, tiny pink violets, and at one point the skeleton of a bear whose heavy thigh bone was so gorgeously and symetrically sculpted I could not resist wrenching it loose and sticking it in my pocket. I came eventually to a long-abandoned farm and wandered around the garden and ghost house, peering into the windows, trying to imagine how anyone might have coaxed a crop out of the few centimetres of soil atop the alvar.

It was only when I got back to the highway and jumped the rusted remains of the farm's fence that I was able to see the front side of a government sign: "Indian Reserve. Positively no entry. Violators will be prosecuted. Minimum $50 fine and one month in jail. The Federal Indian Act."

I walked away, questioning what it is about governments that makes them so determined to create crime, not to mention punishment, out of, say, the gathering of a few sticks in a provincial park or an innocent hike across a kilometre or two of unpopulated land. As Margaret Atwood said of fences, "There's nothing they can keep in, or out." What made the sign doubly memorable, I thought, was that the bureaucracy that posted it had spent a century or so attempting to integrate, not separate, the country's aboriginal and white popula- tions—only to arrive at this threat to send interminglers to jail. My own attitude was that if the aboriginals of Manitoulin didn't want me on their land, let them say so. But don't leave it up to a bureaucracy that in the words of a seditious Native friend, "no self-respecting Indian would bother to piss on if it was on fire." The truth is I have never met a Native person, either in the United States or Canada, who did not welcome me onto his or her reserve.

I would have kicked the sign over entirely had it not been for my hasty realization that even Manitou laughs. Because directly across the highway another sign said, "Experience our Heritage. Stop in. Next left. Ojibway moccasins, quill crafts, birch bark. Catch the Spirit of Manitoulin!" (Will the real Spirit of Manitoulin please stand up?)

Where the highway crossed back over the Narrows, I crawled beneath the bridge (undoubtedly breaching another set of statutes) and watched a hundred or more torpedo-shaped suckers, big fellas, sculling in the current, motionless except for the flicker of fins and mouths as they gathered in minnows and bugs. I dropped in a pebble (surely breaking yet another law) and saw my subterfuge rewarded when one of the fish inhaled it, quivered slightly, and shot it back out.

By the time I got back to Little Current, it was 11:00 P.M., and a dense wet snow was falling. The twenty-kilometre walk had been arduous, but my knee had held, despite my having left my knee brace in the motel. George later told me that Peter had quite seriously questioned my *compos mentis* when I had told them to go on without me. It wasn't as if I had been obliged to finish what I had started. Twice while I walked, Native drivers had stopped and offered me a lift. But I didn't want one. More than ever these days I was enjoying the intensity and satisfactions of the road—as well as a revitalized awareness of myself.

George had told me one night that he was afraid I was getting too isolated in my endeavour. Despite our occasional differences, he was doing what he could to prevent that—and I appreciated it. But I was feeling increasingly comfortable and self-reliant during the long bouts on my own.

If anything, I wanted to be on the road even more than I was—and ironically, as my fitness increased, I took ever-greater pleasure in getting *off* the road, in the feeling of spentness and exhaustion that came at the end of a long day of walking.

As I came into Little Current, I stopped at Farquhars Dairy, an island institution on the north side of town, and treated myself to a thirty-ounce milkshake and a pair of five-dollar banana splits— modestly restorative appetizers for the party-sized pizza that George and I picked up at a local restaurant and ate in the room before I collapsed unconscious on the bed.

WET AND HUNGRY, I limped into South Baymouth at about supper hour the following day. The next morning, we would board the S.S. *Chi-Cheemaun*, an immense 150-car ferry, and sail fifty kilometres across the main channel that separates Lake Huron from Georgian Bay to the resort town of Tobermory on the north tip of the Bruce Peninsula.

We pitched the tent free in John Budd Park, a somewhat gloomy and over-used tenting site a ways north of the ferry dock, where I washed a few clothes, and hung them on tree branches in the rain.

In the morning, it was still drizzling. But we were anxious to catch the first ferry out. So, rather than pack up properly, we simply tore the tent down and threw it, sopping, into the van. And at nine o'clock, we clanked up the gangway for our passage into the dark heart of Ontario.

For me, the highlight of the two-hour crossing was going into the cafeteria and spotting a friend of mine, Jackie Field, a dreamy, some would say mystic, young woman who the previous autumn had taken a creative writing class from me at Lakehead University. We had had, since the beginning, a candid and communicative friendship—talked easily about writing, about matters of the spirit, and about the ongoing conundrum that is life on earth. She was travelling with her dad, John, who was helping her move home to southern Ontario. When the three of us had talked for perhaps an hour, Jackie got up, wandered off, and it was only as we were heading into the staircases to our vehicles that she appeared out of the ship's gift shop, happily holding two small wrapped parcels, one for George, whom she had met in the meantime, one for myself. As it turned out, she had spent the better part of half an hour selecting books for us—George's a sketch book or diary, which he put to use immediately; mine *The Lone Pine Field Guide to the Animal Tracks of Ontario,* hand-inscribed with the hope that "the tracks of the Spirit" would guide me "safely through" and that I would "sing lightly" as I walked.

The rain had stopped during the crossing, and it was in the spirit of this serene goodwill that I headed down the famous Bruce Trail south out of Tobermory. The walking trail follows the Niagara Escarpment for some 740 kilometres down the Bruce Peninsula and across central Ontario into the Hamilton area, then southeast to within a few kilometres of Niagara Falls. The trail was cleared and developed during the early 1960s and is considered a model of what can be done by devoted volunteers of the sort who keep it marked and maintained to this day. It is also a model of "stakeholder" participation, in that much of the trail crosses privately held land whose owners long ago consigned passage rights in perpetuity to the Bruce Trail Association.

For more than four years during the late 1980s, I lived with my wife and son, Matt, on the wooded lip of the Niagara Escarpment near Dundas. The Bruce Trail ran smack across the frontage of our rented house, and we were at times a kind of "mission to hikers," providing water, phone, directions, first aid, and occasionally, rogue parking. Every once in a very long while, a hiker who had walked all the way from Tobermory, perhaps five hundred kilometres to the north, stopped to talk. These were not the sort of people who needed directions or Band-Aids. On a day in perhaps 1987, one such hiker told me about the portion of the trail that runs east then south from Tobermory along the high limestone cliffs of Georgian Bay—about the "Mediterranean" spectacle of its beaches and rock pillars, and of the forty-kilometre views over luminescent turquoise water. He said it had been the pinnacle of his experience on the trail, and at that point I decided I would one day walk it, too.

Now, fifteen years later, here I was, striding along a shoreline that on a sunny afternoon in late spring might have been taken for the glory spots of the Aegean. But it is not the Aegean parts that you see first. The trail twists out of Tobermory through dense mixed forest, spongy underfoot, or over well-weathered rock. By the time it reaches the water at Little Cove, eight or ten kilometres southeast of town, you have been long enough in the tunnel of foliage that you are ready for the thrill. And you get it. The water is greener than anything you might have imagined—and bluer too, the colours swirling and stretching into a mottled map that blends gradually into the foiled silver of the horizon. It is dream country. Towers of sculpted limestone, bleached as white as Lot's wife, rise out of the shallows and off the beach, some to the height of the trail, perhaps forty metres above the water. Moss and scrawny spruce grow in pockets between the ledges of rock, and tiny twisted cedars, some said to be two hundred years old, corkscrew out of the cliffs.

The surprises come one after another—mostly scenic. But at one point, a hawk screamed angrily at me from behind. A skunk threw me into a quick pirouette, and a heap of greenish bear poop, well cut with seeds and newly dropped, had me squinting into the undergrowth and glancing over my shoulder. The scat of a fox or coyote was, for reasons I couldn't fathom, as green as the bear's.

Where the trail cut inland, I walked through hundreds of scattered trilliums, both white and pink, and fields of forget-me-nots. I felt a gentle tweezing on my neck, and picked off a ladybug with twenty spots.

A sign along the trail said "200 METRES TO THE LARGEST SINKHOLE IN THE AREA," and an arrow pointed up a side path. I might have preferred to dance a slow one with Faye Dunaway or Sophia Loren, but because there is something faintly arousing about the thought of the planet caving in, off I went (quickly discovering that, as in life, the trail to the sinkhole was more alluringly marked than the main chance). A sign halfway said, "YOU ARE HALFWAY TO THE SINKHOLE."

On the off chance that you make the trip, I will not spoil it for you by describing what I discovered at the end of the path—except to say that it is a large plain hole in the ground. And like a typical Canadian male, I took a pee into it. And like a typical Canadian male writer (as defined by Margaret Atwood), I have now written about taking a pee into it.

By mid-afternoon, the day had turned hot, and I took my shirt off in the sun and wind. At the most seaward point of an elaborately eroded promontory, I scrambled down five or six natural stone steps onto an anterior ledge. My intent had been to sit for a while and watch the water, but in no time I had my T-shirt folded into a pad for my head and was stretched out on the moss. And was then briefly, sweetly asleep as the water crashed forty metres below.

Fools are always well treated in paradise, and I could hardly have known as I lay there that within an hour I would be hopelessly, lamentably lost.

During the late afternoon, I began looking for Cyprus Lake, which was connected by several paths to the trail on which I was walking and where I had arranged to meet George. But when I got to a lake that I believed to be Cyprus, the paths weren't there—not one of them.

For several days I hadn't carried the cellphone because there had been no service on Manitoulin. But on this day I had it with me—and now phoned George, who had a better map than mine and whom I suspected would be able to tell me where I was if I described the lake.

I might have been right. Unfortunately, in the dense bush we could not keep our phone connection for more than a second or two at a time. I'd phone, he'd answer, and the phone would go dead.

During a dozen or more mini-calls, I urged him to drive the van to higher ground, where we'd have a better chance of connecting. But I couldn't tell whether he was getting the drift of things. Or for that matter, whether higher ground existed in the area.

Finally, I simply assumed that the water before me was Cyprus Lake—assumed incorrectly—and leaving the main trail, headed off around the shore of the lake through forest heavily blocked by undergrowth. Within fifteen minutes I had picked and plowed my way around a beaver swamp at one end, forfeiting entirely my sense of direction, and was as dead lost as I have ever been. As for directional clues, I could not tell how far I had come around the lake because its densely forested shoreline looked the same from any angle. Moreover, the sun was still high enough, and the foliage thick enough, that I could not properly tell in which direction the sun was moving.

The psychologist Robert Neel has said that walking in a formally constructed labyrinth is an invocation first to silence, then to meditation, as well as to clarified senses and consciousness.

It would be a stretch to call any part of my overall route a labyrinth. But there were times certainly when there was a hint of the labyrinth or maze—for example, during decision-making over which turn to take to stay on course, or when assessing how the map corresponded to the terrain. Even on the Trans-Canada, where only one route existed, the walking could stimulate an internalized labyrinth of memory and imagination. So it should have come as no surprise, now, where my walk most approximated an actual labyrinth, that I felt a sense not so much of concern or frustration as of vigorous stimulation. Even during the late afternoon, when I was still unable to differentiate one point of the compass from another, my inner radar was on full alert, sparking an exaggerated awareness of my surroundings and myself.

The blackflies alone were frustrating, to the point where I realized that if my luck dissolved completely and I had to spend a night in the bush, I'd need a strategy against them—such as burying myself in leaves. At one point, I remembered what Walter Twoboy, a Cree trapper from northern Manitoba, had said about being lost in the woods—fundamentally, that it was impossible, because you couldn't be lost in your own home. And he was at home and could survive, at any time of year, even in the deepest part of the forest.

I was, of course, not at home and was permitted my calmness in part by the knowledge that no matter what happened, or when, I had to be within seven or eight kilometres of the Lake Huron shore or a road or highway or dwelling of some sort. And as the sun arced over into the west, I knew, of course, that by following it, I would eventually come out to Highway 6—and wished, perhaps, that I was more legitimately and honourably lost.

WHEN I HAD WANDERED AROUND for perhaps an hour and a half, I came upon a faint two-lane trail, obviously unused, but which had clearly once borne traffic and would lead somewhere if I just followed it away from the lake.

To prevent a lengthening story from turning into the wanderings of Odysseus, I shall say only that, indeed, after forty minutes—of swamp, of standing water, of forest at times so dense that I could barely see the sky—the trail widened into a one-lane road, and I was able to talk briefly to George by phone. By this time, he had consulted the provincial police and had commandeered the help of a young woman from the national park, who now came on the phone. When I told her I had just passed a rickety cabin, she said, "Oh, my God, you must be on Roper's Road! There's no way we can go in there."

I said, "Who is Roper, and what's the problem?"

If it had been a movie and I its director, I would have edited the script at this point, as it veered sharply into cliché. Then again, life is cornier than the movies—before she could answer me, the phone went dead.

I dialled again (close-up of finger punching buttons). But this time I could not reach her.

Understandably, the woman's comment put a new jump in what was rapidly becoming a very weary step. By now the sun had swung far enough into the west that I knew I was headed toward Highway 6, and kept expecting it to appear. But another hour passed before I heard distant traffic and came finally to a swampy clearing by the highway, where George was sitting in the van drinking a beer with the windows up to keep the blackflies out. He was exhausted, impetuous, anxious to explain how he had had to follow this fast-driving young woman, who after she realized I was on Roper's Road had been kind enough to lead him to this spot.

But she had spooked him—in large part by telling him that under no circumstances should he drive in to get me. Roper apparently didn't mind the odd hiker using his road to escape the bush, but took a hostile view of people driving on it, especially any sort of government or park official. We never did find out what Roper might have been up to, presumably in the cabin I had passed—quite possibly nothing more than reading Plato or refining heroin or plutonium. Nevertheless, both

George and I were happy to vacate the locale, from which we drove up the highway to the national park and, without registering (because there was no one on duty to write up our names, addresses, and licence plate number in triplicate and put us in the database and advise us about fires and not feeding the animals and what to do with garbage and how to display our site documents and sell us wood and present the water advisory and the park map and calculate the provincial and federal taxes), we simply drove in and lit a little cooking fire and pitched our tent.

ONE OF THE MANY REASONS I care deeply about George is his acute malapropian subversion of the language. His is a world of *Canudians* and *Kookeranians* and *lebasians,* and of writers named *Dostiofsky* and *Kokshwenkle* and *Gurthy,* and a country named *Zamboobaway.*

As we ate that evening, he began telling me about a herringbone jacket his dad had bought for him when he was a teenager—transposed in the tale to "a hambone jacket"—and how proud he had been of it, had worn it to the prom, and so on.

I said, "Are you talking about a herringbone jacket?"

"Ah, you private-school guys," he shot back, knowing as always that I would feel obliged to remind him that I had never attended a private school. But rather than do so, I reminded him that it was he, not I, who had taken a master's degree in a subject no less rarefied than fine art, in a city no less sophisticated than New York—this compared to my own efforts in humble botany and zoology at the University of Toronto. "You're an elitist," I told him. "And I'm getting tired of the condescension"—at which he busted out laughing for perhaps the first time in three days.

My friendship with George has always been a bit crotchety and on our current travels was rarely more fractious than when we accompanied one another on shopping ventures, as we did the following morning in Tobermory. Where food was concerned, I tended to want more and bigger and better quality. George, on the other hand, wanted less and smaller, but was more bullish on plastics and metals; he believed we "needed" a better dishpan, a proper kettle, a new paring knife, a length of rope, paper towels, snap-top containers for leftovers, a wooden spoon, new pot scrubbers, a fishing rod, a Rubbermaid juice container. He had acquired a big steel pot and a better frying pan at the Value Village store in the Soo. And ceramic mugs. And more cutlery. And a more efficient corkscrew. I said, "George, do we really need all this stuff?" and I quoted Thoreau to the effect that "a man is rich in proportion to what he can afford to do without."

"Don't tell me about doing without," snapped George, who had done his share of doing without during thirty years on the financial fringe.

The debate came to a good-natured head over George's suggestion that we get "a couple of cans of creamed corn for emergencies." Which we did, despite my speculation on what sort of emergencies we might get into that could be solved by a can of creamed corn. I exaggerated only slightly by telling George that, for me, facing a puddle of creamed corn on a plate *was* an emergency.

6

The Big Dark Heart
of Ontario

Until now, we had had very few route choices to make. There had been one highway east, the Trans-Canada, and one highway south across Manitoulin and down the Bruce Peninsula.

Now, for the first time, as I approached the base of the peninsula, there were any number of highways and backroads that could take me into Toronto.

Destination NYC was still pretty much an imponderable—in sharp contrast to the endpoint of most contemporary travel, during which route and journey are entirely sublimated to destination. As air passengers, for example, we don't even think to ask what our route might be. The airline decides, and the journey is little more than a mild, time-consuming inconvenience (made less tedious, ironically, by the screening of movies as often as not set in land-scapes of the sort that once gave context to those "tedious" journeys on the ground).

In some ways, I would like to have stayed longer on the Bruce Trail. But because the trail is so tortuously indirect, I found after a couple of days that I was walking forty kilometres of it to get ten kilometres closer to Manhattan.

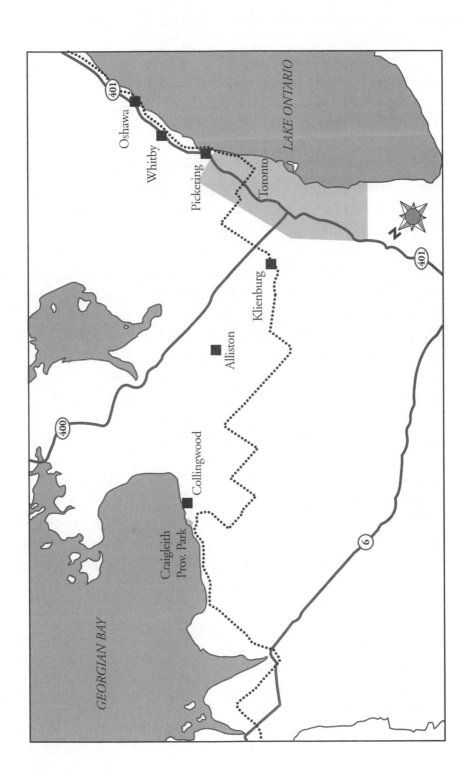

So at Ferndale, I switched back to roads, and by the evening of May 30 had reached Craigleith, at the south end of Georgian Bay.

George and I pitched camp for the night at Craigleith Provincial Park, west of Collingwood—the first provincial park in which we encountered something approximating a crowd. Just south of the park, Blue Mountain and its adjoining ridge of hills rise precipitously, then fall away gradually toward the lower Great Lakes. Firewood was hard to come by along this populated stretch of waterfront, but with a few scrounged sticks and a piece or two out of our cache, we got a little fire going and cooked up a couple of half-kilo rainbows that George had caught in the A&P in Collingwood. At dusk, our youngish female neighbour—another elusive Gloxinia—put on a tiny bright-beamed headlamp that enabled her to wash her dishes and split some wood, using both hands. The entertainment started when she crawled into her tent and hung the lamp on the back part of the frame, throwing a vivid one-woman shadow-play, Matisse-like silhouettes, against the tent's front wall: Gloxinia blowing up her air mattress and making her bed, Gloxinia straining one way and another to get her clothes off, Gloxinia tucking in, reading, drinking her nightcap.

As i walked south along County Road 19 toward Blue Mountain on Sunday morning, a man's voice came sharply out of a grove of lilacs to my right: "Would ya take a dump fer cryin' out loud! I'm gonna be late for church!" I turned to see an elderly man in a white suit, with hair the colour of Old South, standing over a Chihuahua dog.

"Take a crap!" he hollered. "I've gotta get to church!"

This is ski country, and on the slopes closest to the bay, as many as forty or fifty ski and snowboard runs dropped like streamers of greeny blue velvet from the mountaintops.

I walked steeply uphill for ten kilometres under a cloudless sky, with a frigid north wind at my back. The view over Georgian Bay gets more spectacular as you climb, and for stretches I couldn't resist turning and walking backwards, taking both the scenery and the wind in the face.

As I pressed uphill, four immense women in an old Mercury Topaz drove out of a lane in the maple woods and settled in alongside me heading upward and south. But the car's engine was so weak, the hill so steep, and the women so ample that the car simply couldn't get going and, for a hundred metres, putted along, engine straining, at exactly the pace I was walking. Far from being embarrassed by this triumph of load over acceleration, the women laughed and hooted until the car shook. When I began to pull ahead of them on a particularly steep stretch, one of them rolled down the rear window and hollered, "Can we offer you a lift, sir?" Eventually, on a flatter stretch, they picked up speed and disappeared over the next hill.

THE SCENERY atop the high rolling plain that extends south off the mountains was as idyllically pastoral as any I'd seen, and at times throughout the morning and afternoon, I was reminded of Wordsworth on his walks through the fells and fens of the English Lake District. However, where Wordsworth saw sheep, stone fences, and daffodils, I saw sheep, stone fences, and dandelions—fields of them, yellow to the horizon and as impressive to the eye as anything I saw in the Lake District when I walked there during the early 1970s.

One thing you don't see in Canada or the United States but see routinely in England and western Europe are dozens, if not hundreds, of other walkers, often with knapsacks on their backs—in the mountains, in farm country, on forest roads and trails. I have read that millions of British citizens go hiking on warm-weather weekends. By comparison, I saw just five other serious hikers on some 2,100 kilometres of road and trail between Thunder Bay and New York City. Walking is taken so seriously in England that a decade ago the multi-million-member Ramblers' Association began what it called "Forbidden Britain" mass trespasses in an attempt to clear out remaining impediments to walkers on private land. The block of votes represented by British hikers is so strong that the British Labour Party recently honoured a well-noted election promise by passing extensive "right to roam" legislation. I do not think I am far off in suggesting that any North American political party that campaigned for the rights of rural walkers would be dismissed as pinko heretics, in violation of the rights of property owners, not to mention the television-automobile extravaganza, and that it would not need a computer, or even a string of beads, to total its votes.

As a result of the ferment in England, centuries-old trails through the countryside and forests remain open by law to hikers. In countries such as Holland, Sweden, and Spain, citizens retain wider rights yet to open space. The result is that Europeans are perhaps more intimate with their geography than are most of us in the United States and Canada, where land is more rigidly divided into recreation and production zones and where legal right of access has never been an issue.

As I walked downhill into the village of Feversham, I passed a busty middle-aged woman out digging her garden in work boots and a bathing suit rendered preposterously informal by its almost totally deteriorated elasticity. Her hair was as blond as Monroe's, and she had an Export A lodged in the corner of her mouth. As I eyed her, fascinated, she called out, "Preview's up, buddy! Ten cents a minute!" And she exhaled an explosive Export-A laugh. We chatted briefly, and when I told her I was walking to New York, she took the cigarette out of her mouth, looked at me skeptically, and said, "Yeah, and I'm digging to China." And again she pressed out her throaty cavitating laugh.

George and I camped for the night near Alliston at Earl Rowe Provincial Park, about as tame an operation as you are likely to find among campgrounds controlled by the Province of Ontario. Mowed lawns, man-made beach, no fear of wildness—unless perhaps your neighbour goes berserk at finding he has to walk fifty metres to pick up his *Toronto Star*.

During the late evening, I took a lingering shower in the park's conspicuous wash house and then sat outdoors under a three-hundred-watt spotlight, fending off mosquitoes as I trimmed every bit of dysfunctional skin from around the lesions and calluses that blanketed the bottoms of my feet. As I did so, a good-sized porcupine hauled his prehistoric caboose into the light, twitched his nose at me, and having decided he preferred nature to Earl Rowe, waddled off into the trees. I rubbed antibiotic cream into my toes and sores and then allowed myself what had come to seem pretty much the ultimate in self-pampering. I unwrapped a new pair of terrycloth socks, one of several I had bought in Sault Ste. Marie, and gently pulled them on. I would exchange them in the morning for polypropelene, but for now it was as if some ultra-subtle masseuse, some tiny-tentacled magician, were applying the best of her love and talent to precisely the spots where I needed the attention most.

THE PROBLEM was both practical and symbolic (and farcical, too), but on my route down Highways 18 and 8 toward Toronto, I had increasing difficulty finding discreet places in which to pee. And given that I was drinking as much as six litres of water and Gatorade a day, urination was more than an occasional concern. I couldn't just duck into the woods as I had been doing for the better part of a thousand kilometres. There were no woods.

Between Mansfield, some seventy kilometres north of Toronto, and Bolton, perhaps fifty kilometres farther south, the landscape is largely open fields interspersed with modest schools and churches, outlandish "executive" homes, plus the occasional gravel pit, restaurant, or lilac bush. From Bolton south into Vaughan Township (the site plan for which seems to have been plagiarized pretty much whole out of *The Inferno*), there exist, in no particular order: enclaves of individual homes (constructed mostly when there was still an elm tree or two around); mudlots (where "AFFORDABLE ESTATES" will eventually rise); construction sites (where "AFFORDABLE ESTATES" are already rising); and of course, "AFFORDABLE ESTATES" in the form of chock-a-block tracts of unlivable-looking town and row houses.

The result is that you have to invent pee sites—by, say, plastering yourself against the backside of the last-standing rotten maple, or squatting in the ditch with a solemn look, as if to suggest you are searching for whatever sort of lizard it was that stole the trees and put up all those AFFORDABLE ESTATES.

On June 2, at Wildfield, west of Kleinburg, having run out of inventions and needing desperately to pee, I walked onto the lot of the Value Plus gas bar and asked politely if there was a washroom I could use. The attendant, a lumpy little misanthrope of perhaps thirty-five, who was heading indoors after serving a customer, glared at me and blurted, "Do I look like a toilet?" And he pushed past me and yanked the door shut behind him.

It occurred to me too late to mention that there did indeed seem to be a hint of the latrine in his aura. And later that afternoon, when I told the story to Coleen Walsh, the delightfully insubordinate producer of CBC Radio's *Metro Morning*, where I was to be interviewed the next day, she said immediately, "You mean he was a shithead!" Which pretty much caught the spirit of the thing.

Later, at the Shell "convenience" centre on Highway 50, I asked an otherwise reasonable-looking female clerk for the washroom key and was told it was only for those who "get gas."

"I have gas," I told her, and without so much as a raised eyebrow, she asked if she could see my receipt.

As anyone might understand, there is a temptation in these circumstances to utter witless threats—for example, to tell such folk that you will never enter a Shell station again or that you intend to write to the president of the company (who will surely consult his board of directors post-haste). In this instance, however, under the constraint of a hyperextended bladder, I told the corporate robot before me simply that since I would be urinating *somewhere* within approximately thirty seconds, perhaps she could advise me as to where on the lot, or in the store, she would suggest I do that.

While her eyes said, *Oh, please, just go away,* her mouth said softly,

"I guess we could make one exception." And she hustled over to the counter and returned with the key on a foot-long fob dangling from the end of her outstretched arm.

I WOULD LIKE TO BE ABLE TO SAY that finding a place to take a leak was the greatest of my challenges on this section of my route. Unfortunately, it was one of the lesser obstacles on the sixty kilometres of highway that took me from rural central Ontario into a suburban dead zone as charmless and as heedless of pedestrians as any I have encountered.

Even on the worst stretches there were, of course, moments of redemption, sometimes when I expected them least—a whiff of sweet grass, the glimpse of a flicker or finch, the lilacs or honeysuckles that had somehow escaped eradication.

And there were creatures worse off than myself—such as two gorgeous snapping turtles, perhaps a hundred years old, crushed on the pavement by the Mad River south of Avening. Or the fawn so recently dead that I was sure its nerves twitched as I passed. And the endless numbers of dead cats, skunks, dogs, porcupines, groundhogs, raccoons—all part of a body count I might have expected to decrease as I approached Toronto, but which in fact increased sharply in proportion to the increase in traffic.

Where Highway 18 crosses into Dufferin County, some forty kilometres north of the Toronto suburbs, a sign pointed out that since 1978, there had been "1,280 accidents on this road. Thirty deaths." More than these rural commuter highways, however, or even the sixteen-lane freeways well into the city, it was the middle zone, the dense arc of outer suburbia, that described best for me the fierce and inviolable contract that, as a society, we have with the car. Indeed, picking my way through Toronto's walk-proof outer suburbs made hiking into New York City, as I would do three weeks hence, the comparative equivalent of a stroll in the park.

In much of Vaughan Township, for example, there are no side-walks. In places, there are not even shoulders on the roads—just curbs immediately adjacent to the ditch. You choose the most benign-looking little grey line on the map as a potential route into the city (red lines signify main routes). But when you get to it, it is four lanes wide, has a speed limit of 80 kilometres an hour (everyone is going 110), and there are sixty vehicles a minute in each direction, many of them gravel trucks, dump trucks, or eighteen-wheelers. The ditches are afloat with septic sludge, old furniture, clothing, Tim Hortons cups, cigarette packages, McDonald's and Burger King wrappers, as well as mufflers, fan belts, and burned-out headlamps.

As a walker, I could not have been more isolated out there. Unlike the drivers on rural highways, no driver on these suburban trunk roads even looks at you. The closer I got to the city, the more I felt that most of the drivers would not actually have seen me if they *had* looked. In Arizona recently, a Catholic bishop drove into a pedestrian and killed him, then drove home with his windshield smashed, claiming later that he thought he had hit a pothole. In another part of the southern United States, a woman left a dying pedestrian embedded in her windshield in the family garage, and went inside and made dinner.

In the comfort of one's easy chair watching television news, such stories are difficult to comprehend. Out here, however, in rush hour, they become morbidly comprehensible. For a thousand kilometres, I had watched every vehicle that passed; it was my defence against the driver who might have nodded off, or had turned briefly to scold the dog or adjust the baby's bottle.

Because I watched so carefully, I ascribe a degree of validity to my conclusion that the majority of the rush-hour drivers on the day of my walk into Toronto fitted one of two psychological profiles: they were either impatient (or downright angry), which is easily deciphered, or they were in some sort of low-level trance.

"Trauma-based mind control" is a psychologist's term that describes, among other things, torture methods designed to overstimulate the senses through exposure to, say, endless loud music or bright light.

The result is that the senses eventually shut down in confusion, and the victim becomes bewildered and vulnerable.

By the end of a day spent largely on Highway 50, I was, in a sense, such a victim—exhausted, disoriented, decidedly less confident than usual in my middle-aged faculties. As I approached Highway 27 outside Kleinburg I took note of a sign that pointed the way to the McMichael Art Gallery, where I was to meet George, a sign aiming me straight ahead. However, by the time I was fifty metres on, I had fumbled the sign's information to the degree that I was sure it had instructed me to turn right on 27. Which I did—increasing my day's effort by some four kilometres, a distance that amid the dust and heat and noise felt like twenty. For forty minutes or more, there wasn't a break in the succession of SUVs, minivans, and trucks—all of them travelling at speed, all within half a metre of a shoulder that in places was little more than a metre wide. What's more, most of them were occupied by one person (as if it were not clear already why the Western world needs control of the Iraqi oil fields).

Beyond this, of course, the vehicles were loud—some had no mufflers. And they raised dust. And burned oil. And spat debris. As Walter Bond had told me at Montreal River Harbour, every little rock or metal fragment becomes shrapnel beneath the wheels of a gravel truck or transport.

I had expected nothing less. At the same time, I had not anticipated the intense impact both on the psyche and body that this sort of traffic would have.

I would not have corrected my mistaken right turn when I did had I not come to a highway hotel and, suspecting by now that I had gotten off course, ventured in to ask my way. If the highway was an affront to a walker, this benighted concrete inn was an outright indignity. Its sole entrance was a tinted glass door that led not into a lobby or reception area, but into a morbid and airless little forespace, perhaps two metres square. As I reached to pull open a second door, presumably to the innards of the hotel, a voice sounded out of a speaker, telling me to "step back from the door" and, essentially, to state my business.

"May I come in?" I said.

"Not without a key," said the voice. "Rooms are $119. What is it you want?"

I said, "I'd like to get to the McMichael Art Gallery."

"Never heard of it."

My initial instinct was to try to persuade the voice that *surely* it had heard of the McMichael. But as quickly as the thought came, it went—and with it any notion of introducing the voice to the foundations of Canadian art.

I said, "How do I get into Kleinburg?"

"You walk straight out the door across the highway," the voice said (I must at least give it credit for succinctness), "and you keep going."

A short walk along Major MacKenzie Drive did, indeed, take me to Kleinburg's main street and eventually to the McMichael, where a fair portion of the work of Canada's famed Group of Seven—plus the work of other Canadian landscape painters—is housed. A number of those artists (J.E.H. MacDonald, A.Y. Jackson, Lawren Harris, Frederick Varley, Frank Carmichael) painted the most famous of their canvases in areas where I had recently walked, including the Algoma hills and along the north shore of Lake Superior. More than once during the 1920s, Jackson and Varley rented a boxcar from the CPR and lived in it for months, as far north and west as what is now Lake Superior Provincial Park. So well known are the resulting canvases (reproductions of them appear by the hundreds of thousands on Christmas cards and calendars, and hang on the walls of virtually every elementary school in Ontario) that, for me, there were days in that wilderness when the unfolding grandeur of the scenery had evoked a succession of iconic paintings, one after the other.

I had not visited the gallery in perhaps a dozen years and was disquieted by how much the wooded grounds, once so vast-seeming and free of civilization, had been squeezed by the spread of the suburbs. A sign out front described the gallery and its surroundings as "the Spiritual Home of the Group of Seven." Compounding this implied irony was a seven-part iron sculpture spaced out along the road into the grounds, each part of which was a two-metre-high letter of the word *BABYLON*—a pertinent echo perhaps of the city's northwest suburbs, but hardly of the "spiritual home" of geniuses the likes of Tom Thomson, Fred Varley, and Lawren Harris.

Even so, the footpath into the park was cool and green and therapeutic—a kind of tunnel through the cedars and pines—and by the time I reached the only vehicle left in the parking lot (which is to say my own overripe van), I was feeling a little less frayed.

George, who was sitting on the grass drinking beer out of a Tim Hortons cup, had spent his afternoon in the gallery and said immediately that "the problem with the Group of Seven" wasn't their paintings, which he liked well, but "all that soupy prose" that everybody always wrote about them. He said, "Here are these guys whose work said something worth saying about the land, and along come a buncha writers determined to resay it with bad adjectives."

I explained to George that, at that point, I myself felt modified by a bad adjective or two—say, *frazzled* or *freaked* or *fed up*. George is, as Van Morrison put it, "long-time hurt" by the culture's deepening disrespect for tobacco, and as he listened to my battle stories, he postulated that cars, far more than his beloved cigarette packages, should be obliged to carry images of the damage they do: broken bodies, mangled dogs and deer, people sick from breathing carbon monoxide. To say nothing of the ecological impact of road building, iron mining, manufacturing plants, oil wars, and refineries. "They should put a picture of you on there," he said, meaning, I think, of my pale and emaciated likeness after a day of being keel-hauled by transports and gravel trucks.

IN HER BOOK *Wanderlust,* Rebecca Solnit points out that while the suburbs have limited our opportunities to walk, it is "the suburbanization of the North American mind" that has done most to knock a culture off its feet. Her assessment certainly fits any evidence I am aware of. As a seven- or eight-year-old, I thought nothing of walking a mile or more to school, or to the river to swim, or to town from our summer cabin in north-central Ontario. And I was told I was a softy compared to generations past.

And I was. My dad walked fifteen kilometres round trip to get to school during the Depression, sometimes in 40-below weather. By comparison, my teenaged son, Matt, and his friends, while quite happy to hike into the Nor'Wester Mountains with their snowboards or to board for hours at the local ski resorts, insist when I drive them to the hills that they be dropped off within metres of the ski chalet so as not to have to walk across the parking lot.

At home, they sit for hours guiding hunters and hitmen through the jungles and ghettos of cyberspace *on foot*. But unlike the virtual walkers that are their alter egos, the boys themselves are reluctant to walk a mile to the video store to rent or return the games.

As adults, we have little to feel smug about. We drive twenty kilometres to where we can take a three-kilometre walk on a sanctioned trail. Or we drive to the gym where we climb onto treadmills, apparently indifferent to the rollicking social parody that is the solemn sweating man or woman striding frantically toward nowhere. Had John Bunyan written his famous allegory, *Pilgrim's Progress,* in the twenty-first century, he might well have put Pilgrim on a treadmill. Or on the daunting trail that leads through the mall.

Clearly, many, if not most, contemporary North Americans prefer the trail through the mall to the one along the riverbank or through the woods. Why go outside when nature can be witnessed perfectly well on television? The mall, too, of course, can be experienced on TV, in the form of the Shopping Channel. Mall lite. While many of us acknowledge the mall's stultifying environment, few of us, once inside, seem to harbour any longing for the dogs and birds and panhandlers, the trees and breezes and sunlight, that once gave character and nuance to a shopping expedition. Nor do we seem to miss the kinds of stores that in another era competed as aggressively to be different from one another as mall stores seem to compete to be the same.

GEORGE AND I ESCAPED back to Earl Rowe Park, where George threw together a revitalizing pork-and-pepper stir-fry. But for the first time in perhaps three weeks, I could not shake the effects of the day's walk. Forty kilometres of traffic and road dust had beaten up on me. But if I was looking for a break, it would not come tomorrow, as I had already promised cellphone reports to both Toronto CBC's *Metro Morning* and CBC Thunder Bay between 7:00 and 9:00 A.M.

So I was up at 6:00, and by 6:45 was booting it east along Major MacKenzie Drive on a stingy little cow path that had been worn into the weeds perhaps twenty centimetres from an ankle-high curb that was all that separated me from non-stop, high-speed traffic. I had agreed to meet George in downtown Toronto at the home of my old friends Dan Diamond and Carol McLaughlin, some thirty kilometres away. And it was not until I had walked for nearly an hour that I could claim the luxury of a sidewalk, the first I had travelled since the Soo, some seven hundred kilometres back. Though made of concrete, it was as appealing as a country lane, and I did my interviews in relative comfort as I marched east toward Yonge Street, where I would turn south into the city of my birth.

If there was a flaw on this otherwise sunny summer morning, it was that, in retrospect, I was unhappy about my interview with Andy Barrie on *Metro Morning*. Whereas I had wanted to be ebullient and funny and anecdotal, I had settled for the truth and had been caustic in my assessment of suburban Toronto. In short, I had griped. About everything from roadkill to the absence of footpaths or sidewalks to the banality of the strip malls and housing. If I had anything to feel good about, it was that I had told perhaps a hundred thousand listeners about the jerk at the True Value gas bar who had refused to let me urinate in his pot. Also, for fifteen minutes or so afterwards, motorists who had heard the interview honked and waved or, in several cases, rolled down their windows and shouted out greetings.

At Highway 400, I found myself within sight of a southern Ontario landmark called Canada's Wonderland—an amusement park made conspicuous, if not alluring, by its fifty-metre-high fake mountain. Wonderland's chief reason for existing is, of course, to make money. But for those willing to pay the $39 entry fee, it exists so they can "thrill" themselves on hellish upside-down roller-coasters or on "death drops" or tied to rapidly descending bungee cords. Such thrill-seekers are undoubtedly unaware that you can traumatize yourself more economically simply by walking forty kilometres along the roads of Vaughan or Peel Township.

In fact, your chances of suffering true trauma—or the Ultimate Trauma—are far greater there than on even the hairiest roller-coaster. In Toronto, an average of fifty pedestrians a year are killed, the majority of them on what the Metropolitan Toronto Council refers to as "major suburban arteries." In Canada and the United States there are nearly seven thousand pedestrian deaths annually—more, it might be noted, than occur worldwide in plane crashes.

And yet any assertion of the rights of the human body on foot over the automobile is held suspect. While much of science, not to mention philosophy, would have us believe that flesh and bone, not spirit, are the ultimate and perhaps only validation of what it is to be human, we have, judging by the evidence, lost faith in flesh and bone. Laura Robinson, an Olympic cyclist turned writer, says that if we believed in our bodies, we'd have designed a world that better accommodated and gratified them.

"Instead," she says, "we accommodate cars."

BY THE TIME I HAD WALKED several kilometres south on Yonge Street I was so tired that at the Finch Avenue subway station I decided to quit for the afternoon, take the train downtown, and return when the day got cooler.

I spent the afternoon sacked out in the guest bedroom at Dan and Carol's, and having tried unsuccessfully to persuade Dan, then George, to accompany me that evening, returned alone to Finch Avenue at about 8:30 P.M.

From there I marched south into North York in what I must admit was a version of private glory.

I had made it to Toronto.

If I was walking under a constraint, it was that I had been so long in the wilderness and on backwoods highways that, now, on Yonge Street, every effulgence or sign of urban humanity, virtually every storefront, absorbed my attention and stopped me in my tracks.

At Church Avenue, I stepped into a teensy gated cemetery, whose dead were mostly Pennsylvanians who had arrived in Toronto—or York as it was then called—during the very late 1700s. Half of them, it seemed, had died young, a fact that greatly impressed a soulful teenaged girl who was touring the cemetery with her mother. At the grave of Eliza Jane Johnson (1826–1843), the girl put her hands over her mouth in quiet dismay, and then read aloud to her mother:

> Read this vain youth as you pass by.
> As you are now, so once was I.
> As I am now, so you must be.
> Prepare for death and follow me.

"That is so creepy!" said the girl. And it was. And it was hard to avoid considering that whatever had killed the teenager could almost certainly have been cured today with a prescription for antibiotics or a bit of surgery.

Across the street, the lavish North York Arts Centre was advertising, as I recall, *Showboat,* now in its forty-fifth week—or was it 145th? Next door, above a vast and unsightly mud hole, straddled by a rickety wood structure and a few scraps of sheet plastic, a sign advertised "Toronto's Most Exclusive Condominiums."

At the Silver City theatre complex, a sign for Dunn's Montreal Deli got me fantasizing that I could perhaps get a couple of Montreal-style bagels to chaw on as I walked. Jessica, the teenaged waitress, said she had just started at the restaurant and didn't know whether it sold Montreal bagels—in fact, didn't even know what Montreal bagels were (they are, as connoisseurs know, hand-rolled boiled bagels, baked in birch-burning ovens and doused in sesame or poppy seeds—"white" or "black" as they say in Montreal's Jewish quarter).

As my query hung unresolved, a lanky, nattily dressed gentleman appeared out of the kitchen. "Of course we have them," he brightened. "Will you sit down?"

I told him thanks but that I was walking, etc.

Would I have the bagels toasted? With butter? Would I take a coffee?

As Jessica prepared the order, Moishe Smith explained that he had the franchise for, I think, a trio of Dunn's outlets, and when Jessica reappeared to ring up the sale, he waved her off with a quiet "No charge." He shook my hand and, as if addressing a man in transit to Valhalla, said softly, "I don't know why you're walking to New York, and I won't ask. But I support it."

I told him in return that I didn't know why he owned a restaurant, but that I supported *that*.

"Sometimes," he smiled, "I myself don't know why I own a restaurant. And I'm not always sure I support it."

EVEN A HANDFUL of generations ago, the sort of walking I was doing that night would not have been possible in a large city. Actually, it *would* have been possible in Toronto during the latter half of the nineteenth century, since at that time Toronto was not a large city, at least by today's standards. Its population in 1850 was a mere thirty thousand people.

Like country walking during the Middle Ages, however, strolling a big city's streets and riverbanks was, during the seventeenth and eighteenth centuries, simply too dangerous. Until the mid-1800s, the streets of Paris, for example, were dirty, unlit, and infested with rats and thieves. There were no proper sewers, so the pavement (where it existed) was filthy with excrement and garbage. Early sidewalks were narrow and so close to the busy thoroughfares that pedestrians were commonly mangled, or even killed, by speeding horse-drawn wagons or carriages—invariably without reprisal. Moreover, pedestrians were apt to get sewage or slops dumped from upper-storey windows into their paths, and anyone of obvious affluence or "breeding" was considered pretty much an open target for a bucket of dishwater or urine.

John Gay's 1716 poem "The Art of Walking the Streets of London," points out that in London, as in Paris, Brussels, or Amsterdam, an underclass of "criminals and desperate souls," many wasted by cheap liquor, proliferated in the alleys and backstreets. According to Betty Friedan, if a woman was out walking in London, Paris, or any other large Western city during the late 1700s or early 1800s, it was all but assumed she was a prostitute—which for women, needless to say, greatly limited the democratic practice of walking, with its varied benefits and inspirations. In New York City, the streets throughout the 1800s were alive with drunks, prostitutes, pickpockets, muggers, and gangs. In fact, well into the nineteenth century, parts of Lower Manhattan were all but a death trap for anyone innocent enough to go wandering through on foot.

Most cities in Europe began improving their paving and sanitation during the Renaissance. However, only in the nineteenth century were most cities large enough—"unknown" enough to their own inhabitants—to invite the sort of exploration for which, say, Dickens and Kierkegaard became famous in London and Copenhagen.

Gradually, of course, things changed. Gas lamps came to the large cities of Europe and eventually electric lights. Streets were paved. Sidewalks were widened and converted from wood to concrete. Traffic signs, stoplights, and road markings came into being, and laws and policing were introduced to protect pedestrians. My great uncle

George MacBain, who lived in Toronto off and on through the first fifty years of the twentieth century told me once that there wasn't a street in the city on which he wouldn't feel safe walking at any hour of day or night. It would never have occurred to him that a city capable of building safe streets in the 1930s and '40s—streets safe from drivers as well as thugs—would, by the end of the twentieth century, be building thoroughfares on which the well-being of pedestrians was more fragile than it had been at pretty much any point during the most lawless decades in the city's past.

SAVOURED IN SMALLISH BITES, the bagels lasted me all the way to the McDonald-Cartier Freeway—the 401—which, at Yonge Street, is so many lanes wide that you walk perhaps the length of a football field to get across it.

South of Hogg's Hollow, I looked wistfully into the window of the old Sloan's Shoe Store where, as a student during the mid-1960s, I had bought Clark's desert boots for sixteen dollars a pair, at that time considered a significant investment in shoe leather. And more wistfully yet into the Melmira Bra Boutique, whose window was an artful gallery of some of the filmiest coordinates I had had the opportunity to gaze on in some time. And the Painting Restorer ("Bring us your dirty paintings"). And a doll boutique (where a hundred little faces inspired an almost tearful dose of longing for my daughters, Georgia and Eden). And stores for Inuit art, Canadian pottery, Belgian truffles, Scottish tartans.

And, of course, dozens—hundreds—of restaurants: Greek, Thai, Jamaican, Ethiopian, Danish, Italian, Middle Eastern. It occurred to me to wonder whether "Canadian" restaurants exist in, say, Thailand or Japan. And, if so, what they might offer in the way of typical Canadian foods. Lasagna? Enchiladas? Dim sum?

There were coffee joints, two to a block: Timothy's, Second Cup, Starbucks, Coffee Time, Country Style, Baker's Dozen, Tim Hortons. Plus any number of independents.

And another Tim Hortons. And another.

And stores in transition—a bonsai shop becoming a sub shop, a sub shop becoming a skateboard hangout, a skateboard hangout becoming a pet grooming salon.

Later that evening, my friend Dan spoke of Toronto's "almost reptilian urge" to replicate itself financially. "Wherever you go on any artery—even places you think have no appeal—there are people taking a shot, trying to realize a dream."

Dan is a talented publisher with a passion for language and for literature. He is also a walker who not long ago did a solo trek through rural Ireland, covering as much as fifty kilometres a day. I have known him since the mid-1970s, when he co-founded *Winnipeg Magazine* and I was hired as its first editor. Carol is by training a psychiatric nurse, but has worked in the specialty food business and now sells houses. During the past few years, however, she has devoted much of her time to urban ecological projects, most recently the "unearthing" of Taddle Creek in central Toronto and the creation of a park on the site of the old Wychwood Carbarns.

Dan and Carol are both, in their ways, high-arc eccentrics whose interest in animals is such that they keep a crow in their house on Wychwood Avenue—in fact, have closed off part of the ground floor so that the bird, Joker, has a place to fly around and conduct bird business.

AT 3:00 A.M., two hours after I had come in from my walk, Dan and I set out again to walk their two large collies around the St. Clair Avenue Reservoir. As we climbed a dirt path up onto St. Clair, Dan told me that in a wooded gully behind the St. Clair West subway stop, a young homeless man with whom we had chatted the previous autumn about life on the street had recently been murdered in his sleep.

Being on foot breeds an increased awareness, even an empathy, for those who sleep in parks. While I am separated from them by a chasm, it has never seemed beyond possibility that an old writer, or

even a young one, could end up living on the street. So it should
hardly be surprising that as I walked east on Danforth Avenue the
next day, the young murder victim was in my thoughts—or that as
I passed Danforth Avenue Baptist Church I felt inclined to sit for a
while with a wiry white-haired street dweller who was sprawled on
the sidewalk taking care of a sleeping bag, two chair cushions, an
aging bicycle, and three or four dishpans and bowls. Which is to say,
everything he owned. His name was Bob, and when I asked how he
had ended up where he was, he explained patiently that he had been
"burned out" twice, had lost everything he owned in fires in 1989
and 2000. He was fifty-seven years old, and after the first fire,
having no energy for work, he had lost his job as a stockroom clerk
and gone on welfare. After the second fire, he was told by the
welfare department to go back to work. "I told them I couldn't," he
said, "and they cut me off."

Bob was bony, with sharp features and a savage tan that in places
on his face and arms had puckered into sores. He had optimistic blue
eyes and hands that looked as if they had been chewed on by dogs.
He had, he said, six or seven broken teeth, but the key feature of his
physical presence, and clearly his pride, was a long well-combed
beard, largely white but, from a steady diet of Export A cigarettes,
stained an unsavoury yellowish brown around his mouth.

Bob spoke of the fires that ruined him as if he were watching them
on a private screen in the back of his skull. In the first, he lost fifteen
hundred vinyl records, a lifetime's collection. In the second, he lost
two thousand taped movies.

The day was Bob's 640th in succession on the sidewalk. "I come at
eight in the morning," he said, "and I'm here till eleven at night. I'm
out here in blizzards, lightning, and rain. I've had one terrible winter
and one mild one. People say, Why don't you go somewhere else? And
the answer is, Because there's no place else to go. I can't sit in front of
a store or a restaurant—I'm bad for business. I could sit in the park,
but there's no money in the park."

Bob suspected that one of the more devious local store owners had been responsible for slashing his bike tires a while back and for stealing his sleeping bag twice.

"Danforth Baptist," he said jerking his head over his shoulder, "is my second home. Well, since I don't have a first home, I guess you could say it's my first home. The members tell me that even though I never go in, they consider me a part of the congregation."

Since the beginning of May, Bob had been sleeping in nearby parks. However, in winter, he sleeps in a city-run shelter.

I said, "Are the shelters as bad as they say?"

He looked at me as if considering the question for the first time and said quite innocently, "Who's 'they'?"

I said, "The media," at which he cackled ruefully and said, "I'll say this for shelters, that if they didn't exist, I'd have been frozen to death long ago. Worst thing about them is they stink. All those guys taking off their shoes at once. And some guys are sick. You're more likely to die of asphyxiation than of a knifing." Bob felt that if he were going to get knifed, it would more likely be in a park. "That's why I don't tell anybody where I sleep. Even the cops don't know. And they're my friends. They respect me. They know how hard it is out here."

Bob said he knew guys who slept in cemeteries, in churchyards, in garbage Dumpsters, by the Don River, under bridges, on subway vents, and right on the sidewalk. "And women, too," he said.

When I told him I was walking to New York City, he assumed I was doing it because I had no place else to go. He said, "Shit, man, you should just stay here!"

Bob was saving, as he put it, "to get back on his feet." But in the half-hour I sat with him, no one except me put any coins in his dishpan. During the four hours before I arrived, he had "earned," as he put it, just over three dollars in loonies, quarters, and dimes—all of which would go toward his daily tobacco habit.

Was he lonely?

"No," he said, adding with no betrayal of irony, "I'm very well connected." During the time I sat with him, at least three people, including a young black woman, whose backside Bob described as "eye-popping," said hello to him by name. But none threw him a bone.

Was I bad for business?

"Probably," he said. "People see I'm preoccupied talking to you, and they know I can't put the hook on them, so they sneak by. But I don't care. I'm not in this for the money."

I HAD BEGUN THE DAY walking southeast from Wychwood Park and then across the Don Valley on the Bloor Street Viaduct. The latter was embedded in my consciousness at the age of thirteen when my dad explained that after returning from World War II, he had felt confused and empty to the point that as he walked home from university one night, he stood for half an hour on the viaduct weighing whether or not to jump. Had he done so, of course, I would not exist—at least in this particular juju.

What had saved him from jumping, he told me, was that in the depths of his confusion he had started to pray. "I prayed my way out of it," he said. And when he walked off the bridge an hour later, it was with a renewed sense of spiritual purpose and clarity.

I was born in Toronto perhaps a year after that fateful occasion, lived briefly within blocks of the viaduct, and left the city with my sisters and parents at the age of two. However, I often visited, and returned eventually to finish high school at East York Collegiate before spending four years at the University of Toronto during the late-1960s and early-1970s. During that period, I lived just north of Danforth, so that my walk that afternoon was, in effect, a kind of homecoming.

For twenty minutes, I stood on the viaduct looking south down the valley, once considered an environmental catastrophe with its freeway, rail lines, hydro towers, and paper mill—and with the filth of the Don River flowing through it like toxic molasses. Nature, of course, is irrepressible, meaning that my predominating impression of the view was not so much of lingering contamination but, as the novelist Jim Harrison put it, of love among the ruins, in the form of huge willows and ash trees along the riverbank, fields of tall grass, stretches of purple loosestrife and pink rocket, the sight of a red-tailed hawk cruising the flood plain in search of a rabbit or groundhog.

By smudging the visuals a little, I located a mental image of my mother as a child, sledding and skating in Riverdale Park and a decade later walking up Broadview to catch the streetcar to her job at the St. Clair Avenue Bakery. And of my father ambling back and forth across the viaduct on his way to and from the University of Toronto.

I poked around the East York neighbourhood where I went to high school on Coxwell Avenue. And located the site of the Beau Brummel mens' shop, where, as a teenager, I had bought tailored wool bell-bottoms at the irreproachable price of ten dollars a pair. And the Hogan used-car lot, where, at the age of twenty, in the face of my dad's intense resistance, I acquired my first (and to this day only) memorable car. I have not driven that 1962 Alpine in more than thirty years, but remember to the molecule the lusty, leathery, gearboxy smell of its black interior on a hot summer day.

Just east of Victoria Park, I took an unscheduled detour south along Anndale Drive, past number forty-one, the home of a university sweetheart, every detail of whose presence and person (and passion) came roiling back.

Danforth in the sixties was an all-but-institutionalized ribbon of commerce lined with car lots, cleaners, garages, lumber yards, drygoods and hardware stores, fast-food joints, appliance dealers, the occasional pharmacy or clothing store. With its stores and streetcars and subway trains, the avenue was a kind of marshalling principle for the working neighbourhoods to the north and south—families of British and northern European extraction, and blue-collar Italians and Greeks.

At the time, an African or Asian would have been regarded as a curiosity in, say, East York or Riverdale. I seem to recall one Chinese and two black kids in a population of some sixteen hundred students at East York Collegiate.

Farther east, in the pathologically white suburb of Scarborough, a black or Asian would, during the sixties, have been regarded, at best, as a curiosity, at worst as a foretaste of spectres to come.

Today, on east Danforth, the rarity is to see anyone who is *not* Asian, Oriental, or black—while Scarborough is perhaps the biggest black enclave in the country. Meanwhile, Danforth between Broadview and Pape, far now from its utilitarian roots, is a Toronto standard for arty boutiques and trendy restaurants and bars.

At one of a half-dozen Chinese grocery stores east of Broadview, I bought two pounds of Montmorency cherries and spit pits into the street all the way to Woodbine. At Pharmacy (as my tastebuds convalesced from their umpteenth Montmorency orgasm) a Pakistani kid had a barbecue going and sold me, for a buck, the best-tasting cob of corn I had ever eaten (for the record, it was husked, then grilled, so that the kernels were ever so slightly browned, even caramelized—the whole of it doused in butter, curry powder, and lemon juice).

As in the north suburbs, practically anywhere you look in Toronto's East End, someone is building, or at least advertising, "Elegant Condos," "Gracious Semi-Detacheds," "Lifestyle Towns and Splits," "Elegance Under 200" (thousand), and in one notable case, "Low-Cost Elegance" (as opposed, one might guess, to "medium-cost" elegance: indoor plumbing and so on, frills easily renounced without crucial loss of *savoir faire*). The results, needless to say, are often anything but elegant. And are sometimes, I understand, far from "low cost." As I had walked with Dan the previous night, we came across a group of townhouses in the Bathurst–St. Clair area, each of which had been pre-sold for a half-million dollars. Dan pointed out that the cladding on them was sheets of two-inch Styrofoam sprayed with a thin layer of stucco, that the heavy masonry of the front steps—perhaps two tons of concrete block work—had been set directly on the soil without a foundation or drainage, and that the blocks in those steps had been put together with industrial glue—yellowish contact cement—rather than proper mortar.

Danforth eventually merges into Kingston Road, at which point it meets a vast cemetery, where I had worked for four months after my second year of university—cutting lawns, weeding gardens, preparing and tidying grave sites, whatever needed doing. Out of a kind of reverse nostalgia for a job I had hated but had found fascinating, I arced up through the cemetery, recalling vividly the Fellini-like cast of characters with whom I had worked, as well as the lunatic practices and unspeakable practical jokes I had witnessed and in which I had occasionally participated (think irresponsible boys unsupervised around open graves).

I recalled less frivolously helping exhume the body of a much-heralded female murder victim; stacking up "dirt nappers" in the un-air-conditioned chapel during a heat wave while we awaited the resolution of a city-wide gravediggers strike; and early one morning as I cut grass on an industrial riding mower, nearly cutting the feet off a wino as he slept off a bender beneath the wisteria bushes by the cemetery fence. I will say in the interest of decorum that the dead themselves were never (intentionally) violated, although some went down with unlikely bedfellows (a dead cat comes to mind) and attended by rather bizarre funeral rites.

WHILE I WAS BUSY WALKING, George was downtown busking on the waterfront, where he had hoped to have a carefree, profitable day. But when I met him around dinner hour at Guildwood, way out by the Scarborough Bluffs, he was more exhausted than I was—from the heat and from the physical effort of fiddling for four or five hours. Plus, he was fed up with what he called "all the millionaire tight-wads"—families out for a Sunday stroll "dressed in two thousand dollars' worth of clothes," but reluctant to drop a coin into his violin case. At one point he had, in his words, "stooped to playing 'Amazing Grace,'" the busker's last gambit, a piece that if sung soulfully by a bassett hound is guaranteed to wring a dollar or two out of even the most abject backslider.

Later, as he stood outside a liquor store playing blues improvs, a convertible pulled up full of self-absorbed young men who parked within a couple of metres of him. Such is the regard for any sort of "real" music these days—or at least for George's real music—that when the young men jumped out and went into the liquor store, they left not only their engine running, loudly, but their stereo thumping at such volume that it entirely drowned George out.

THE SCARBOROUGH BLUFFS are sixty-metre-high cliffs of gradually eroding sand and clay above a wide apron of marsh, beach, and concrete rip-rap that has been dumped along the Lake Ontario shore over the years to prevent further erosion. In the lore of the East End, the bluffs have always had a slightly portentous reputation, occasionally featuring in stories of foul play (bodies being found, etc.), or as the site of terrible accidents in which kids fell to their deaths or landslides took backyards into oblivion. Beyond this, they are legendary as a trysting grounds and are one of Toronto's few nude swimming areas.

Despite George's day, he felt lively enough to descend the bluffs with me and walk three or four kilometres along their base. I had no sooner expressed my surprise that we hadn't run into any nude bathers on such a hot evening when, across a ridge of piled boulders, there they were, a well-tanned, middle-aged couple, as bulgy as water toys, lying sunny-side up on the sand.

We sat for a while where a flock of Canada geese nestled along shore, occasionally diving into the shallows after bits of seaweed. But their fearlessness of us, even at three or four metres' range, did not extend to a Labrador retriever whose approaching presence, at fifty metres, sent them scattering up the shoreline or out onto the water.

LIKE MANY PEOPLE, I tend to view large cities as unresolvable tangles of forces and distances that can be met only, or most effectively, with the aid of cars and buses and subways, or at very least bicycles. What a revelation it was, therefore, to realize that I could cross the whole of Toronto, which had once seemed so vast and complex, in a couple of very manageable sessions on foot. As George and I sat by the water, I remarked to him that I would have thought having to walk such a city would make it seem even bigger and less forgiving than it is, just as there were days north of Lake Superior when I might have been convinced the world *was* Lake Superior and that I was destined to walk its shores forever. Toronto, on the other hand—the city proper—had become not only considerably smaller than I had imagined or remembered but, compared to the great tracts of wilderness to the north, was positively benign.

Toronto's sprawling eastern neighbours, however—Pickering, Ajax, Whitby—seemed no less daunting than they ever had, perhaps because I tended to view them as the eastern equivalents of the horrific northwest suburbs I had encountered earlier in the week.

And had I ended up walking the eastern suburbs in any conventional sense, I might well have felt walloped by them, too. However, from a walker's point of view, a nice thing happens as you move east out of Toronto. At Pickering, you come into miles of newly made waterfront parkland, with well-developed cycling and walking paths that take you clear through Ajax to Whitby, a distance of perhaps fourteen or fifteen kilometres.

The ninth of June was the hottest of my now forty-four days on the road, and in the relaxed ambience of the park, with terns and gulls drifting overhead—and with the lake sloshing lazily in the haze just ten metres away—I was in no particular hurry. At times I walked with my T-shirt off and on a couple of occasions took advantage of park benches to stretch out and catch a few winks. Most happily, there were no cars and no roadkill. The word *heavenly* comes to mind, except for the usual reminders that where there is heaven, hell is often, as the song says, "just a kiss away." Several kilometres into the Ajax part of the park, for example, I came across a young man and woman with

spray bottles on their backs, wearing protective masks and blasting a
heavy mist of herbicidal poison onto a decidedly weedless lawn. The
area was well staked with signs that warned pet owners and parents to
keep their various charges off the sprayed areas for, I think, forty-eight
hours—in other words, until the toxins were safely in the soil and
water table, not to mention in the lake, where fish and birds would
cache them for a while before they worked their way out into the larger
food chain. It might be said without undue sarcasm that in the old
days, it was the job of one's enemy to poison the food and water
supply. But now that the enemy is dandelions (with their poor track
record as adversaries), apparently we must poison the food and water
ourselves.

Over the years, I have drawn my share of electricity out of the
Ontario power grid, so am in a poor position to get peevish about the
Pickering Nuclear Plant. But when I passed it in the shimmery haze of
the morning, it, too, had a certain "kiss of hell" quality about it, its
eight domed reactors seeming to suggest the bone vaults of some
godless medieval cult.

George met me briefly near the reactor site, and as we talked, a man
of perhaps sixty came along with an African grey parrot on his shoulder, its wings clipped so it couldn't fly.

It is perhaps indiscreet to say so, but the parrot's owner, a one-time
transport dispatcher, was so spectacularly ill-informed on every subject
except parrots that talking to him became an only slightly embarrass-
ing delight. When George told him he was from Winnipeg, for
example, the man pointed at the lake and said quite studiously, "Now
Winnipeg—I've heard of it, but is it on this body of water?"

He twice referred to atoms as "those little gizmos that everything is
made out of," and when I told him I had walked from Thunder Bay,
he exclaimed, "Oh, good lord! What year did you start?"

To the east, along the lake, there were familiar-looking half-built
housing developments, the descriptive word *estates* having been
supplanted in these parts by the word *shores*—as in Whitby Shores,

Lynde Shores, and Lakeside Shores. Development is not entirely unopposed. Along Shoal Point Road, where H.A. Hornung Investments was planning to drain a lovely little lagoon and marsh to build sixteen "luxury homes," there were signs on the lawns of several modest old houses that read, "Save Our Wetland—No More Houses Here."

On the same road at—of all things—a donkey sanctuary, six or seven sweet little grey donkeys, of a sort that in this culture are typically seen only on Christmas cards, munched impassively on a patch of long grass.

At about three in the afternoon, hot and starved, I stopped at Pierre's Burger Bus, just across the municipal line in Whitby. As its name suggests, the place is a converted bus, something of a culinary landmark I came to understand, owned by Gilles and Georgette St. Pierre.

I ordered their biggest double cheeseburger, asked if they'd fill my water bottle, and prompted by Georgette's questions, divulged that I was walking to New York. "What *for*?" cried Gilles, looking at me as if at a three-legged circus freak. But before I could respond, Georgette (think Alice Cramden) blurted, "I've told you a thousand times, Gilles, if you'd walk to the store for smokes, instead of driving, you'd see that it's a totally different neighbourhood than you imagined! You see things! That's why he's doing it! Right?" she said, shooting me a glance.

Georgette eventually presented me with *la chose choisie,* onto which I piled everything from Dijon, sauerkraut, and horseradish to hot peppers, sweet peppers, and chop-suey sauce—you know, to please Georgette. Then I sloped off toward Manhattan.

But I hardly got a kilometre down the road when I was thirsty again and stopped at the Burger King, where I made the mistake of drinking a large iced tea and an even larger chocolate milkshake, which was not a milkshake or even chocolate in the old sense, but a kind of granular grey mortar, about a litre of it, that for the next couple of hours sloshed in me like a kilo of uncured concrete.

By Oshawa, I was nauseated to the point of dizziness. And was made more so by the squirming course of County Road 22 as it twists four lanes wide and furious with traffic through this hard-headed and left-leaning old union town; over and under the train tracks, around factories and warehouses, past the GM auto plant, with its four hundred stacks, and the flaming Lasco Steel plant.

Where 22 falls in parallel with the MacDonald-Cartier Freeway, I walked between the two roads on a metre-wide median of steeply inclined grass, clinging as a form of life insurance to a chain link fence so I would not tumble into speeding traffic.

At a modest shopping plaza on the east side of the city, I stretched out on a wide embankment of grass, no longer able to stay upright. And there I slept in the cool evening breeze—and woke up refreshed. And walked south to Lake Ontario, into Darlington Provincial Park, where George had pitched camp atop the lakeside bluffs.

The night was breezy and humid, and an occasional streak of lightning spidered up off the horizon, perhaps fifty kilometres away. We ate a bad pizza that George had bought in Oshawa, and sat watching as the darkness settled and the lights of Toronto bristled into silvery green luminescence to the west.

I had survived the city with its endless traffic and concrete, and felt good about it. But the heat was more insidious, and I had not yet adjusted. For one thing, my appetite was not what it had been. I could sense that I was losing weight and vowed I would increase my intake of calories—especially in the morning, when it was cool and I could most easily metabolize my food. "You should drink more beer," George said.

Notwithstanding that this is his remedy for just about anything that could befall a human being—emotional, physical, professional—I took his advice and split with him a one-and-a-half-litre bottle of decidedly gassy Olde English ale, or Olde English Swampe Pisse, as George called it. (When he had taken a bottle into Dan and Carol's two days earlier, Dan had exclaimed quite seriously that he "didn't

know anybody actually drank this stuff except out of a paper bag!")
But it was fine—it was good—and being the sort of drink that quickly
erases any standards, I split another with George and believed I could
feel the goodness seeping into my muscles and organs.

"Now," said George, taking his newly discovered curative to the
prescriptive phase, "what you're going to have to do is give me forty
bucks, and that way we won't get caught short, and I can make sure to
have some decent beer, some Guinness or something, waiting for you
when you come off the road." I might have inquired about some
decent pizza or steak, but in the spirit of the moment agreed that his
plan possessed wisdom and was in the act of forking over a pair of
twenties when a pulsing roar, its volume rising rapidly, erupted out
of the darkness to the east. Within seconds a gazillion-watt search-
light appeared above the water coming toward us, fast.

While at first we were confused by the suddenness of the assault,
it quickly became clear that an immense military helicopter—I
believe a Sikorsky Labrador—was airborne along the waterfront, just
a few metres above the height of our elevated campsite. It may have
been a training exercise or search, or some kind of security patrol,
perhaps related to the Pickering or Darlington nuclear plants. But
when this formidable flying battleship came virtually into our campsite, it occurred to me that maybe we were the object of the mission.
For a minute or more, the wind came so hard off the aircraft's blades
that I was sure our tent was going to be ripped from its pegs and
blown away. In all, the scene might have passed for something out of
sci-fi Hollywood—our astonished faces, our hair blown into tufts, the
light casting our campsite in an otherworldly glow. At the height of
it all, perplexed, annoyed, somewhat intimidated, both George and
I skittered for cover under a nearby red pine and waited, crouched,
George holding fast to his jug of Olde English, as the helicopter
made a second low-altitude pass and then abruptly sped out over the
lake and was gone.

LAKE ONTARIO contains less than a tenth of the volume of water of Lake Superior. And its shores support roughly sixty times as many people. The numbers alone would suggest that the ecological pressure on it is six hundred times greater than that on Superior. Lake Ontario suffers coal-fuelled power plants, nuclear reactors, dense airborne contaminants, and industrial sludge. What's more, it is a catchment lake for the toxins of all the other Great Lakes.

And yet when the wind and sun are right, and the eyes of the beholder are willing, it is still a gorgeous sight—inspiring in its fury, calming in its tranquility. During our four-day journey to Kingston, where we would cross into the United States, George and I would see it in both extremes.

The walk from Darlington to Presqu'ile, a distance of some eighty kilometres, was a languorous two-day aberration. The heat was allayed by a soft breeze off the lake, but no more than enough to put a fleeting afternoon cat's paw on the sunlit surface of the water. The occasional funnel of white smoke from a bulk freighter rose somewhere beyond the horizon. But for the most part, the haze erased the line between silver lake and silver sky. In the fields, the corn was waist high, and in country gardens, the peonies and irises were luxuriantly in bloom. The ditches were full of buttercups and Queen Anne's lace.

This is railway country, and at no point on my walk had I been more aware of trains—which in these parts are engaged in an endless shuffle of passengers and freight between Toronto and Montreal (or more broadly Quebec City and Windsor-Detroit). The Canadian Pacific and Canadian National Railways have long referred to this most travelled of their routes as "the corridor," and sometimes four or five trains an hour, or even more, go rocketing past, pulling cars from all over North America. East of Bowmanville, I stood on a bridge and looked down onto some two hundred rattling flatcars, gondola cars, cattle cars and boxcars, each with its load of plywood, two-by-fours, Ayrshires, gyprock, steel beams, bulldozers, concrete and plastic pipe, hydro poles, "container" boxes, and, pretty much as always in this country, tons of Durum Number One bound for the muffin mills and Wonder Bread bakers to the east.

Air travel has made us relatively nostalgic about the passenger train. But for all the sweet memories that are inspired by coaches and dining cars, we are well reminded that trains, too, played their part in walking's decline. *Life* magazine wrote in September 1998,

> For most of human history, all land transport depended on a single mode of propulsion—feet. Whether the traveller relied on his own extremities or those of another creature, the drawbacks were the same, low cruising speed, vulnerability to weather, and the need to stop for food and rest. But on September 15, 1830, foot power began its long slide toward obsolescence. As brass bands played, a million Britons gathered between Liverpool and Manchester to witness the inauguration of the world's first fully steam-driven railway.

North America welcomed the trains less than fifty years later, and despite the enormous amount of land available in the nineteenth century, people often built their houses within twenty or thirty metres of the railway tracks, accepting the roar of steam engines in the night as the tolerable cost of the convenience and "company" of being situated where they were.

What struck me most about this region's adaptation to the railway was that, as in decades past, so many of the inhabitants had located within the proverbial stone's throw of the main line. Undoubtedly, the night whistle or the mere rumble of the 12:40 ripping through from Montreal is as significant a sound for these country dwellers as the factory whistle might have been over the years for town or city folk, or the school bell for children—a tolerable purgatory within the broader reassurance of being connected to the whole.

More striking yet about the residences was the outrageous aesthetic code of the regional *nouveaux riches*. In some cases the buildings seemed less like houses than private museums devoted to just about anything that could go awry in the realm of taste. One monstrosity was surrounded by an acre or so of green-painted concrete. At another, the entryway was flanked by life-sized polished reproductions of medieval armour and at another by painted concrete lions as big as those in Trafalgar Square. Yet another house had a false front and roofline, castellated as if to conceal archers, and a pair of ten-metre false turrets on the front corners. At a more discreet lakeside home in the village of Port Granby, 105 champagne bottles had been lined up in rows beside the blue recycling box.

I WALKED THROUGH THE TOWN of Port Hope, familiar with the Victorian sensibility of the place—the lawns, the statuary, the old brick buildings, all more or less typical of small-town southern Ontario—but decidedly immune to any excitement over the specifics of the courthouse, opera house, or old churches, or of the effete colonial implications of the cannons in the downtown park. Perhaps ironically, I was more impressed by the immense cemetery on the town's outskirts, which I would guess accommodated more bodies than the town, with its twelve thousand living souls (and undoubtedly exerted more influence over the souls of the living than might be the case in a place a little less obviously defined by the perhaps self-delusional mores of its past).

George, on the other hand, did not get through Port Hope so readily. By the time I caught up with him that night, near Cobourg, he was in a ghastly mood, disgusted with and railing about what he perceived as the town's stodgy and self-righteous pretensions, its British correctness, its Orangemen, its eight brick Protestant churches, and about my own Protestant upbringing. More than anything, he had been offended by a piece of public statuary that he said he had at first taken as "no more than the usual waste of bronze" spent in honour of those who had done "the dirty work" of empire. But closer examination had revealed that the celebrated figure, Lieutenant Arthur T.H.

Williams, had "gallantly led the victorious and decisive charge" at the Battle of Batoche, routing Riel's recessionists and slaughtering hundreds of George's adoptive Métis forebears. The monument had been erected in Williams's hometown "by his admiring countrymen throughout Canada assisted by his companions in arms, and the Government of Canada."

"Admiring countrymen," scoffed George. "These guys were executioners! Culture killers! I'm in the land of the enemy!"

I thought it mildly ironic, and said so, that George was attempting to drown his sorrows with a bottle of Olde English ale.

"It's all an old Métis can afford!" he complained. What's more, it was apparent that his sorrows were learning to swim. Certainly they were still flailing half an hour after he picked me up. "The Métis never marched against Port Hope," he grumbled as we sat in the Cobourg Tim Hortons. "But these ... these ... rancorous volunteers from the town of eight Protestant churches—these guys thought it was their God-given right to go out and kill them. To kill us. And I say *us* because they killed the future, too. After that, the Métis never got it back together."

He was silent for a moment, then said, "And the Canadian government's stooge in all this was T.H. Wilkins from Port Hope."

"Williams," I corrected.

George tossed me the notebook in which he had recorded his traumatized response to the afternoon, plus an ink sketch of the bronzed and dauntless "T.H. Wilkins," sword raised, colonial eye resolute, as he prepared to lead the charge against the Morrissettes of old.

What interested me almost as much about the notes was a nearby comment that "firewood had to be found to cook a steak, because the Highway Walking Man demands protein to keep up his strength." And below that, a note to the effect that "Walking Man" was "doing forty klicks a day, despite the heat" and how, when finished for the day, "he glows with pride, like a rod of uranium at work in the Pickerskill [*sic*] nuclear plant."

THE NEXT MORNING, in Cobourg, I mailed a parcel to Georgia, Eden, and Matt—odds and ends that I had been picking up in stores since way back at Sault Ste. Marie: CDs, candy, firecrackers, Beannie Buddies, a skateboard hat, a knife. In a brief phone chat with Betty the previous night, she had strafed me for promising the kids a parcel and then not sending it immediately. So I was determined to get it mailed. On account of which I was late starting that morning and by nightfall was still a dozen kilometres from where I was to meet George at Presqu'ile Provincial Park.

It had been another day of Floridian light and heat—of listless haze hanging low over Lake Ontario. I felt strong if a bit sinewy, but was having difficulties with my feet. I had noticed the previous day that two of the toenails on my right foot had turned white, but otherwise seemed normal. But that morning as I had prodded them, one had almost come off in my hand. When I fiddled the second one, it, too, lifted like a trap door on the soft pink flesh underneath. The prospect of simply yanking them off was unendurable, so I did my best to tape them into place. After a few hours' walking, however, the lesions, the tape, the perpetual low-level discomfort, began to change my gait—an adjustment that, by dark, had become a detectable limp.

The clear skies of the past couple of nights had by now been erased by a stormy southwest wind and a blanket of clouds, so there was not so much as a star or a ray of reflected light visible on the gravel road I was following along the lake.

Under the circumstances, I could not help thinking about what it must be like to be blind. Basically, like this. However, even in so brief a darkness, nature went to work, and in no time I felt my other senses beginning to compensate, the surrounding sounds and smells becoming heightened—the chirruping of frogs, the waves lapping ashore, the smell of lilacs coming across a field. More subtly, I believed I could tell when the surrounding poplars gave way to cedar or swamp or open fields.

Suddenly, in the inky dark, not five metres away, a harrowing two-pitched yowl erupted out of the blackness, followed by the sound of crunched bone and the frantic quacking of a duck, perhaps in its death throes. As I limped on down the road, this gruesome little symphony led me to postulate that a raccoon and fox had met unexpectedly at a duck's nest, thieves without honour, and had had to fight one another before hitting Jemima, who undoubtedly perished with her ducklings.

The road into Presqu'ile Park added three or four kilometres to my day, and since I had neglected to take my phone, I had no contact with George and hadn't a clue where he might have pitched camp in the vast and labyrinthine campground. Then, as if on cue, a pair of headlights swept into view. George had made several trips out to the park gate, had now found me, and in no time we were sitting by our picnic table, lashed by an inundating wind as the waves crashed onto the limestone rip-rap three or four metres below us. George, who is not easily embarrassed by material inadequacy, explained the relative humiliation he had endured pitching the old tent in a cartoon battle with the wind, under the amused scrutiny of our mostly elderly neighbours, all of whom were now safely asnooze in their $60,000 RVs. (But it was we who got the last laugh, in that, by morning, while our enfeebled house stood pegged and upright if a little wobbly, their more sophisticated canopies and bug shelters had in a number of cases been ripped loose and sent flying down the road or, in the case of a light screened picnic shelter, into the shallow water, from where its owner was trying unsuccessfully to retrieve it by swearing at it and, between bouts of profanity, casting a lure with which he hoped to hook and haul it ashore.)

While I had been walking that afternoon, George had visited an asparagus farm, a place worked by Mexican migrants, where he bought ten pounds of fresh-picked asparagus for the agreeable price of forty-nine cents a pound. So dinner that night featured asparagus—five pounds of it, boiled, buttered, and sprinkled with lemon juice and cayenne. I was into my third or fourth plate of this appetizing treat when I spotted a shadow in the passenger seat of the van, the sliding door of which had been left open to shed extra light on the campsite.

I got up to investigate and was taken aback to see a monstrously fat raccoon sitting there practically making love to our prized loaf of home-baked bread from Cobourg. Seeing me, he bolted back between the front seats, out the sliding door, and off into the night—carrying the bread bag and everything that remained of the loaf. A few minutes later as I ingested my ration of Olde English, I turned, thinking to speak to George, and there again was the raccoon, now sitting beside me, eyeing the butter, perhaps having found the bread a little dry. I jumped up with a yelp of surprise, and again sent him waddling into the night.

A minute later, a wire of lightning split the southern sky, and we hastily packed away the food and shut ourselves into the tent. And were barely asleep when a cymbal-like clattering erupted within metres. By pointing the flashlight out the tent's back flap to the picnic table, I could make out, through the rain, the form of our fat and fateful companion, his ring-tailed rump pointing heavenwards out of a three-gallon pot from which he was greedily slurping the water in which George had cooked the asparagus.

7

The More Easily
Kept Illusions

The undertaking of a pilgrimage has, for centuries, been a vital exploratory possibility for those wishing to give physical expression to an inner or spiritual journey—to make a display, however humble, of commitment. Every year, pilgrims stream to Mecca, to Jerusalem, to Chimayo, to Lourdes, and to Benares. Or they simply walk where their feet lead them, in the manner of the Peace Pilgrim, an otherwise nameless American woman who in 1953 set out from Pasadena, California, to walk 40,000 kilometres in the interest of world peace. In the end, she walked 120,000 kilometres in twenty-eight years—without an address, without a change of clothing, accepting money, accepting food and accommodation as they were offered, and espousing causes that ranged from civil rights and nuclear disarmament to peace in Vietnam.

Thoreau said every walk is a pilgrimage of sorts. Yet I was never quite sure what to say when people referred to my own journey in such terms. And people did. Particularly reporters and broadcasters, who often wanted to know "what kind of a pilgrimage" I was on.

Was it spiritual? Of course it was (as the yogi said, Remember that you are not a human being having a spiritual experience, but a

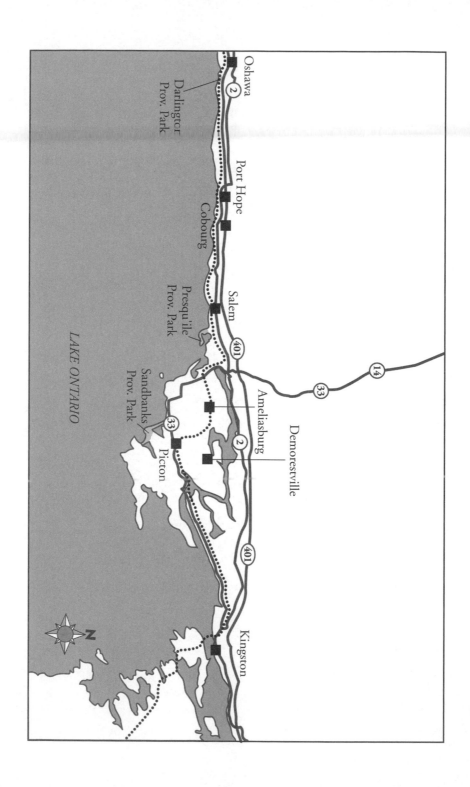

spiritual being having a human experience). And yet somehow the concept of myself as a pilgrim on a spiritual quest seemed a little too rarefied for an endeavour into which I was constantly factoring the likes of fat raccoons, a rotting tent, and Olde English Swampe Pisse.

I could relate better to a less elevated notion of pilgrimage—the sense, perhaps, that exertion and privation are in the end rewarded by a feeling of spiritual well-being. I had been fascinated to read about pilgrims who, in the spirit of privation, deliberately made their journeys more difficult—by going barefoot or crawling or putting stones in their shoes. A while back, I had read about a Native man who had run backwards across the United States, wearing tiny rear-view mirrors attached to his glasses.

However, if one thing more than any other attracted me about traditional notions of pilgrimage, it was the suggestion that the spiritual is not just of the air and of the unseen but of the earth underfoot, that there is a transcendent, if not mystic, power in the mountains and forests and waters themselves, and even in the streets of the city. The idea that we absorb the best of the earth's energy through our feet is a correlative here—as is the notion that in dancing on the earth, the soles of the feet are a conductor between the energy of the planet and the spirit of the dancer.

All of this resonates with the Native belief that the entire natural world—rock, water, fire, wildlife, trees—is in some way an embodiment of spirit. I have tended to resist the collateral belief that every pebble, pine needle, and raindrop has an individual spiritual essence. But there is undeniably something redemptive in the knowledge that the sacred has earthly location and that, as Rebecca Solnit points out, we are able to move physically toward spiritual destinations that are more elusive, more difficult to comprehend, when approached in the abstract.

If beyond locale and privation my walk bore the earmark of the old-style spiritual journey, it did so largely, I would say, in its provision of the chance to reflect, to rediscover, and to re-arm against the pressures and pessimism that are so much a part of contemporary life.

In addition, I several times picked up intimations of pilgrimage in my desire to seek out specific towns or people, as when, on the morning of June 15, I walked east across Prince Edward County, intent on visiting Ameliasburg, where Al Purdy, often considered the greatest of Canadian poets, had lived for more than forty years. Purdy had first caught my attention when I was a student, in an essay on his war experience where he referred to himself as "a soldier who couldn't be trusted with a wooden gun." This was a soldier to whom I could relate.

I reached Ameliasburg, hungry, miserable, in hard rain, and met George at the little white-frame Al Purdy Library—recently named so, and with a swishy new sign out front, surrounded by petunias. Al had apparently spent some time in the library, although its collection was surely not much bigger than his personal library. But the teenaged girl on duty didn't remember him and could point us to just two or three of his books. And she had no idea where we might find his home. In a back corner of this tiny place, we discovered a number of clippings and photos about Al's presence in the town, about the rededication of the library in his honour a year or so earlier, and about his recent funeral, which had been attended by a contingent of the more recognizable members of the country's literary grind show.

Purdy's work won him a wide and appreciative readership, and fomented friendships and extensive correspondence with, among others, the American poet Charles Bukowski, the Canadian novelist Margaret Laurence, and Purdy's one-time hero and inspiration, the Montreal poet Irving Layton. Purdy was also, perhaps, the last Canadian writer to have had a friendship with the hard-drinking English novelist Malcolm Lowry, while the two were living in Vancouver during the early 1950s.

But in a sense it was Ameliasburg that had made him as a poet. He moved there, still in obscurity, in 1957, because it was close to his hometown of Trenton. And there, in the earth, fields, and crumbling architecture, he discovered a sense of his own constitution and past that began immediately to redirect his poetry. With his friend the poet Milton Acorn, he built a house out of scrap lumber on the shore of Roblin Lake, adjacent to the town. He spent time there sporadically through the late 1950s, and in 1960 he and his wife, Eurithe, spent their first winter in the house without electricity or plumbing. They lit oil lamps to read and chopped through a metre of ice for water. During the coldest months, Purdy set the alarm to wake him every two hours to stoke the cast-iron stove that was the building's only source of heat.

"While living there—trapped, if you like—I was forced to explore my own immediate surroundings," he wrote in *Maclean's* magazine in 1971. "Wandering the roads on foot or driving when we had money for gas, I got interested in old buildings—not as an expert, but with the idea that houses express the character of long-dead owners and builders."

Purdy wrote that he kept finding roads he had "never noticed.... Leafy and overgrown some of them fading to a green dead-end at run-down farmhouses, abandoned long since but still containing the map of people's lives."

What I had enjoyed particularly about Purdy's work was this insistence, line after line, poem after poem, on the link between a person's inner make-up and his or her landscape and surroundings.

I had met Al a couple of times, and once, during the late 1980s, had dinner with him and a few other writers after a publisher's function in Toronto. He was tall, big-boned, ornery, somewhat intimidating, and he talked loudly and drank heavily—for all of which reasons, he wasn't the easiest guy to get comfortable around.

George and I went into the dismal village store, a place half-lit and with half-empty shelves, where a woman emerged from the back room, unsmiling, to sell us camera batteries that were two years past their expiry date.

"You don't have anything newer, do you?" I said, instigating an exchange that might have been lifted out of a Harold Pinter script.

"Newer than what?"

"Well—than these!" I said, holding out the dusty, faded package of batteries.

"Expiry dates only matter for bread," she said, snatching them from me and, without so much as a glance at them, ringing up the sale.

As I took them back, I asked if she knew where the poet Al Purdy had lived, but she shook her head no, giving the impression she had been asked the question a hundred times already that day.

I said, "Did he ever come in the store?"

"Did who ever come in?"

"Al Purdy, the poet. He lived on Roblin Lake—for forty years."

"Well then he must have come in. What did he look like?"

I attempted a description, and she asked if he still lived in Ameliasburg.

"No," George butted in. "He's past his expiry date. With poets, it matters."

George and I toured the road around the lake, peering through the rain at this cabin and that, but could not identify Purdy's.

Purdy wrote of how the roads around Ameliasburg possessed what he called "this endearing quality of never going anywhere important, certainly not to a city; of being an end in themselves, as if at any place where you might care to stop the car you have already arrived."

We followed precisely such a road (coincidentally named Al Purdy Lane) down a wooded embankment onto a flood plain where the little river that flows through the village meanders past the Ameliasburg cemetery. And there, in the rain, we hauled open the creaky graveyard gate and advanced like ghostbusters through the longish grass, scanning the grave markers until we came to the riverside where a shiny slab of black granite in the shape of a book had been erected over Al's remains.

"The Voice of the Land," said the inscription, inspiring George to modest oratory on the nature of landscape and our inability to understand time—how perhaps we merely create time as we need it, as believed by certain African tribes and, perhaps, George thought, by Purdy himself.

I took George's photo, and having thus paid our respects, we beat it back to the car and back up into town, where we sat in the van, hulling strawberries and listening to a tape of Al's own rich voice speaking of "a land of quiescence and still distance" where a man could

make room

enough between the trees
for a wife

and maybe some cows and
room for some
of the more easily kept illusions.

The rain came harder against the windshield, and a few minutes later I was back on the road, moving a step at a time toward Picton, toward Manhattan, certainly toward some of the more easily kept illusions—such as the feeling of progress, the feeling that I was gaining perspective as I gained distance and was perhaps somehow the better for it.

Prince Edward County, I should mention, is distinct among southern Ontario landscapes, in that it is not part of the province's mainland but is a sprawling, sparsely populated island—a palette of limestone and varied soil that extends nearly halfway out into Lake Ontario, and is separated from the lake's north shore by the narrow and elongated Bay of Quinte.

It was a curiosity to me—certainly a coincidence of a high order—that I had now visited the homes of both of the county's legendary modern residents, the first having been the hockey player Bobby Hull, with whom I had spent a day on a journalistic assignment ten years prior at Demorestville, northeast of Ameliasburg, where since his earliest days as a Chicago Blackhawk, Hull has raised cattle and kept a modest house. Though the two men might not, at first glance, appear to have much in common, I discovered while interviewing Hull that he has a lyric, sometimes wistful, sensibility and, like Purdy, not only loves but enjoys rhapsodizing about the local landscape. As a boy, he travelled the farms along the Bay of Quinte in summer, haying, threshing, and throwing stooks on the horse-pulled wagons. And toured the countryside on Sunday afternoons with his family in their 1930 Model A. "I'd see those red-and-white Herefords out there on the green meadow," he told me, "and they looked kinda nice to me, and I thought that if I was ever able to afford some, I'd buy them, and buy some land out here to go with them. And as soon as I could, I did."

It is perhaps the influence of the limestone or the stinginess of the soil, but Hull and Purdy shared other traits—among them their gruffness, their creativity, their stubbornness, their refusal to bow to convention, and their stated need to get away regularly from the remoteness of the island and go into the city. On a more gustatory level, both were passionate about beer (Purdy made, drank, and wrote about it; Hull both drank and promoted it—indeed, was representing an Ontario brewery at the time of my visit and broke out a twelve of the product when I arrived at 8:45 A.M.).

And they both loved hockey, which Purdy once referred to as a "combination of ballet and murder."

And they loved women—Al mostly poetically, I suspect, whereas Hull took a more functional approach. In fact, at the time of my visit, the great wingman was fantasizing his memoirs, and solicited my advice on how he might diplomatically handle the complexities of his life with what he called "babes," of which there had been a staggering number. Fortunately, I told him, writers didn't have such problems and encouraged him to be honest whether or not he told the truth.

WHEN I HAD GONE about a kilometre up the road, George passed me with a beep, narrowly missing a twenty-kilo snapping turtle that was enjoying a mid-afternoon shower in the centre of the pavement. Determined that the old reptile's long life not end under the wheels of a speeding vehicle—at least not today—I took a stick out of the ditch and, using a method I had employed before, attempted to get the turtle to chomp down on it so I could drag him to safety. I prodded him gingerly with my toe, pushed at him ineffectually with the stick, and then, realizing there was no other way, simply grabbed his shell by the edges, jerked him off his feet, and as he swam and snapped at the air, carried him to the swampy ditch and plopped him into the muck.

GEORGE AND I FELT anything but unique eating in a Picton fast-food joint that claimed to have served "billions and billions" of the self-same grease bombs that we ordered. But our purpose had been to get out of the rain, and we accomplished it.

When the sun came out during the early evening, I decided to dry out by walking the dozen kilometres to Sandbanks Provincial Park, where the extent of our plans was to consume another five pounds of asparagus. My injured toes had recuperated (or had at least toughened and shed their nails), so I was having none of the difficulty that I had had the previous day.

Between Picton and the park, I passed a commercial strawberry field from which I liberated a dozen good-sized berries. But when I stepped across the ditch for another dozen, a gun blast sounded from the middle of the field (I have for years coveted an opportunity to write "a shot rang out," and am not about to pass it up now). I was informed later that most of the local market gardeners used automatic blank detonators to scare away crows and raccoons, but at the time I could think only of picking buckshot out of my posterior, so beat it back up onto the road.

Farther along, I stopped at an old country house and stared in at gardens that were lush almost to the point of decadence. In particular, I was attracted by a thirty-metre bed of irises, thousands of them, hybrids, in colours from the dreamiest parts of the spectrum. I walked along in front of them on the lawn, reading signs that bore names such as Interpol, River Hawk, Knock 'em Dead, Icefield, Sultan's Palace,

Dusky Dancer, After Hours, Prissy Miss, Forge Fire, and Lara's Affair. Several of them bore blooms that were as close to pure black as anything the plant world can produce.

A lanky, gentle-mannered man appeared behind me and introduced himself as Jack Laundry, a former elementary-school teacher for the Prince Edward County Board. Apart from teaching, Jack had devoted his life to the growing and hybridization of flowers, in particular irises, 137 varieties of which stood before us in the bed. He had developed most of them personally, by a process he called "rhizome grafting," and had named them himself.

"At one time," he said, throwing an arm behind him to take in several acres of yard, "I had 15,000 gladioluses here—250 types. I had 500 rose bushes, 120 kinds of day lilies." But he was into his sixties, was stiff in the joints, and was losing sight in one eye. So he had cut back.

"Well, they're still the best gardens I've ever seen," I told him, to which he said (typical of those who have lost all sense of proportion), "They're really not much."

And when, in turn, he enthused over the length of my walk, I said (typical of those who have lost all sense of proportion), "It's really not much."

For comparative purposes, I told him I'd heard the average human being walks a hundred thousand kilometres in a lifetime.

He said, "And I've added another five thousand on my knees, crawling up and down these rows pulling weeds."

8

A Walk on the Wilder Side

ifty days on the road, at a walker's pace, had impressed upon me the intricate natural continuity of forests, mountains, beaches, water, air—the endless knitting of habitats and species ranges. Of sunlight, soil, and seeds. Of streams making lakes making clouds—making rain and spruce sap and moose blood.

I had been impressed, too, during 1,700 kilometres, by the endless fragmentation of that oneness into townships, districts, counties, municipalities, police precincts, political ridings, conservation zones, Native land, Crown land, parkland, private land, everything down to adopt-a-highway and snowplow zones: the world as jurisdictional game board, all stops more obsessively championed than is the indivisible world of nature, or even art.

I had crossed every line, and none had given me even remote cause for concern until early on the afternoon of June 18, at Kingston, as George and I sat in the terminal of the Wolfe Island Ferry, psyching up to cross the St. Lawrence River to Wolfe Island and, from there, the U.S. border into New York State.

George, more than I, had come to view the passage as an impending calamity. Above all, he was convinced that under the telepathic

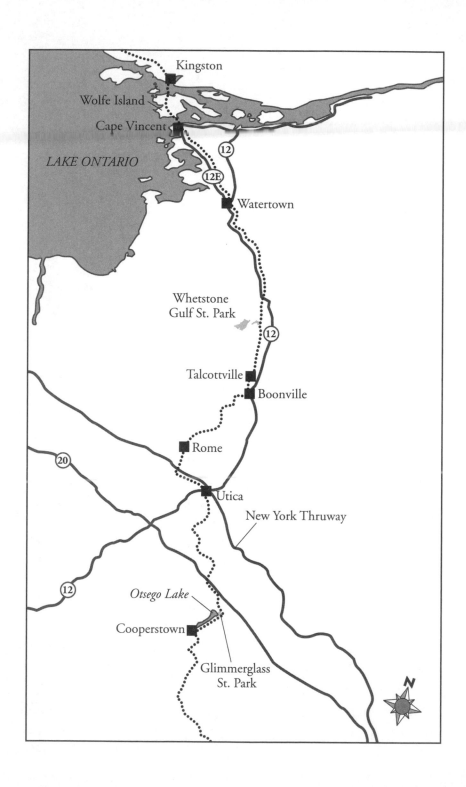

Kingston

Wolfe Island

Cape Vincent

LAKE ONTARIO

(12)

(12E)

Watertown

Whetstone
Gulf St. Park

(12)

Talcottville

Boonville

Rome

(20)

Utica

New York Thruway

(12)

Otsego Lake

Cooperstown

Glimmerglass
St. Park

N

scrutiny of border guards, we'd be exposed as moral or cultural heretics—at very least as rat-ass Canadians, or socialists, committed to medicare, welfare, gun control, writing, *walking*—all of which he construed as implied insults to the sort of people who were likely to be defending the world's most famously "undefended" border.

Moreover, he suspected that his dozen years of illegal residency in New York, his years without a green card, would in the intervening years have been discovered and at immigration would leap out of cyberspace, and that he'd be turned back if not arrested and thrown into ill-lit durance while his fate was decided by what he referred to as "Bush voters."

Even if all else went well, he believed that some fragment of illegal substance in the seams of his borrowed luggage would be sniffed out by dogs. For that reason, in Toronto, he had gone to elaborate lengths to wash the big nylon bag in which he was carrying most of his gear. "Look at me," he had said that morning as we broke camp, "I even look like a terrorist." And he did. His swarthy face, his moustache and goatee bore a striking resemblance to the mug shots of Muslim terrorists we'd become accustomed to seeing on television.

Much of his concern—our concern—was, of course, ignorance and the fact that neither of us had been in the United States since the Twin Towers had come down. George, more than I, had bought into the much-heralded media construct of post-9/11 America as a paranoid backwater—racist and survivalistic to the point where its border authorities would distrust anyone engaged in such an arcane project as ours. George was further convinced that in the aftermath of 9/11 New York State would be akin to a military or vigilante zone. Against my protestations that I had always had peaceful travels in Upstate New York—in particular in the Adirondacks as a child—George responded that I was naive; things had changed; New York State was more violent and heedless than anything we were accustomed to in Canada. I had annoyed him one day by saying that I suspected no part of New York would be any worse than his hometown of Winnipeg, where drug gangs all but own the north end of the city, where arson and murder are commonplace, and where winter alone constitutes such a violent, unlivable compression of forces that by comparison the Adirondacks, Catskills, or Hudson River Valley would seem like idylls of the peaceable kingdom.

Beneath all this was the unspoken knowledge that if we were stopped at the border, our adventure—this unwieldy, poorly planned hallucination that we had nurtured out of the wilderness, this thing we had come to love—would be over. George might have been just as happy to reroute to Montreal or Quebec City. But for me it was Manhattan or nothing, and I had gone so far as to consider entering the United States illegally if we were doused at the border. I have friends on the St. Lawrence River at Cornwall, where I lived from age ten to seventeen, and could easily have arranged to cross the river in a powerboat, as we had done as teenagers. But that would have meant carrying on without George, in that he wasn't up to walking the necessary distances in the absence of the van.

It would also have meant horsing twenty kilos of gear on my back, pitching camp in whatever field or thicket presented itself at the end of a day's walk, carrying fewer clothes and shoes, no books, a vastly reduced pantry, and a flyweight tent instead of the reassuring canvas nine-by-nine. As I would not have taken the camp stove, and wouldn't always be able to light a fire, it would have meant lots of uncooked meals.

Above all, of course, it would mean no one to confide in or listen to—or share the fire with, or rag on, or trust.

Against such eventualities, I had bought new passports for each of us and had, months ago, conferred with the U.S. Immigration office in Toronto as to how to ease our entry. On their instructions, I had had my editor, Diane Turbide at Penguin, write me a letter explaining the nature of my endeavour, stressing that I wouldn't actually be working in the U.S.—wouldn't be writing—but would simply be observing, taking notes toward an eventual book. I was particularly sensitive about the issue in that once, years earlier, as I crossed at Detroit to visit Gordie and Colleen Howe, about whom I was writing a chapter in a book, I was detained for hours at the Ambassador Bridge, while a female border guard consulted an official in another city on whether there was someone in the United States who could do the job I was on my way to do.

"But it's *my book*," I had complained. "How can someone else write my book?" Which was exactly the question that had sent her into consultation.

Diane had also written a letter for George—or at least signed one I had written—describing the Pollyanna nature of his participation in the trip and his all but fetishistic fondness for America.

It took me a good two hours to cross Wolfe Island, which like St. Josephs Island, is a throwback to Eden, or at least another century, with its fenced farms and narrow shaded roads. When I reached the south side of the island, George was waiting, and we drove back inland to an old rural cemetery, where we took every item of luggage, camping gear, and food—every tool, book, and roadside treasure—out of the van and consolidated it, leaving us with a thigh-high stack of boxed refuse, including firewood that George had husbanded all the way from Pancake Bay. There was no trash can around, so I took the pile out among the graves and constructed a neat tombstone-shaped heap that I assumed would eventually be discovered by the township graveyard keeper and carted to its reward in the local landfill or incinerator—or simply dumped into a grave, as we used to do with refuse during my summer at the cemetery in Toronto.

In the interest of respectability, George had had the van's severely cracked windshield replaced in Trenton, and at Sandbanks Park a couple of days earlier we had done our first machine laundry of the trip.

I drank a quart of Gatorade in the shade, while George had a beer or two, then I ran a dishpan of water from the public faucet and let it heat for ten minutes in the sun. Carrying soap, mirror, razor, and towel—and entertaining vague thoughts about the handiness of death—I walked to a high pink stone at the back of the cemetery and commandeered it as a wash and shaving stand.

Tarted up and tidy, we drove the van onto the listing four-car ferry—a barge-like conveyance as funky and dilapidated as anything one could hope to avoid on open water—and heaved out onto the south channel. I had originally planned to cross at the Thousand Islands Bridge at Gananoque, unaware of the teensy port of entry at Cape Vincent off Wolfe Island. But I had discovered the latter on the map one day, and when I learned it is the smallest customs post in the United States, I switched plans and now highly recommend Cape Vincent to all neurotics wishing to enter America.

When we were perhaps fifty metres from shore, I spotted a great blue heron standing placidly on the dock in front of the customs shack and had a sudden presentiment that everything would be fine.

The bespectacled immigration officer who appeared at the van window as we eased off the ferry was, I would guess, in his mid-sixties, was fit in a dapper military way, and wore a big grey push-broom moustache. He examined my letter with approximately the concern one might afford the directions on a shampoo bottle, deconstructed the pathos before him, and said, "Well, fellas, you're in the right place. I'm a distance man, too—except I'm a swimmer."

From that moment on, he avoided even the appearance of looking into the back of the van, of "inspecting" us, as if to do so would violate the faith that he clearly believed existed between "distance men."

He worked his way down from important "distance men" questions about pace, exhaustion, nourishment, fluid consumption, and gear, to inconsequentials such as whether or not we were carrying hand guns or explosives, or had ever been indicted on a federal offence.

"Got maps?" he said.

"Not really."

"Well, you better come in then. I'll draw you one to Watertown, get you started in the U.S.," and he led us into the grungy little shack from which he guarded his homeland.

If ever there was a positive emissary for the customs and immigration industry it was Peter McAfee. During the next ten minutes, this one-time FBI agent drew us a detailed map to the American Automobile Association office in Watertown, where proper maps would be available; explained every crossroad, bend, and point of interest between Cape Vincent and Watertown; and delivered a succinct but compelling review of his years as a drug cop, college instructor, and distance swimmer. He had several times swum the Hudson River at its widest point amid brisk tides and ocean freighters, held records in any number of swimming events at the annual U.S. Law Enforcement Games, and had rigged his registration for the upcoming Police Games in Lake Placid so that he would be competing, as he put it, "mostly against a bunch of old farts." As he spoke, an ornery little cocker spaniel stood within inches of his feet, yapping so enthusiastically that at every new volley, it sprung about four inches off the floor. "At ease, Pearl!" Peter blurted at each outburst. "At ease, now!"

"You boys enjoy yourselves!" he called as I walked, and George drove, away—about as sage a piece of advice as anyone could have bestowed upon us as we entered the final phase of our journey.

I left Cape Vincent to the chimed accompaniment of the grand old hymns of Christianity, hair-raisers, broadcast electronically from the bell tower of a local church: "How Great Thou Art," "Peace in the Valley," "It Is No Secret," "O for a Thousand Tongues to Sing." The lot of them are so deeply ingrained in me from childhood that to this day I have no rational resistance to them—am happy to let them sift undeflected through my radar, straight to where I am most submissive and defenceless.

Juiced by the music and by the freedom of having gotten to where I was, I booted it southeast along 12E, past derelict motorhomes, unpainted wood shacks, the crumbling barns of cattle and dairy farms, hayfields cut and baled, toward the muted peaks of the Adirondacks glowing a bluish greeny grey in the distance. With their long winters, thin soil, and stony ground, the borderlands of Upstate New York are by no means God's gift to agriculture. And yet from tiny Cape Vincent in the west to the scruffy village of Rouses Point, where New York meets Vermont meets Quebec, the land is gloriously in the shadow of the Adirondacks and within the sustaining spirit of the St. Lawrence River.

With few exceptions, the houses along the 1,700 kilometres of my route had raised little in the way of architectural curiosity. But it puzzled me now as to why the old limestone farmhouses along 12E resembled so decidedly the rural stone dwellings of, say, Quebec's Eastern Townships, or even of rural Bordeaux or Provence. Several such dwellings, with their steep roofs, tiny dormer windows, and teetering, covered verandas, might have been lifted whole out of the rural Quebec paintings of Clarence Gagnon or Marc-Aurèle Suzor-Coté.

I found the answer at Chaumont, where in the vestibule of the post office an interpretive brochure explained that in 1797 Benjamin Franklin had sailed to France to raise money and military resources for the Revolutionary cause. Count Jacques LeRay de Chaumont, fresh from the Revolution in France and sympathetic to democracy (and, one would assume, ever-willing to kick English butt), loaned Franklin a million dollars and three warships for John Paul Jones's fleet.

When the American Revolution ended, and the debt was due, Franklin and the co-signators of the Declaration—by this time low on funds but with oodles of prime real estate at their disposal— offered de Chaumont and his family land instead, with the result that the count's son bought for a pittance most of what is now Jefferson County in Upstate New York.

I was not aware until later of the bitter and bizarre outcome of all this—specifically that the Frenchmen opted for land on the latitude of Paris, believing such territory would enjoy the same supernal climate as the French capital. You might think they'd have had some knowledge of the French settlements that had been in Canada for a hundred years—and within miles of Upstate New York. If not, didn't anyone, including Franklin and his confreres, think to tell de Chaumont about the Adirondack winters? Or should we assume it was in the Americans' best interests *not* to tell him, to allow the French to settle far off in what was then wilderness, as opposed to claiming Switzerland-sized chunks of Massachusetts or the Delaware Valley?

Whatever the case, in the summer of 1802, de Chaumont sent master stonemasons to begin cutting local limestone and building the French-style houses that to this day exist in varying condition as far south as Boonville. It was only when winter rolled in with its intense cold and Adirondack blizzards that it was clear a mistake had been made—a big one. The uninsulated stone of the houses, no matter how expertly cut and mortared, sucked heat from the interior faster than the inhabitants could cut wood to stoke their inefficient French hearths. Wash water froze overnight. Children shivered in bed. Whole families caught pneumonia and died.

The settlers might have cried *oncle* and gone home, except that Napoleon's brother and several high-ranking scions of the new French Republic had come with them to establish a presence in Upstate New York—though they came with servants to cut *their* wood, having missed at least part of the revolutionary message.

A macabre-looking stone monument at the entrance to Chaumont Memorial Park bears the words "This park is dedicated to the STRENGTH OF THE HUMAN SPIRIT, and to our INALIEN-ABLE RIGHTS as legitimized by the PRINCIPLES OF THE AMERICAN and FRENCH REVOLUTIONS."

To a Canadian, the sentiments seemed a BIT OF A STRETCH, and were lent an indisputably ironic twist by the presence of Big Dick's Market and Gas across the street.

George and I bought sirloin, corn niblets, and canned potatoes at Big Dick's, and having scarfed down our meal at Long Point State Park—all the while avoiding profuse droppings of goose poop—

exercised a version of our inalienable rights by parking the van in a no camping zone on the fringes of the park and curling up inside for our first night's sleep in the U.S.

Up at dawn to avoid discovery, we drove back into Chaumont, steering through a suicide mission of sandy brown bunnies, dozens of them, hopping disastrously this way and that across the highway. A half-dozen herons fished the weeds along Chaumont Bay, off Lake Ontario, and red-winged blackbirds swayed on the cattails.

A teenaged boy had beaten us out of bed, and was walking along 12E with a stringer of black bass. We stopped and asked if he wanted to sell one. "For a ride into town, I'll give ya one!" he announced. And five minutes later, he handed over a fat three-pounder that we gutted and fried à la Veracruzana (cayenne, onions, canned tomatoes) at a rotting picnic table in the parking lot of an abandoned motel.

Before leaving Thunder Bay, I had promised to phone the Warwick Hotel in New York City when we were nine or ten days out of Manhattan. Now I placed a cellular call to the hotel's redoubtable sales manager, Ray Slavin, and confirmed what had often seemed more than a little improbable—that we were getting close to New York City.

"We can't wait!" Ray intoned genially (he intones everything genially), echoing my own excitable sentiments of the moment.

I WAS HALFWAY to Brownsville, perhaps ten kilometres southeast of Chaumont, before the sun fired a first golden tracer above the distant mountains. By 9:30, the temperature was in the mid-nineties Fahrenheit and my feet were a mess. As I sat on the steps of the Brownsville General Store airing my blisters and eating a lemon pie, dog-style, off its plate, a woman whose T-shirt said "My sick days ran out, so I phoned in dead!" ground to a halt in her pickup truck and shouted gaily out the window that she'd seen me on the road—did I need a lift? No thanks, I explained, I was walking into Watertown. When she showed interest, I added that, in fact, I'd walked from way up in Canada and was heading for Manhattan. She stared at me for a few seconds, shrieked with laughter, and said in a protracted whisper, "Hollleee shhhhit."

Of the hundreds of people I met during my walk, this slim, dishevelled woman was the only one who saw in me some feeble potential for celebrity and acted on it by asking for my autograph—because, as she put it, she was sure some day I *might* be "a famous dude." She lit a cigarette, and when I had signed her address book, I took the opportunity to ask about the French in the area and whether they were still a presence. She responded unself-consciously that she knew "absolutely no history," having skipped most of her history classes in high school. "All I can tell ya," she laughed, "is that this is Napoleon country," adding that she was pretty sure Napoleon and Josephine had been friends of George Washington, "or somebody," and might even have lived around here "about two hundred years ago."

AMERICAN GRAVEYARDS have always been showplaces of patriotism, and as I wandered through the extensive Brownsville Cemetery, I saw my first evidence of a new species of patriotic hero, the U.S. fireman, who in the glare of 9/11 has achieved pretty much the status of the American military vet. I counted a miniature version of the Stars and Stripes on some twenty-five graves. More than thirty, however, were marked with the firefighters' predominantly yellow mini-flag with its red likenesses of a pick, ladder, and fireman's helmet, and the motto "Loyal to our Duty."

As in Cape Vincent and Chaumont, the houses in Brownsville were festooned in commemorative bunting and flags, in banners proclaiming, "America, we love you" and "Land of Hope and Glory," as well as sundry Bible verses, mostly on the theme of vengeance against the unjust, and the unimpeachable "God Bless America."

Here and elsewhere, the Stars and Stripes were painted onto shutters, wishing wells, doghouses, fences, boulders—and in a few cases onto plywood cutouts of Snoopy and Charlie Brown or Homer and Bart Simpson. At an old frame duplex in Lyon's Falls the next day, a

version of the flag had been painted directly onto the siding, in triplicate, like a Jasper Johns extravaganza. One little place in Brownsville
was in such catastrophic shape beneath its patriotic decor (two front
windows blown completely out) that anyone might have concluded its
inhabitants were more loyal to the cause than perhaps the cause had
been to them.

Not that I witnessed a unanimity of patriotism in northern New
York State. A few miles down the road, at Lowville, I saw in the
window of what appeared to be a student residence a poster of George
Bush depicted as a pinheaded marionette whose strings were being
worked by a couple of hyena-headed oil men; and outside an
Episcopal Church near Boonville, a four-by-eight-foot plywood sign
showing Bush above the slogan "Terrorist Against Terrorism"; and a
billboard near Rome, sponsored by a peace coalition, showing a crowd
of gleeful Arab children watching a red, white, and blue bomb descend
into their midst. Later, in New York City, I saw a trio of fit young
women wearing tank tops bearing the unambiguous "Fuck Bush."

FOLLOWING PETER MCAFEE'S HAND-DRAWN MAP, I crossed Interstate
81, which leads south into the belly of the beast, and made my way
downhill into Watertown—past carpet stores, fast-food joints, and
playing fields, eventually to a sharp left turn at the nineteenth-century
brick prison that stands, bars and all, at the edge of the oldest part of
the city. Watertown is a virtual museum for the grand Victorian frame
houses—big gothic cubes with back kitchens and widow's walks—that
you see, mostly in lapsed condition, throughout Upstate New York.
There was at one time significant wealth in Watertown, and it has left
a legacy not just of fancy wood houses but of neo-classical banks,
archives, and government offices—and best of all, a marble-fronted
library, palatial and gracious, on whose wide steps George took my
picture wrestling one of a pair of immense marble lions. However, the
commercial heart of town—hotels, department stores, theatres—looks
as if it has been through a war. Which in a sense it has, hit not by a

"smart" bomb (apparently so-named because it targets buildings, not people) but by let us say a "dumb" bomb, an economic bomb, that has left the empty buildings intact but has made a "surgical strike" against the people.

Except for a few post-industrial stragglers—walkers—who frequent the desultory restaurants and dollar shops that do business in what were at one time prosperous multi-storey department stores, the core of this city of perhaps fifty thousand people is deserted. The city is, in fact, a mini-version of what cities such as Detroit, Pittsburgh, and Cleveland had become during the 1960s and, with effort, have recovered from. The "real" life of such places—as defined by television, the car, and the mall—goes on, of course, in the suburbs, where walking is as dead as Jacob Marley.

And yet I was, and am, fascinated by Watertown, due largely to a brilliant trilogy of books by Watertown's best-known writer and cultural saboteur, Frederick Exley, whose autobiographical *A Fan's Notes* appeared in 1969, followed by *Pages from a Small Island* and *Last Notes from Home*. Each of these books is a testimonial both to Exley's brilliance and (happily in these days of fettered dissent) to the principle of free speech, inasmuch as the books are a robust strafing of most of what it was and is to be North American during the late twentieth and early twenty-first centuries.

However, to describe Exley as Watertown's "best-known" writer is, in its way, absurd, in that he is perhaps "worse known" in Watertown than he is even among the rest of the reading population of North America, where perhaps 999 out of a thousand people have never heard his name let alone read one of his books. Which endears me to him even more. To be an Exley follower is to feel the exclusivity of a cult.

From his books, it was as if I knew Watertown, knew a version of it, almost as well as if I had lived there: the New Parrot Bar, the Olympic and Palace Theatres, the Jefferson County Sanatorium, Coffeen Street hill, Willie Gee's Chinese restaurant, the St. Mary's Street pool, Watertown High School, the *Watertown Times* office.

As we walked around, I recalled for George a scene from *A Fan's Notes* that was of particular pertinence to the spirit of our travels—namely, Exley's description of a two-day snowstorm that had shut down the city, leaving only the young people (the walkers) mobile, while it paralyzed the car-dependent adults. "Their faith in the supremacy of the Detroit product was lamentably touching," Exley wrote. "Middle-aged men shovelled furiously, at risk to their hearts, attempting to loosen their Fords from Nature's perverseness, as if those automobiles were extensions of themselves without which they could not live." While Exley and his friends were young and undoubtedly callow, they were, he said, "acute enough to know that though Detroit owned America," Detroit didn't yet own them.

What I wanted, I had decided, was to see the house on Moffet Street where Exley had lived, and which he referred to repeatedly, though never by number, in his work. It seemed a modest enough ambition, and to that end (the library being closed), I asked a succession of thirteen Watertown adults, likely looking types, if they knew anything of Exley or had encountered his books. But not one of them had so much as heard of him, despite his having transported their burg to readers around the world and, in the process, won a National Book Award and a Guggenheim Fellowship during the early 1970s. Meanwhile, municipal politicians and small-print artists—any record of whose contribution lies long unexamined in the minutes of the local council—are named on street signs, buildings, and parks; indeed, stand ten feet high in bronze in the town square.

We were mystified that Exley could be so utterly unknown—vanished—in the town where he had been born and lived his life.

I was doubly frustrated to know that, like so many gifted artists, Exley had put most of what he was and had into his (selectively) celebrated works, and had died during the late 1980s, in debt, dissolute, alcoholic—in his case spitting blood from the lung cancer that was killing him as he lived out his days, writing, at his mother's home in Alexandria Bay on the St. Lawrence River north of the city.

That said, it gave me satisfaction to sit for a while on the library steps, where he had undoubtedly come and gone hundreds of times over the years, and get a first-hand sense of the lovely, hypocritical little city that had inspired the heresies that are his legacy to the world.

Guided further by Peter McAfee's map, George and I made our way to the office of the American Automobile Association, where an alluring young woman in a sleeveless cotton dress searched patiently for every map—in the end a total of ten—that might possibly help us between here and New York City.

She said that during her three years of employment at the AAA, I was the only person of the thousands she had served who was *walking* somewhere, as opposed to driving or cycling or flying.

Watertown is appropriately named, in that it is bisected by the inky Black River and because it was water in the form of hydroelectrical production—and as a mainstay of the local papermaking industry— that originally brought wealth to the town. But as I stood in the AAA office, I did not know this. And when I asked my bare-shouldered benefactor where the wealth had come from to build what had obviously once been a splendid and prosperous city, she leaned across the counter and said surreptitiously, "I probably shouldn't tell you this. I could get fired. But I'll tell you anyway."

I leaned in, ear to the oracle.

"It's all Mafia money," she whispered. "Don't tell anybody I told you."

After a quick bit of mental Rolodexing, I said, "But there wouldn't have been Mafia up here in the late 1800s, would there?"

"Everywhere," she said.

"Why could you get fired?" I said.

"Because it's discriminatory to Italians."

Adding inanity to this already absurd skulduggery, I thought to ask, "Are you Italian?"

"Of course," she whispered. "Everybody in Watertown is."

To this day, I do not know whether she believed what she was telling me or whether she was a prankster's step ahead of me and was simply bored and imaginatively at play.

ON A WHIM, I had brought along an old Sierra Club manual on the American Environmental Movement. But for eight weeks it had languished in the "library box" in the back of the van. This ragged document explained, among other things, that the movement had been founded not by environmentalists in the scientific or academic sense but by people who believed in walking. Chief among them was John Muir, who during the 1880s and '90s walked thousands of miles in the California Sierras and in 1901, out of his interest in preserving wilderness, formed the now-famous club. For thirty years during the early twentieth century, Muir led countless Sierra Club members into the mountains and forests, where they enjoyed the recreational benefits of walking and, of course, were exposed to Muir's conservationist credo.

As I walked south from Watertown that evening, George read the entire manual, and at dinner by the fire in Whetstone Gulf State Park, he told me that, while he was appreciative of the movement's aims, what disturbed him about "these Sierra Club types" was that they were all affluent and educated and had "the luxury of being *able* to be concerned about the environment," and take weekend hikes in the mountains. The poor, he said (and he did not exclude himself), had neither the time nor energy to worry about ecology, much less to go hiking, when the best of their resources were constantly being consumed by mere survival. "Even if they wanted to climb mountains," he complained, "they couldn't afford proper shoes," and he told me that as a kid growing up in wartime St. Boniface, he had never had "anything decent" to put on his feet.

There was a curious and plaintive irony to all this, in that, even now, George was not wearing the shoes he had brought with him from Winnipeg—a pair of lightweight sneakers that wouldn't have lasted fifty kilometres on a mountain trail, or even on the highway—but a pair of high-end English walking shoes that had been owned by my father who had died less than a year before. These well-made shoes were one of a number of pairs, barely worn, that I had scooped from the closet at my dad's vacated apartment specifically to give to George, who I knew from previous transfers wore my dad's size. My father, who was a lifelong walker, would have been fascinated by our trip, indeed, would have loved to be with us. So, in an amused but heartfelt way, it pleased me that these most apt and personal remembrances of him were along on my travels, "tramping out the vineyards," so to speak, even though he was not.

I pointed out to George that at least a branch or two of the historic Underground Railroad, the escape route of the slaves, had come up into northern New York State—that, in fact, there was a statue commemorating John Brown and the slaves in nearby Saranac Lake. I said I doubted the slaves had worn any shoes at all.

"They were running for their lives," grumbled George. "We're not."

There was a silence, and suddenly we were both laughing at what was hardly as indisputable a comment as it might have seemed.

With $800 worth of hiking shoes in my gear, albeit provided free, I could hardly deny that proper shoes were costly. At the same time, as I pointed out to George, virtually every ghetto kid in North America these days seems to own a pair of $200 basketball or board shoes.

I wondered aloud whether specialty shoes were necessary at all for long-distance walking and mentioned an acquaintance of mine, Dr. Dennis McPherson, a professor of Native studies at Lakehead University, who in an effort to raise awareness of Native rights issues, had recently walked 1,400 kilometres from Thunder Bay to Ottawa in a simple pair of street shoes—over ordinary dress socks. His one concession to the grind was to put a pad of fresh moss in his shoes, daily, in the manner of the early aboriginals, thereby adding cushioning and a natural deodorizer and antiseptic.

Later, as we washed the dishes, I offered up an unsolicited monologue on the exploits of John Chapman, America's first and perhaps greatest distance walker, whom I had originally encountered in one of my childhood storybooks, then later in the essays of Edward Hoagland, who called Chapman "America's John the Baptist," a voice crying in the wilderness, Chapman left Massachusetts in the late 1700s and for fifty years tramped the wilds of the northern U.S., preaching love and wearing a metal pot or "mushpan" on his head. He is best known, however, for planting apple seeds anywhere he could find receptive soil—which led not only to his famous nickname, Johnny Appleseed, but would seem to qualify him as the continent's first environmentally motivated walker. What had always impressed me most about Chapman, I told George, was that he invariably walked barefoot—covered an estimated 400,000 kilometres that way and in winter wore a single boot with which he broke trail.

But my recounting all this was, in a sense, a superfluity, in that I believed, as George did, that the poor, with or without shoes, were unlikely to hike or to get involved in ecological politics. Their participation, George said, "would do nothing but help perpetuate a world that had already failed them." And we agreed that whether as individuals or as societies, the wealthy, who would seem to have the most to preserve in this life, are generally as unconcerned as the poor about saving the planet. In fact, unlike the poor, they seem for the most part on a runaway course to destroy it.

I told George that some of the apple trees I was seeing along the roads—knotty, unpruned old things—might well be descendants of those Johnny Appleseed had planted more than two hundred years ago, when he ranged across the northeastern United States with a twenty-kilo bag of seeds on his back. George said he could relate to some aspects of the man's vision—for example, his sense of "democratic access to healthy food." But he considered Appleseed's affectation of a "porridge pot on his head" to be beyond even George's standards of reasonable eccentricity.

My plan all along had been to walk through the village of Talcotville (population two hundred), about sixty-five kilometres south of Watertown—a place I knew through the books of that town's most famous inhabitant, Edmund Wilson.

Coincidentally, Wilson, too, was an impassioned walker and environmentalist, who refused to drive, never held a licence, and felt that big highways (and their attendant industries) were ruining the American landscape. Toward the end of his life in Talcotville, during the early 1970s, he fought a draining battle with the New York State Department of Highways over its plan to straighten and widen the curvy road in front of his house, ostensibly to make it safer. In the end, to Wilson's consternation, the highways people did as they intended, cutting off ten feet of Wilson's treasured front yard and garden, increasing traffic, and the speed of traffic, and not surprisingly, creating as many accidents as the straightening might have prevented.

I had first read Wilson's *Memoirs of Hecate County* as a teenager in perhaps 1964. The fictionalized memoir is a rich, sometimes racy, book about Lewis County, through which I was now walking—about its villages, swamps, and wildlife, and of course, its people and their passions. It is also a book about sex, presented with documentary—almost voyeuristic—detachment, fascinating to a teenaged boy. "What astonished me most," Wilson wrote at one point in the book, "was that not only were her thighs perfect columns but that all that lay between them was impressively beautiful, too." And on he plunged into "all that lay between"—building story and sensibility in such a way that John Updike would eventually call the work "the most intelligent attempt by an American male to dramatize sexual behaviour as a function of, rather than a suspension of, personality."

In the fall of 1947, with the world still under the shadow of Hiroshima and Nagasaki, the book was brought to trial on obscenity charges in the Supreme Court in New York City and, absurd as it might seem in the light of today's liberal tolerances, was judged both corrupt and corrupting.

Wilson is routinely described as the greatest modern American "man of letters." He was an editor of both *Vanity Fair* and *The New*

Republic, and after a trip to Russia in 1935—a trip stimulated by his fascination with socialism—wrote *To the Finland Station,* which is still something of a standard in university history courses on World War I. He wrote numerous books of literary criticism, as well as a study of the decline and desperation of North American aboriginals, whose condition he considered an American and Canadian disgrace.

With the great man's home as my target for June 21, I walked southeast from Martinsburg along gravel roads through the undulating farmland that forms the western foothills of the Adirondacks. Lewis County has one of the highest rates of unemployment in the U.S., and the towns, with their empty mills and decaying Victorian houses, exude a wistfully shabby elegance. The best of the old houses, the big frame wedding cakes, have, here and there, been spiffed up and converted into bed and breakfast joints or funeral homes, an ironic afterburn to the spanking prosperity that once existed in the area. But such places are outnumbered a dozen to one these days by trailer-park shacks and by dilapidated hotels that with their neon Genesee and Utica Club signs contribute a ray of colour, if not of expectation, to the scene.

During a five- or six-kilometre stretch, mid-morning, I passed half a dozen deserted century-old farmhouses, great boxy skulls, their barns and sheds in heaps, their manure piles nourishing five-metre saplings and generations of twitch grass and raspberry canes.

Alas, gravel roads are not the best surface for a walker. They require harder work of the ankles, inasmuch as the feet get angled this way and that on the stones. Had it not been for the extreme heat, I would have compensated by wearing proper hiking boots. As it was, I could hardly stand wearing socks and had on those prissy little sockettes (minus the pompoms) that women wear to play tennis. Still, my feet were sweating what must have been several ounces of moisture an hour and by noon or so were half-skinned and fried. The heat of the sun beat through my hat and burned the perspiration off my shoulders as fast as my body could produce more.

Do not get me wrong—it was a halcyon day. And I could not have been happier, walking purposefully alongside ripening fields, in the shadow of the mountains, my senses primed, my muscles alive and in motion. The buttercups were bright; the smell of sweet grass and alfalfa was intoxicating. The only sounds apart from an occasional car were the twittering of finches and the whirring of grasshoppers and cicadas.

At Grieg, where the roads are a mishmash of possibilities, I asked directions of an elderly woman, who glanced at me suspiciously and said, "You'd better ask at the post office."

I did and was told by the postmistress that I should "drive back to" such and such a place, and …

"I'm walking," I interrupted, and in the silence that ensued, "to Boonville … through Talcotville."

"Talcotville!" she quacked.

"How far is it?"

"John," she called into the back. "How far to Boonville?"

"Twenty minutes," came the disembodied answer.

"In miles," I called. "I'm walking."

"Walking!" cried the voice.

That Talcotville is no longer named on the state map might have been a clue to its advancing insignificance. Even so, I was unprepared for its lack of any commercial endeavour or any reference to where Edmund Wilson had lived or to his prodigious career. Considering that he was thirty years dead and had been among the most influential writers of the twentieth century, I had imagined that at least a plaque might exist, or that a street or road might have been named in his honour. The irony of my searching out Wilson's house was that in doing so I was knowingly aligning myself with the literary idolaters whom Wilson once described as "falling somewhere between blubbering ninnies and acutely frustrated maidens."

But I didn't care. And cared even less when, about halfway along the village's main and only street, I experienced a twinge of inner pleasure at recognizing the old stone manor—the "farm house," as Wilson always called it—in which he had lived during the summer for much of his life, had written his books, and during the fifties and sixties had thrown legendary parties and entertained dozens of international writers and thinkers: Lillian Hellman, Dashiel Hammet, W.H. Auden, Stephen Spender, John Dos Passos, and many more.

The house is one of the most elegant of the area's limestone relics, with its high pillars, its balcony and portico, and thirty or more wooden-sashed windows with twelve panes of glass each. On the windows of the upper back rooms and hall Wilson invariably asked visiting poets to inscribe a poem with a special diamond engraving tool that he kept for the purpose. (Ten days hence in the New York City Public Library I would find on display the pane on which W.H. Auden had written in a tiny gin-addled script all twenty-seven lines of his poem "Make This Night Loveable.")

In a lane across the road I chatted with a paunchy snaggle-toothed farmer named Art Bailey, an impeccably good-natured man, who told me, among other things, that as a kid he had mowed Wilson's lawn and that Wilson paid him five dollars a cut, about twice as much as anybody else ever gave him for similar work.

Bailey had read Wilson's autobiographical novel *Upstate,* published originally in *The New Yorker* during the 1970s under the title "Talcotville Diaries." The book deals extensively with life in Lewis County and, according to Bailey, raised the hackles of Wilson's farm relatives up the road, not because of the scandalous sexual innuendo that had alarmed others in the community but because Wilson's narrator had some less than flattering things to say about the mentality of his rustic relatives. Plus, he referred to the "goose shit" he had to walk through to get to the fictionalized version of the relatives' farmhouse. "They didn't mind it being mentioned. But it wasn't goose shit," Bailey laughed. "It was turkey shit." And for years afterwards the family ridiculed Wilson about not knowing the difference.

Wilson died in the house on June 12, 1972, and within hours was laid out in his pyjamas and dressing gown on his iron bed in one of the main-floor rooms while a brief funeral was enacted before a dozen or so friends and neighbours. Then he was carted out the front door on a wooden pallet and taken down to Boonville for cremation. It was claimed by his daughter Rosalind that even before his ashes were buried in Wellfleet on Cape Cod two days later, souvenir hunters had begun to dig up the lady's slippers that he had painstakingly transplanted from the woods to the gardens around the house.

When I asked if Wilson had left any sort of legacy in the community apart from his literary reputation, Bailey reflected for a moment and said he thought Wilson had recognized that his rural neighbours "had an intelligence and wisdom" of their own, and that he had always acknowledged and valued them. "And, of course, we valued him, too," Bailey said—a significant epitaph to a man who was often perceived to be something of an elitist.

Did the current owner have any interest in Wilson's legacy? "The house is just real estate now," Bailey said. "In fact, the owner doesn't even like people coming around inquiring"—which perhaps explains why Wilson is publicly unrecognized in the village.

GEORGE AND I RETURNED for another night at Whetstone Gulf State Park where I asked an enthusiastic young park ranger by the name of Luke Webster if I could plug my laptop into the phone jack in his office to get my emails. We talked about writing and seeing the world, and later that night, he came unexpectedly to our campsite, apparently somewhat burdened. He said he loved his work in the park, loved his family, loved his infant daughter who lived with a former girlfriend, etc., but that what he really wanted to do with his life was have adventures and write. But he wasn't sure *how* to have adventures and write, how to break free of the ruts and expectations that seemed to be all around him. This led to a discussion about fulfillment, risk, and so on, and I told him I thought we were all pretty much in the same boat, how a couple of months back people had told me I was nuts to head off walking to New York (that it was no project for a guy my age, etc.). I told him that if I had listened to those people—arguably the voices of reason—I would have denied myself one of the most invigorating experiences of my life. The way to have adventures, we decided, was pretty much to go and have them. As for writing, same thing—those who get it done tend to be those who decide to get it done.

Weeks later I got an email from Luke, via CBC Radio, thanking me for my encouragement and telling me that he was writing and, as a result of our talk, was making plans for a mountain-climbing expedition to Nepal.

BY CHANCE the next morning at Boonville, I picked up the southbound Black River Trail along an old network of deep stone-sided canals that had once been feeders to the famous New York and Erie Canal system. Through much of the nineteenth century, the waterway carried boats and trade from New York City to the St. Lawrence River via the Hudson and Lake Champlain, or westward from Albany across New York State to the lower Great Lakes. For a time after the Revolutionary War, when the Appalachian Mountains were still an all but insurmountable obstacle to westward expansion, the canals also functioned as a kind of interstate migration corridor, allowing hundreds of thousands of settlers to get to the fertile soil of the Midwest, and on to the Rockies and the Pacific.

I have been accused of being mulish, and now on the Black River Trail was quite literally following in the footsteps of mules—beasts that in the early days had beaten out the recessed path along the canal bank as they hauled loaded bateaux from one town to the next. The mule path ran within inches of the canal's edge, through miles of overgrown orchards and fields, knee-high buttercups, hawkweed, clover, asters, daisies, half a dozen kinds of grasses—all of it an extraordinary sensory salad.

In a little grove of alders, I was thrilled to see a bluebird, the second of my life, having seen the first as a child when my father stopped the car on a country road near Napanee and told me to *look over there,* because bluebirds were rare, and it was perhaps the only one I would ever lay eyes on.

Relative to the previous day's gravel, the footing along the canal bank was so soft and cool that as the temperature rose gradually into the high nineties, I found myself blissing off into something approaching a dream state, taking care not to get too dreamy for fear I'd fall twenty feet into the ancient slime that, in some parts of the canal, was the only "water" left.

Just north of Pixley Falls, at a point where the trail veered close to the highway, I heard a child's voice and turned to see an eleven- or twelve-year-old boy, a kid with Down's syndrome, standing by the asphalt at the top of a gentle rise to my right.

"Where ya going?" he called.

"Rome," I called back, slowing my pace.

"Why you walking?"

"Because I want to," I told him. "You live around here?"

Without speaking, he thrust a stubby arm back toward the highway in the direction of a teetering frame house that had not seen a brush load of paint in perhaps fifty years.

Maybe five steps farther along, I yelled back, "Be careful on the highway!" to which he answered, "I love you!"

It was undoubtedly little more than a rote response, a kind of glad-hander, from a kid who, despite his limitations, had learned to play the angles. On the other hand, there was the possibility he knew something about the need for connection and the importance of expressing that need that the rest of us had overlooked.

Whatever the case, his words went through me like a bullet, and in the swollen seconds that followed, I could not help considering that I had walked nearly two thousand kilometres, some two million steps, all of it timed in such a way that, on a remote stretch of rural trail in

Upstate New York, my path would intersect with that of a fatefully disinherited kid whose message for me, no matter what I chose to make of it, was that he loved me.

"I love you, too," I yelled over my shoulder, and with adrenalin rising in my chest, I began to jog—down a grassy slope, through a little clump of trees alongside the canal, and out onto the flats beyond.

Intermittently, my afternoon reverie was clouded by the knowledge that my own family had in the early days of the Erie Canal, followed it northeast on a belated "escape" from Salem, Massachusetts, where, during the late 1600s, my aptly named ancestor Bray Wilkins had been a fiendish participant in the New England witch hunts. He was a noted Puritan zealot, a landholder, who made accusations against several Salem "witches," including a number of teenaged girls who were suspected, among other things, of reading tea leaves, playing with the early equivalent of a Ouija board, and conducting mysterious moonlit rites at the time of their first menstruation.

More consequentially, the old man made accusations against a member of his own family, his granddaughter's husband, John Willard, whom Bray, the family patriarch, had never welcomed into the clan. Finding himself suspected of satanic practices, Willard had gone to Bray seeking advice and asking that Bray pray with him for wisdom and deliverance. Not wanting to be associated with a man under suspicion—and having no love for the man anyway—Bray refused, and eventually claimed that when he had next seen Willard, the latter had given him a "piercing glance," with preposterous effects. "My water was immediately stopped," Bray testified at Willard's trial. "I had no benefit of nature, but was like a man upon a rack."

The "stoppage" was considered evidence that Bray had been dealt a wizard's curse by John Willard, and it wasn't until Willard was safely in jail that Bray was able again to urinate. When Bray's grandson Daniel died mysteriously a few days later, Willard's wizardry was confirmed—he had hexed the family—and largely on Bray's testimony, he was eventually burned at the stake.

Two written histories of Salem reveal that, of the twenty or so men in the large Wilkins clan of the day, only one, Thomas Wilkins, Bray's son, had the guts to speak out against the old man's charges. And for that, he was ostracized from the family, as were generations of his heirs. It was not until the Erie Canal came into being, however, that Thomas's scions packed their New England bags and, with this new opportunity to cross the mountains, headed west and north to Canada where they, my ancestors, established themselves in the wool weaving industry at Hespeler, Ontario.

All of which horror and redemption was intermittently on my mind as I walked along the canal bank, as I crossed the main canal at Rome the next day, and eventually the Hudson River.

DELTA LAKE STATE PARK, north of Rome, where George and I spent the night, is surely one of the purest insinuations of hell ever surveyed and gated by any recreational agency. School was out, in both the figurative and literal sense, and the park—a featureless geological sump covered with packed clay and loosely spaced maples—was bristling with big-wheeled pickup trucks, overpowered runabouts, hundred-pound dogs, stone-throwing kids, and benighted moms and dads, in some cases as many as twenty people to a tent site.

George, having selected the campground, was a trifle apologetic when I walked in at perhaps 9:00 P.M. "It's not Whetstone," he said, and described in Goya-like detail how during the early afternoon our neighbours, camped ten metres away, had launched a two-hundred-horsepower "bass" boat of some sort—a craft twenty feet long and done up in military camo—and spent the mid-afternoon stoned, tearing up and down puddle-deep Delta Lake, terrorizing swimmers and filling the air with an apocalyptic motorized wail. When I arrived, fourteen of them—six adults, eight kids—were sitting around an unlit firepit, staring solemnly at the ground, incinerating cigarettes and shouting minute-by-minute commands (mostly "Shut up!") at an immense St. Bernard dog tethered to the bench of the picnic table.

The backdrop to all this was an unbroken blitzkrieg of the heaviest of heavy metal music played at such a volume it all but smoked from a pair of hundred-amp speakers in the back of an aging pickup. When the children picked up a Frisbee, the dog, anticipating action, leapt up tore the table bench off at the spikes, and went racing toward the lake, dragging the two-metre plank behind.

As if to nurture me amid the surroundings, George made perhaps the finest meal he had prepared in eight weeks—a garlic, ginger, white-wine, chicken stirfry that he cooked with loving attention as I tended to my feet and scribbled out two or three pages of notes in the twilight. I had torn up another toenail, and the blisters of the previous day, rather than peeling and falling away as they had in cooler tempera-tures, had reconstituted themselves into a sort of epidermal mush and had bled for the better part of the afternoon, leaving the soles of my socks a sodden browny red.

Whether drawn by foot smells or by the fragrance of ginger chicken, the St. Bernard, now chained to the picnic table's leg, began with minimal effort to drag the table toward us as a horse might drag a four-furrow plow, prompting his owner to scream, "Don't be an idiot!" and then, "Okay, *be* an idiot!" and finally, "You're an idiot!" and to tie the dog to a tree.

In the heat, I was able to sleep with my feet outside my sleeping bag, so that by 7:00 a.m. they were pretty much dry and serviceable. Again, I left George to decamp and, by 9:30, had walked ten kilometres to the city of Rome. It would hardly have surprised Edmund Wilson, who anticipated the worst for America, that during the years since he regularly visited the city, Rome, like Watertown, had been gutted by post-industrial malaise, leaving closed mills, potholed roads, and derelict schools, as well as an inescapable sense of futility.

At Pucci's Italian Deli on the main street, I gulped a quart or so of ice water and a meatball sandwich as a young man at the next stool explained that he and his wife had been unemployed for more than a year and that his last job had been in a funeral parlour in Buffalo. I said, "It wasn't one of those mob places with the double coffins, was it?" (a reference to the legendary Buffalo gangland practice of compressing unwanted bodies into sub-compartments of otherwise regular coffins). He stared at me and said solemnly, "How the hell d'ya know that stuff?" and I told him I'd worked in a cemetery, among guys who knew everything there was to know about illicit burial practices.

"Well, that's exactly what it was," he said softly, adding that when he started at the place, he had been told never to say anything to anybody about it. "And they meant it," he said. "And I never have. And I'm not going to now. I mean, I don't even know who you are or why you're sitting here beside me."

He said the only work in Rome these days was "shit crap—worse than Buffalo," and if you wanted something beyond minimum wage, you had to go to Syracuse or Albany, where local job-hunters were heading farther south yet into New York City and New Jersey.

AFTER A COUPLE OF HOURS walking through the depressed rural uplands south of Rome, I reached Interstate 90, the New York Thruway. My plan all along had been to stay strictly on smaller highways, but now, on a perverse whim, I decided to follow the interstate east for ten or twelve kilometres before cutting south of Utica down to Highway 20.

It perhaps goes without saying that it is illegal to walk on the shoulders of an interstate highway. However, the terrain west of Utica is mostly unfenced hills and fields, so for the roughly three hours I was out there, I was able to stay twenty or thirty metres off the actual turnpike and still get a good blast of the action—though *blast* is far too insipid a word for the violent high-speed roller derby that, at all hours of the day and night, plays itself out on the major-league highways of America.

As absurd as it now seems, America's vast network of freeways was originally a dream of the U.S. Defense Department, which early during the Cold War perceived a need for an easily accessible system of roadways that would provide a means of escape from American cities during nuclear attack. The result, the hundred-thousand-kilometre U.S. interstate system, was completed during the early 1970s, by which time its purpose as an escape route had become ambiguous at best. But its meaning to the burgeoning trucking industry was clear, and a revolution began in what is now the continent's largest and most visible heavy industry.

I spent six weeks riding transports in 1997, have good friends in trucking, and as a result have learned more about the long-haul industry and interstate system than I will ever need to know. For example, that excluding major cities, the interstates are among the few human creations, including the Great Wall of China, identifiable from outer space. And that while the interstate system would seem endlessly accommodating to traffic, if the continent's 3.5 million tractor-trailers took to it in single file, they would cover its entire hundred thousand kilometres, lined up with less than a cab length between them.

According to a 1999 survey published by Layover.com, the continent's several million long-haul drivers include nearly forty-six thousand graduates of accredited American and Canadian universities (among them more than six hundred Ph.D.s and two thousand M.A.s), more than a hundred former college and university professors, some seventy-five thousand convicted felons, and more than three hundred thousand women. The same survey claimed that on average these drivers read more than twice as many books as do lawyers, doctors, or high-school teachers, many of them borrowed from the unofficial exchange libraries that are a feature of many of America's thousands of bustling truck stops.

WHERE STATE HIGHWAY 49 crossed the thruway, I went up and stood on the bridge overlooking four lanes of traffic. As each truck exploded out from underneath me, it was as if the bridge itself were about to be swept away, and me with it.

After two or three minutes, I found myself disoriented not just by the racket and hot air, but by a kind of perceptual backwash, as if I were in motion above the pavement. During a five-minute period, 1 counted 151 transports passing beneath me in both directions—an average of one every two seconds.

At a truckstop about a kilometre farther along, I bought a quart carton of milk and strolled out into the cafeteria-style seating area. By the windows, I spotted a loose-limbed man of perhaps forty-five, wearing an orange Hawaiian shirt and distinguished from most of those around him by the fact that he was reading—an ecological book, no less, by the American writer Annie Dillard. I walked up to him, apologized for intruding, and asked if he'd mind if I sat down.

"Not at all," he said and, after I had told him what I was up to, "If you want to *ride* into New York I can have you there by this evening."

Neil Jessop had a detailed and intelligent take on the trucking industry and told me among other things that it is a rare driver these days who is willing to go into New York City at all. The freeways and streets are too hectic, the loading docks too tight, the delivery schedules a nightmare. He said drivers are paranoid because some eight hundred American truckers a year are taken hostage by armed hijackers, most of them in either Los Angeles or New York, where hijacked loads can be driven quickly to the docks and onto ships. "The funny thing," he said, "is they're not just after computers and televisions—they take beef, pork, turkeys, that sort of thing. In Japan, all that stuff is as valuable as computers and a lot harder to trace."

Neil said that during a two-week period the previous year he had hauled peanuts from Valdosta to San Diego, lettuce from the Salinas Valley up to Indianapolis, pork from there out to San Francisco, grapes to Dallas, beef up to Philadelphia, tomatoes back to Cleveland, plums to Dallas, and so on. "In the days when I was hauling dry, I'd pull VCRs from New Jersey to California, computer stuff back east; I'd haul makeup, bathtubs, caskets, every commodity and contraption you can think of." He had hauled lethal viruses, live reptiles, nuclear waste. "The spent plutonium," he said, "travels in plain white trailers, so nobody knows that a rolling Three Mile Island is zipping along beside their car or sitting in the truckstop or going through their town." He compared tractor-trailers to "ants out there on their rounds," each moving his own little bit of what's holding the colony together. "And by that I mean junk," he said laughing. "We're a culture held together by junk!"

Neil said he thought what I was doing was "one of the sanest things" he'd ever heard of. As for himself, he thought long-hauling was the last occupation in the country in which you could be "a big-time misfit" and still be "right there at the heart of it all, and be valued for it."

As he ate blueberry pie and ice cream, he described a study he had read that showed the contemporary trucking industry is so pervasive, so central to the North American economy, that if it were to shut down entirely most of the rest of the economy (devoid of fuel, building supplies, food, clothing, educational and office supplies, furniture, books, mail, etc.) would seize within three days. After five days, he said, virtually every supermarket in the United States and Canada would be empty of produce, canned goods, and dairy products. And after ten days, widespread malnutrition would be felt in the continent's larger cities. The underlying message was about globalization and consumeristic dependency. More specifically—as in Watertown and Rome—it was about the loss of regional self-sufficiency, once the pride of America's diverse population and economy.

I have nothing even remotely negative to say about truck drivers. Almost invariably during my weeks on the highway, they had been more considerate toward me than car drivers. They had honked and waved greetings, given me wide clearance as they passed, and blasted timely warnings if they were approaching from behind in the passing lane. I told Neil the only trucks I had found offensive were the cattle trucks—because of the suffocating smell of manure, as well as the obvious trauma being inflicted on the jostled and bawling cattle as they rattled toward the slaughterhouse. Trucks hauling wood chips, by comparison, trailed an almost intoxicating redolence of spruce sap.

As I walked Neil to his dazzling blue Kenworth tractor and reefer unit, he told me that when he came out to the truck at night, he generally expected to find "lot lice"—in other words, a prostitute— hanging around, and that not long ago in Nevada he had returned to the truck to find a hooker relaxing topless in his seat behind the wheel.

FROM A PRIVATE STANDPOINT, one of the nice things about being in the United States was that I was no longer being asked, "Why New York City?" For weeks in Canada, I had fended off queries about the validity of the destination, many from professional broadcasters and journalists whose perspective seemed to be that as a destination, New York was too gaudy, too flagrant—a perspective whose insidious modesty seemed Canadian in a way that went beyond even the doziest clichés about northern self-denial and restraint.

Here in the U.S.—even in Upstate New York, a sort of missing page in the contemporary atlas of America—it was well understood why someone with choices might decide to strike out for Manhattan.

THE FOLLOWING MORNING at a greasy spoon near East Winfield, I noticed on a staff bulletin board a computer printoff of two photos, one showing a Boeing 767 like the ones that had hit the Twin Towers, the other a composite of military aircraft—bombers, fighter jets, combat helicopters. To the left, under a likeness of the American flag, were the words "Dear Mr. bin Laden: Now that you have taken the time to get to know Boeing's fine line of commercial aircraft, we would like to get you acquainted with Boeing's other fine products. Sincerely, America."

I stared at it for a few seconds and saw in it, for the first time, the vulnerability of the so-called war against terrorism. The call to arms, it seemed suddenly, was not so much a rallying cry for the self-assured as a fearful but arrogant mantra—*my-father-can-beat-your-father*—bruited as a kind of back stiffener from amid the wreckage of 9/11.

A young man behind the counter—intelligent face, wire-rimmed glasses—saw me looking at the photos and began staring at me as if I were about to steal them (which I was). As I came back into the main restaurant, I said to him, "Do you think they'll catch him?"

"Osama?" he said quizzically.

"Yeah, Osama," I said, and he pantomimed an enormous weariness.

However, a stout, pretty-faced girl behind him piped up, "You can't let them get away with it!"—a comment that by whatever vulnerable inference was playing out in my head, seemed to link me with "them" and seemed thereby as much about men generally as about the elusive moral hologram represented by Mr. bin Laden.

When I had eaten a hamburger, I ordered another and took it with me down the road—devoured it, loaded, in exactly four bites. If my obsession with food had increased again it was because I had become acclimatized to the heat and, at the forty-kilometre pace, was hungrier than ever. For breakfast, I was still eating half a dozen eggs, oatmeal, raisins, and a can of condensed milk—and I was drinking nearly a gallon of Gatorade a day, plus two or three litres of water and whatever beer George supplied. Moreover, I was eating shockingly large dinners and any snacks I could cram in when George caught up with me, or when I passed a restaurant or store—sardines or tuna from the can, bread loaded half an inch thick with peanut butter, milkshakes, whole quarts of buttermilk.

My problem was that I was still losing weight. I had left Thunder Bay at a fairly lean 170 pounds and was struggling now to stay at 148 or 150. The notion of dropping further disturbed me, since any new losses would be at the expense of muscle, which I could not afford.

My appearance was frightful. Despite ongoing applications of sunscreen, my ears and nose were scabby with sun damage, and the sight of myself in washroom mirrors—skinny, sweaty-eyed, skin the colour of an old penny—invariably unsettled me. On the positive side, my stomach and backside were now as hard as they had been since high school, and while a small voice within kept urging me to take a day off just to eat and relax, the walking was compulsive, and the lure of New York City was growing daily.

At a convenience store in Richfield Springs, just two hours after my burgers, I assembled a self-serve hot dog heaped with chili, sauerkraut, cheddar, and three extra wieners—the sort of meal that at my current level of exertion fuelled me adequately for perhaps ten or twelve kilometres.

Thus nourished, I walked east along Highway 20, through gentle hills to Springfield, where I ate a lemon ice-cream cone the size of a softball and, at dusk, headed south along a shoulderless rural road that hugged the east side of Otsego Lake and tomorrow would take me into Cooperstown, thirty kilometres away, where I had long planned a visit to the Baseball Hall of Fame. Tonight, however, my scheduled stop was at the north end of the lake, at Glimmerglass State Park, where, if I was lucky, George would have the tent up and dinner waiting.

However, the park was farther from Springfield than I had imagined, and at perhaps eleven o'clock, despite an avalanche of stars, I found myself walking through blackness so impenetrable it was only when a car came along that I could see well enough to step safely off into the tall grass and weeds that grew right up to the edges of the road. For a while, my only companionship was the occasional howl of farm dogs, which could hear and undoubtedly smell me in the still air. I had learned to distinguish between those that were tied up—non-stop yapping—and those I would soon meet at a lane's end, which tended to bark once or twice then save their energy for the "bowwow powwow," as George had referred to one of my recent meetings with a pit bull.

Otherwise, the aloneness, and in a curious way the freedom, of the road deepened measurably in the darkness, and it wasn't long before I was feeling quite jaunty over my disappearance into the night.

Still a few kilometres from Glimmerglass Park, I went down a hill into a natural lowland and was quite suddenly amid fireflies—at first just a few, but then millions of them, blinking across the low fields on both sides of the road like a shapeless galaxy of green lights or the reflections of stars seen in water. For ten minutes or more, I had the eerie, dazzling sensation of walking through outer space (which, of course, I was, we are, from the perspective of anywhere but earth). I began to wonder why these tiny flying creatures blink or even light up at all. By act of will? Involuntarily? I felt certain it was about mating, about looking for one another in their short, purposeful lives, and despite my aloneness I felt cheered to be in the company of other brief-lived sojourners looking to extend and fulfill themselves—by creating light of all things! The artist's fatal ambition. And perhaps the lover's. Certainly, if I had had a little green lamp within my own pelvis or tailbone, I would at that point have turned it on.

I found George at around midnight, camped on a circular road in the middle of the park, most of whose pruned and grassy tent sites were more like landscape lessons than "nature" and were occupied by thirty-foot recreational vehicles. As an alternative to this civility, George had inquired about the park's advertised "wilderness" sites and had been directed to a half-dozen clearings that varied from the one he had chosen only in the fact that their grass had been cropped not at lawn length but to the "wilderness" standard of ten or twelve centimetres. What, I asked him, did he expect in a park named Glimmerglass, surely one of the all-time candy-ass names for any place on the map?

I had barely gotten my shoes off when he pulled a copy of *The New York Times* from the van, opened it to the obituaries, and presented it to me in the firelight.

"Tiff is dead," he said.

He was speaking of the celebrated Canadian writer Timothy Findley, who had died near his home in France, ostensibly from a fall but more broadly from having worked, lived, and—at least early in his life—partied hard. Findley had been a bosom friend of George's one-time mate Catherine Hunter, a Winnipeg poet and novelist who is an old friend of mine as well and is the mother of George's twenty-year-old daughter, Melody. George had never been a great personal fan of Findley, had found him affected and self-indulgent. And he had at one time been rubbed slightly the wrong way by the degree of Catherine's devotion to the novelist, which began during the 1980s when Catherine wrote her doctoral dissertation on Findley's work. But it was all brushed aside now as we toasted his genius and began a rambling reconsideration of the self-destructive fate of so many renowned artists and writers—Van Gogh, Rothko, Plath, Hemingway, Virginia Woolf, Henri de Toulouse-Lautrec (whose identity George occasionally adopted in jest, referring to himself at such times as "little Too-loose Low-trek").

Not long prior, I had learned that the famous Canadian novelist Margaret Laurence, who was a close friend of Findley, had completed by suicide what a quart of scotch, two packs of cigarettes a day, and subsequently lung cancer had begun.

It was impossible to discuss suicide with George, of course, and not turn eventually to his wife, Winifred, who during the late 1970s, after the family's return from New York to Winnipeg, had in depression and despair taken enough prescription drugs to put herself permanently to sleep. At least a part of her depression had been a result of leaving New York, which she did not want to do. In fact, George and the boys had pulled out of the city in 1972, leaving her temporarily in the care of the Bellevue Hospital psychiatric ward on Manhattan's Lower East Side.

That night, by the fire, George told me that one of his lingering anxieties was the question of whether or not if he had dug in, had listened to Winnie, who was working as a nurse, he could have stayed on successfully in New York and supported himself in the world of art and writing. At the time, he said, he had been exhausted from working full-time at the print gallery, from studying for his M.A., as well as raising his boys and coping with Winnie's incipient disintegration. Beyond which, the city was getting costlier, filthier, more violent. "You'd hear shots all the time," he said. "Even the cops were scared.

They didn't answer calls. The garbage stunk so bad on the streets every night, you couldn't walk past it."

To compound things, George and Winnie and their oldest boy David, then six or seven years old, were forced out of their rent-controlled apartment in a very decent and neighbourly old building on Ninety-second Street because bacterially stagnant water—storm-sewer water that had gathered up the filth of the street—was half a metre deep in the basement beneath their ground-floor suite. The mess was beyond the understanding or control of the building's aging landlord and, according to a local medical doctor, was potentially lethal for David, who had been sick for several months with a respiratory ailment.

When the family moved up into the south Bronx near Yankee Stadium in the spring of 1968, David was one of just two or three non-Jewish children among seven hundred students at the old elementary school across the street. But with the migration of blacks into the Bronx, the Jews largely fled, so that when the family left New York just four years later, David was by that time one of only three or four *non-black* students at the school. Violence and drug use had exploded in the neighbourhood to the point where George had begun to fear for his sons' lives. "You'd find needles and bullet casings right there on the street or in the schoolyard."

In 1971, George left his job at the gallery, which had been sold unexpectedly. To make a living during his last months in the city, he bought a fifteen-year-old Plymouth for a few hundred dollars and, as mentioned, was driving gypsy cab, picking up sometimes gun-wielding passengers in the most violent areas of the Bronx and Harlem. "Sometimes," George said, "I didn't even bother with the fare. Pimps. Heroin dealers. They'd kill you to save three bucks."

The family's last days in the Bronx were full of perplexity and despair. George was weary and broke, Winnie, who refused to leave New York, was in Bellevue, and David and Vincent were chafing for their annual summer trip to Canada. To keep his sanity, George had been spending occasional weekends at a Christian sanctuary farm on the Hudson River at Tivoli. Indeed, when he and the boys left the city by train for good in early July 1972, they stopped there—a sojourn that ended in a panic moment the next day as the three of them went down to the tracks to reboard for Montreal. "I'd lifted them into the coach," George said, "and had gone forward to the baggage car to make sure all our stuff got on board." At that point, the train began ever so slowly to pull out. "I looked up," George said, "and there were their faces in the window, in total terror. They'd been separated from their mother, and here they thought they were about to lose me, too."

Now, heading back into the cauldron, George was looking for clues as to what might have been, knowing that what *had* been for thirty years in Winnipeg—a grind of poverty and death and artistic marginalization—had in many ways been a kind of shadow life, and that despite its traumas and drawbacks, New York, at its best, was the last place he had felt fully productive and alive.

By the time we had talked ourselves out, it was 4:00 A.M., and in the faint first light, a bird or two had begun to sing. As he often did at such times, George pulled out his fiddle. Against the backdrop of his quiet improvisations in the dwindling light of the fire, I ate a thick peanut butter sandwich and a can of unheated beans, and stooped into the tent to sleep.

DURING NEARLY EIGHT WEEKS of walking, I had come across dozens of roadside nooks and byways where it was obvious from the condoms and condom wrappers and tissues—and occasionally the underwear and torn pantyhose—that, in precisely these places, lovers had taken to the back seats of their vehicles or had gotten cozy in the front and had then summarily dispensed with the aftermath. While it isn't clear to me why a woman would abandon her underwear in such a situation, I had come across maybe twenty pairs of panties in all (and, on Highway 6, near Collingwood, a quite nifty lime-green lace bra). I had thought at times I should salvage a pair for eventual placement in the grand assemblage I intended to construct out of the moose bones, driftwood, and so on that I had been collecting since northern Ontario. George liked the idea, at least said he did, then accused me of being a "panty fetishist." Which, considering all I might have been—arsonist, armed robber, assassin—carried the faint ring of a compliment. The panties would, of course, have to be the right panties—preferably to have some distinction as lingerie, and "No skid marks," as Dad advises young Joshua in Mordecai Richler's *Joshua Then and Now*. Some I stepped over, or nudged with my toe, were so old and stiff and mud-saturated—or snapped or faded or just awful— that they were recognizable only to the expert eye as underwear.

I mention all this not out of prurience but because about halfway down Otsego Lake, where my exposure to the summer estates of Manhattan's wealthy had become borderline insufferable, I spotted in the ditch a ZipLoc bag that appeared to contain a pair of mottled silver-and-turquoise panties. I picked it up and walked on, feeling slightly ill at ease and trying to imagine what scenario might have led to a pair of apparently dry panties being tossed out of a car in a plastic bag.

A hundred metres down the road I opened the bag and spilled the knickers gently into a rocky creek. Pleased to note on the slate-coloured waistband that they were Victoria's Secret, I sloshed them around with a stick then beat them on the rocks and wrung them out.

And then gave them a sniff!

To see if they were clean.

And then put them in their bag and in my pocket.

I WAS NO SOONER BACK on the road than a late-model Saab ripped past me and screeched to a stop thirty metres farther along. As in a Laurel and Hardy sketch, an elderly man shouted out the window, "Could you tell me how to get to Cooperstown?"

I might, of course, have told him that a dozen years in the bigs, a .300 batting average, and a reliable glove oughta do the trick, but instead opted for an arm aimed up the road and a command to "Go straight!"

Prophetic words, in that the National Baseball Hall of Fame is about as "straight" an operation as the libertarian in me could hope to unstraighten on a Sunday afternoon. Cooperstown itself is a place where any hint of imagination is safely sublimated beneath prim parks, perfect streets, colonial architecture, public statuary, banal merchandising ventures (mostly on the baseball theme), chi-chi restaurants, tall hardwoods, and an almost preternatural absence of seediness ("No panty sniffing in Cooperstown," as George remarked). One thing to be said for the place is that you can park free on any street, a small democratic concession in a town that on a summer afternoon draws ten thousand or more visitors to its main attraction. The largesse is balanced, of course, by the exorbitant price of a ticket into the Hall of Fame—and by monster cash or credit requirements at the local hotels, restaurants, and souvenir shops.

I took George's photo by a statue of the nineteenth-century novelist James Fenimore Cooper, whose family founded the town and whose romantic novels George had never read but loathed on principle for what he called their "fanciful rendering" of the American Indian.

In going to the hall, I was hoping to revisit my childhood obsession with the Milwaukee Braves of the late 1950s, the source of some of my first tastes of both triumph and despair. I remember standing on the waist-high shelf of my mother's china cabinet, my ear pressed to the speaker of the old Viking radio to better hear the static-obscured broadcast of the '57 World Series between the Braves and Yankees; remember the agonizing wait for a tiny iron-on Braves crest, a jokey scrap of ill-printed cotton purchased mail-order for a dime and two box tops from Post Grape Nuts (the latter a kind of cruel joke unto itself, in that Grape Nuts is the cereal not of children or of play, but of the aged, the constipated, the damned). But I wore the crest no less proudly on the back of the bulky zip-up sweater my mother had knitted for me that summer.

I loved the Braves because they were an underdog, at least relative to the Yankees, who were even then the team of money and success. I loved them, too, because of the almost laughably euphonious name *Milwaukee,* a city located, I imagined, in a cow pasture somewhere out yonder—a name that reminded me of milk, although in those days I hadn't a clue that Wisconsin was America's mythically milkiest state. I had drawn pictures of the Braves, collected their baseball cards, sent them fan mail (unanswered), and in 1958 tracked them daily in the Toronto *Telegram* all the way to their second World Series, which they lost in the most painful way a baseball team can lose— they ran out of pitching.

But I had been lucky the previous year, at an impressionable age, to have my fondest hopes rewarded by a winner. And when I walked into the Hall of Fame just past noon on Sunday, June 22, 2002, it was above all to seek out and pay homage to the players from that inspired mid-century team: Eddie Matthews, Warren Spahn, Hank Aaron, Lew Burdette, Wes Covington, Red Schoendinst, Joe Adcock, and the rest. They were among my first and best remembered heroes.

But of course I didn't find them.

When finally I located the cramped display case commemorating the championship Braves of 1957, I found the photos small, the cut lines prosaic, the mementos trifling—somebody's bat, somebody's spikes, somebody's pulverized glove indistinguishable at a glance from some wretched piece of roadkill that I might have passed on the highway. Warren Spahn, who on two days' rest brought down the Yankees with unhittable left-handed curveballs—who is in fact thought by many to be the greatest lefty ever—is mentioned not so much for his talent, or for the implied thrills he might have given a nine-year-old boy, as for for his military record as a GI during World War II and for his immigrant German past (the lone photo of him shows him in his mother's kitchen eating Wiener schnitzel).

Hank Aaron, who played a star's role with the '57 champs, is celebrated in another part of the hall entirely for his years with the team's successor (baseball's ultimate triumph of money over marrow), the Atlanta Braves.

Lew Burdette, the era's foremost practitioner of the prohibited and deadly spitball—and the World Series MVP in 1957—isn't even mentioned in the display. In a game (in a culture) that has always invited subtle cheating—illegal bats, illegal pitching, parks reconfigured to maximize a home team's strengths—Burdette was a cheater. And cheaters aren't acknowledged at Cooperstown.

Nor are the game's legendary, widely practised cheating mechanisms—no corked bats, no nicked baseball seams (no nail files or emery boards of the sort used by pitchers to rough up the baseball and make it livelier).

So squeaky clean is the whole endeavour, there is not even any mention of the long and intimate allegiance between baseball and beer. Teams past and present have been *owned* by breweries—Busch, Coors, Labatts, Interbrew, and so on. Stadiums have been named for them. The players themselves have for years advertised beer. Fans routinely get plastered on it in the stands.

Except for the presence of a meerschaum pipe presented to Ty Cobb and a display of old baseball sheet music, one piece of which bears a photo of Lou Gehrig smoking a cigarette, tobacco, too, goes ignored—this despite the thousands of players who have pitched, batted, and caught with a plum-sized wad of chewing tobacco in their gobs.

Nor is there any mention of the legendary fatso foods—the hot dogs, french fries, and popcorn—that are the kernel of stadium cuisine (and which I fully expected to see for sale, or at least happily commemorated). No mention of the game's famous oddballs. Or, perhaps understandably, of the ill will of Cobb, the money grubbing of DiMaggio, the penthouse shenanigans of Mantle.

Meanwhile, Pete Rose, "Charlie Hustle," a player who hit the ball more times than any other and during the 1970s and '80s all but defined the game, is denied his place in the shrine because he gambled, in a country whose very governments sell gambling and its possibilities with the same barbaric vigour that Charlie Hustle once sold baseball to the fans.

Even the story of baseball's invention by Abner Doubleday in the Cooperstown field where the local stadium now stands verges on an insult to the intelligence of anyone craving a more nuanced version of reality. Surely, baseball-like games were played by kids everywhere—a thrown ball or horse turd, a stick or club, a base path—and particularly by bored slave kids on the clay flats outside their shacks or in the alleys of Chattanooga.

On the lawn outside, George and I got a kick out of a bronze sculpture of the 1950s Brooklyn Dodger pitcher Johnny Podres delivering an imaginary baseball, at the official sixty-foot distance, to the great Dodger catcher of the era, Roy Campanella. Unfortunately, Campanella and other early Major League blacks are diminished by the hall's story of Jackie Robinson, the first "Negro" to play regularly in the majors. Robinson's tale is presented as a "triumph of the human spirit" rather than an examination of an ugly version of America that, into the 1950s (and beyond), kept blacks in their place not just in sport but in music, politics, education, business, almost any place you cared to look.

At the time (and beyond), Canada, too, was, of course, disgracing itself racially and politically in its attitude toward its aboriginals, as well as other so-called visible minorities. It is a modest tribute to Canadians that when Branch Rickey, the owner of the Brooklyn Dodgers, with whom Robinson broke in 1949, decided to season the rookie for a year on a team in a city where Robinson would not feel the full sting of prejudice, he chose the Montreal Royals. And Robinson was indeed treated well in Montreal, and in Toronto, too. But he was not always as well received in the American cities where the Royals played, either by the fans or by the white players he competed against or even alongside.

In the face of all of this soft-pedalling, it struck me that a competing museum, one featuring a little more baseball Babylon and a little less baseball rebop—not to mention with a less clobbered and restricted sense of play—would undoubtedly do well in Cooperstown.

One thing I liked well about the Hall of Fame was a compelling, if sentimentalized, tribute to Babe Ruth and to his apparently genuine interest in children. There is no mention, naturally, of his Promethean carousing and womanizing—or the fact that the throat cancer that killed him was almost certainly the result of his heavy smoking. However, his irreducible spirit is impossible to disguise—especially in the later photos that emphasize his beer gut, as big as a garbage bag, and his ravaged, party-time face. It was while I was studying the Ruth photos and mementos, taking a long look at the shots of Yankee Stadium, that I realized I would want to visit the place—the House, as they say, that Ruth built.

George and I bought postcards in the hall souvenir shop (some of whose wares were manufactured in that bastion of U.S. values and tradition, mainland China). We bought pizza and drinks in a nearby restaurant and went down to Otsego Lake, where a few families, all white, were picnicking and swimming in the heat. Then we walked along the main street, where a number of the many souvenir shops featured photos and T-shirt images of Pete Rose, who has clearly been to Cooperstown as a tout and may someday get there as a citizen of the hall. However, when we spoke to one shop owner about a signed photo of him shaking hands with Rose, he said, "It'll serve the Hall of Fame right if he snubs them when they do try to induct him."

AT ABOUT 7:00 P.M., I walked southeast out of Cooperstown, luxuriating in the freedom of open country, in the smell of cut hay, and as the evening deepened, in the cicada- and cricket-dense twilight.

I was still thinking about baseball, which Walt Whitman said would "repair our losses and be a blessing" to America.

It was a nice thought.

As far as I was concerned, pro baseball was a goner—at least in its original camouflage as play, or as the heroic and absorbing drama

I had known as a child. Far from repairing losses, it seemed reduced to a mere "indicator," a kind of mine canary, for the common toxins of the culture. And in that sense, it is as accurate a reading on greed and the insinuation of corporatism into every corner of contemporary existence as it was once an indicator of bigotry and the politics of race.

But, hey! If things "aren't what they were," as *Punch* magazine once speculated, perhaps it's because they never were.

At Bowerstown, I took out a half-pound bag of roasted cashews I had bought in Cooperstown and, because I had not eaten a full supper, consumed them in greedy handfuls. All of them. As I did so, the last rays of sun laid a diffuse orangy gauze on the hayfields, hardwoods, and barns—and on the foothills of the Appalachians ahead.

9

A Kick or Two in the Catskills

If two hundred years ago I had been about to cross the Appalachians on foot, or on horseback or mule, I would have considered it a necessity to have a gun—might have expected to meet mountain lions, or "catamounts" as they were then called, and quite possibly bears, timber wolves, or unfriendly Mohawks. I'd have needed four days' food and the strength to clamber up creek beds and slate screes, which were the only "clear" walking in hardwood forests that were undoubtedly deeper, denser, and more snaggled than they are today. I'd have considered myself lucky to meet no other traveller—aboriginal or mountain man—in that there would be a better than even chance I would be hijacked by him, either out of spite or for my mule or the few dollars of change in my pocket.

By contrast, when I left Grand Gorge, within view of the north Catskills, at 7:00 A.M. on June 24, I had the luxury of State Highway 23A, which would take me clear through the mountains' northernmost pass and down to the Hudson River. I had a van to carry my supplies, a companion to make my dinner and supply fluids at the end of the day, and the knowledge that if anything was going to take a bite out of me it would be Fido the dog, not a cougar coming down on me

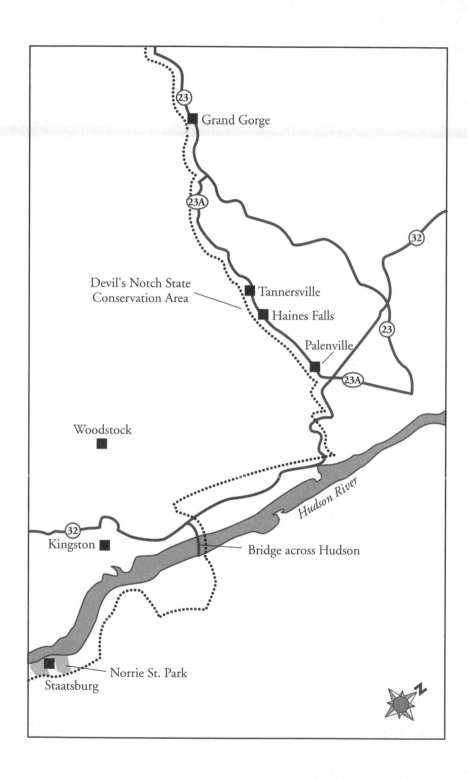

from a tree branch or rock overhang. Furthermore, I knew that if anything actually did attempt to eat me, I could get to a doctor at Tannersville or Haines Falls and that at a convenient halfway point near Hunter, I could sleep in a state-run campground, as opposed to sitting all night by a fire or with my back against a rock cliff to avoid being ambushed by the more rightful inhabitants of the mountains, whether two- or four-legged.

Even now, with every advantage, I was by no means overconfident about what lay ahead. For one thing, it was already nearly 90°F as I began my sunrise approach into the foothills (and within three hours would top a hundred). For another, my feet were as blistered and raw as ever and, I imagined, would be bleeding by mid-morning.

Which they were—initially just a seepage of pinkish fluid. However, by 10:00 A.M., when I took my shoes off, there was a trace of brighter red between the toes of my right foot.

Worse, for the moment, was that I had seriously underestimated my fluid intake, so that by the time I had walked twenty kilometres uphill in the heat, I had drunk every drop of the two litres of Gatorade I had started with. And since at the village of Lexington I had chucked the bottles as an inconvenience, I no longer had even a container to fill. The Catskills this far north, I quickly discovered, were by no means the populous and hospitable resort land that they are farther south. At least until Hunter, some fifteen kilometres away, I would be lucky to find a store, or even a farmhouse, where I could beg a cupful of water. Fortunately, as I slogged uphill in the sun, the road snuggled in alongside Schoharie Creek, a shallow trout-rich tributary of the East Delaware River that runs parallel to the highway right up to the creek's headwaters, some twenty kilo-metres to the west.

The higher the altitude, the longer and more spectacular the views—occasionally of clearings carpeted in wildflowers and blowing grass, but more commonly of horizon-wide slopes of densely packed maple and ash.

The higher I climbed, the greater was the sense that somewhere over the next long incline or the next, I would peak out and be atop the world. But the distances and perspectives are elusive (the bear came over the mountain), and each long ascent opened not onto the rest of the world to the east but onto new stretches of sloped highway, new banks of hardwoods, higher peaks.

After two hours without fluid, my tongue was doing a fair impersonation of a tennis ball and had lost its capability to supply even the sensation of moisture to my lips. The afternoon inched farther into alien territory when, on the gravel shoulder, I came across an immense mottled egg that, had it not been dented on one side, would have had the volume of perhaps a dozen hens' eggs or a twelve-pound round of shot. It hardly seemed possible that a crane or heron had dropped it on the shoulder, or that a fox or any other animal had carried it there intact. Something more bizarre yet seemed afoot when, a hundred metres farther along, I came across a pair of dead snakes that were themselves of mystic dimension, perhaps a metre and a half long, beige-and-black patterned, and as big around as juice tumblers. What was strangest about them was that they were unscarred except for smallish incisions on their bellies, where crows, I suspected, had zeroed in on their livers and kidneys, and had removed these darkest and tastiest of innards (I had witnessed such surgery in the Manitoba Interlake, performed on garter snakes that had stiffened, alive but defenceless, in the overnight frost during fall migration).

What had left these giant fox or milk snakes vulnerable in the June sun was, of course, unknowable. Perhaps extreme heat—intense sunlight, black asphalt. A snake's body temperature is, after all, unregulated. Whatever the case, it seemed certain the snakes had been dead, or were at least comatose, before the arrival of the crows. Otherwise, they would have defended themselves.

At a gravel crossroad where a spidery steel bridge spanned Schoharie Creek, I pulled off my T-shirt and shoes and waded across slimy rocks into the frigid mountain water, bending and scooping it onto my face and hair, going into spasms as the perishing cold ran onto my chest and back. I sipped at the water, then cupped it down as greedily as I have ever drunk.

An hour later, I again fumbled down the embankment, this time nearly stumbling over a teenaged boy and girl in the long grass—and did my best to act casually as they yanked their clothes into place and stared at me as if at some Inquisitional creep.

BEYOND THE PLUSH RESORTS and million-dollar cottages, the Catskills are an unimproved wilderness, where bears and coyotes still have an ecological toehold and where, when the snowboarders and cottagers are gone, an anarchic branch of humanity still traps and chops wood and gathers mushrooms—and sets its own eccentric standards for legality and private conduct. I have always respected anyone who can live by his wits and would consider it arrogant, at best, to apply the word *hillbilly* to even the most socially unevolved of Catskill mountain dwellers. Which said, I was more than a little surprised as I walked past a tarpaper-covered shack, situated down an embankment, to hear a door bang and, when I looked over, to see walking toward me a fiery-looking old man, as bent and scrawny as a straw, with a cubist contortion for a face. Aware suddenly of my presence on the highway, he raised his head, then his hand, in a gesture of greeting.

"Hello!" I shouted down.

"Hello!" he called and, after a pause, "come down here!"

"I'm going to Tannersville!" I called back, thinking to avoid the diversion.

"It's over there," he said, pointing. "Come down here! Come on here! Ya can help me!"

Less than fully convinced, I stepped over the guard cable and eased myself down the bank, through a spectacular garden of lupines. "What is it you need help with?" I said.

"Movin' that old tree blow down," he said, gesturing behind him toward the creek. "Whatcha doing on road, sitcha hot day? Where ya from?"

When he was not speaking, his face, with its deep folds and stubble, twitched through a near-constant series of exaggerated emotional codes—surprise, pleasure, curiosity, puzzlement, dismay.

But when I told him I was from Canada and was walking to New York, it was if he had been hit in the back by a spear, and his face froze in a paralyzed gape.

"New York!" he gasped eventually.

"New York," I said.

"New York!" he said again.

He wore a T-shirt, the armpits of which were the colour of mustard, and his glasses were so deeply encrusted with filth that had I not felt repulsed even to look at them, I might have snatched them off his face and thrown them in the creek for a soak.

"New York!" he exclaimed again, and he told me that, during his seventy-eight years in the shack behind him, I was the first person who had passed "walking all the way," as he put it.

I commented that the highway couldn't have been up to much seventy years ago, and he said, "It ain't much now! 'Course I never had a car, so it didn't matter none. We had that old tractor for skidding logs off the mountain—the only one like it 'tween Lexington and Palenvale." He pointed behind the house to a rusty abstractionist sculpture that in its day had clearly been a machine to reckon with.

He introduced himself as Gimmick, or Ginnick, and led me a few metres up the lot to where a large felled pine lay parallel to the highway. "Came right down rotten off that stump," he said. "Gotta move it around in front of that garden." And with a pair of poles and a piece of stove wood for a fulcrum, we began to lever one end of it across the clearing.

"New York!" he exclaimed again as we finished, and he told me he had been there once with his sister when he was a young man, looking for an uncle who had taken logging money from the family. "Never found nuthin'," he said, and he asked me if I wanted "a shot" for my trouble.

"Of what?"

"Whisky. C'mon in. My sister gonna love seein' ya. She's eighty-eight. She sleepin'—she no good in the heat."

He pulled open the screen door of his dwarfish home, a place constructed partly of logs, partly of boards covered with tarpaper. An antique .22 rifle stood on the dirt floor by the inner door, along with a hodgepodge of rusted stove and machine parts, plastic bottles, cardboard, scrap lumber, cinder blocks, odds and ends of clothing. As I followed him inside, however, I was hit hard by the smell of urine and immediately excused myself and retreated outside. "I like the air," I told him through the screen, and he came back outside, his face twitching through its rounds.

"Do you still log?" I said as I edged back to the base of the embankment.

"Too old," he said. "Just take care'a her."

I was apologizing for not taking the time to meet his sister when, behind him, there was a creaking of the door, and a tiny emaciated crone appeared in the sunlight, more wrinkled and shrunken than her brother and every bit as toothless. As a child, I had had a morbid fear of my grandmother when, at bedtime, she let her long white hair down—and an echo of it kicked in at the sight of the stringy white tresses that fell around the old woman's shoulders.

"Doe," he said leaning toward her. "This fella here—he's walking all the way."

"All the way where?" she whispered, regarding him with suspicion and not casting so much as a glance my way.

"New York," he said, at which point she swung her face toward me, and I realized that her eyes had no appreciable colour and that she was probably blind.

After a longish silence, she said, "That ain't right."

"Why not?" I smiled.

"All that walkin'."

"It's right fer him!" said her brother.

For a few seconds, the three of us stood there, and I thought to ask if anybody ever saw any mountain lions.

"Not fer seventy year," said the old woman. "Uncle ours shot seventeen of 'em once—fer the bounty. One of 'em caught a child over by Hunter, and they wanted 'em outta here. I seen 'em all lined up 'gainst the fence."

"Did it kill the child?"

"Swallered him. I'm goin' in," she said. "It's too hot. If ya want some meat, Gimmick'll get ya some. It's deer meat. He'll show ya. I'm goin in."

Protesting that I had to keep moving and didn't need any meat, I followed my host behind the house to a metre-square trap door—a heavy, medieval-looking thing set in a rotting frame.

"Pull that open," he said.

I raised the lid and eased back as a draft of cool fetid air pushed up out of the pit.

As my eyes adjusted to the darkness, large blocks of ice surrounded by sawdust became visible and—neatly laid out on top, as in one of those gruesome Flemish still-lifes—the skinned carcass of a deer, nightmare head intact, as well as several smaller carcasses. "Coon … porky … rabbit …," he said pointing, and he drew my attention to a bloodsplattered plastic bag in which he was keeping the deer's inner organs. "Deer's got a bone right in its heart!" he said. "Only animal got one."

I told him I'd never heard that and wondered aloud why such a bone might be there.

"Bear got one 'tween its legs," he said. "Right in its sausage."

"That I've heard," I said.

"Raccoon, too," he said. "Little skinny bone."

"What are those?" I asked, pointing at a pair of tiny phallic-looking carcasses.

"Squirrel. They good eating. Doe loves squirrel. Tastes like duck 'ceptin' better, 'cause they eat nuts. I could give you a rabbit."

"No," I said. "I'm not going to take it and waste it."

"Wastin' it's when you leave it on the road," he said with the authority of one who had not had much to waste over the years. He told me that in summer he and a neighbour often gathered up two or three hundred pounds of animal carcasses a week off the highway between Lexington and Hunter. They dressed it all out and either ate it or gave it away—or sold it to jobbers, "at least the venison and rabbit."

Some of it, he speculated, ended up as far away as the high-end dining spots and hotels of New York City.

I asked if they knew it was roadkill, and he looked at me as if reassessing my intelligence.

"They don't pry in," he said. "But you tell me—what would you rather eat, a deer been kilt clean by a car or a pig that lies aroun' breathin' his own ex-*kree*-ment all day and dies paralyzed from electrical shock?"

IT WAS JUST NORTH of here in the Adirondacks that the famous (now debased) sociological study of the Jukes and Kallikaks, two families of mountain "naturals," took place during the early twentieth century. Gimmick and Doe notwithstanding, the groundskeeper at Devil's Tombstone State Campground, south of Tannersville, was as telling a creature of the hills as one might wish to encounter in such a study. George was so spooked by him that on picking me up at Tannersville, he began immediately to obsess over this strange, this eerie, this weird young man who ran what was, by extension now, a "strange" and "eerie" campground.

In reality, it was a gorgeous campground—a place that during the late afternoon was bathed in the remote greenish light that tends to fall through, and even from, old hardwoods.

By the time we had driven from Tannersville to the park, the attendant, who lived in a cabin on the premises, was finished work for the day, meaning that I would not meet him until morning (George meanwhile suspected that he never actually did finish work, that after hours he laboured on, spying on his campers from the recesses of the forest or from beneath the outhouses or somewhere). George had had a few beers, and at dusk, in the firelight, as I sorted out my feet and examined the map, he cooked up a two-gallon pot of what we had come to call "two-stroke" chili—two cans kidney beans, two cans stewed tomatoes, two cans mushrooms, two pounds ground beef, two green peppers, two onions, two garlic bulbs, two plates, two forks, two appetites.

The most complicated part of the dish was the steamed rice (two cups), for which George and I had different cooking methods (two points of view), each of us with an unshakeable commitment to his own. These methods were occasionally the subject of debate, and further debate over which of us really knew how to cook, or knew anything, or was the more stubborn, hypocritical, self-centred, insensitive, presumptuous.

There is a side to George that is just plain galling and uncompromising. And to me, too, of course. "The indulgent fixations of the self," George had called such pigheadedness, while I tended to think of it as the need to tell the story in one's own way. It can be a productive force. And yet so often it finds its vent in issues that, while universal in their recognizability, are almost too trivial to document.

Such as how to cook rice.

Or how a tent gets pitched.

Or a dish washed ("I'm not eating porridge out of a pot with old garlic in it").

One morning recently, we had debated aggressively George's insistent dismissal of *The New Yorker* magazine, which I had read with fascination for thirty years and which George admitted he did not read at all. Nevertheless, he described it as pompous and inconsequential—compared, say, to *The Village Voice,* which he took to be a true validation of the people (this despite its current conformity, and ads every bit as effete and dispiriting as anything *The New Yorker* had ever printed).

To really get us grousing at one another, however, there was still nothing like grocery shopping—as, for example, on the morning after the two-stroke chili, when in the supermarket in Tannersville I resisted buying half a dozen cans of discount pork and beans that had attracted George's attention. "At least get the good ones," I said, at which point George threw the beans back on the shelf and walked away in disgust, ending up in meditative appraisal of the beer in the store's forty-foot refrigeration unit. Eventually he bought a dozen and a bag of ice to keep them cool.

"I'm sorry," I said as we left the store, "but I need good food. I need protein."

"I can't live on protein," he objected—a passable reassertion, I thought, of the Biblical injunction that man cannot live by bread alone.

At a park where we had a sandwich before I started walking, George meticulously installed the beer in the cooler with the ice, leaving at best a few cubic inches for the cubic foot or so of perishable food we were carrying. "What about all this stuff?" I said, indicating a carton of eggs, a quart of strawberries, cheese, grapes, a quart carton of milk. Without a word, he scrunched the half-empty milk carton into a shapeless bolster and rammed it in among the ice and beer. Then he stuffed in the cheese and, having ripped the Cellophane off the strawberries, began wedging them individually between the ice cubes and beer cans. When he picked up the grapes, however, I snatched them away for the road, and then watched as he administered the *coup de grâce,* the placement of the eggs, one at a time, amid the ice, beer, and berries.

Finally I said, "Too bad we don't have a pound of bacon that you could lay out in strips on top of everything."

"You wanted your food packed, it's packed," he said, and he slammed the cooler's lid into place.

We drove in silence back to the highway, where I jumped out and ambled off down the road, having urged George (who remained noncommittal) to pick me up eight hours hence where Highway 23 meets the New York Thruway just west of the Hudson River.

But all that came later.

On the night of June 24, at the Devil's Tombstone State Campground, on the edge of sleep, we heard from somewhere off in the mountains the single lingering howl of a wolf or coyote. Then from another part of the forest, a response. Before long, the night was a shrill, predatorial chorus that I was sure must have signalled a kill, a sort of tribal invitation to dinner. Or maybe it was about mating or just gathering the clan. It went on for two hours or more and then stopped abruptly, and the next sound out of the distance was thunder, and we were quickly into violent lightning and rain.

Within minutes of my crawling from the tent into the well-scrubbed light of the morning, a truck stopped on the road and a thick-muscled man in early middle age—unmistakably the exotic upland Popeye who had so impressed George—got out and ambled onto the site, wishing me good morning and holding out a form on which he said we could submit a report on how we liked what he called "my park."

I said I'd be happy to, and we had a stewardly conversation that produced among other nuggets of information the fact that his wife ran a campground in another part of the north Catskills, that she had been given a newer truck than his (which he called "the crappiest in the state"), that the first-aid box in the park office contained a saw with which an arm or leg could be amputated, and that it was no easy gig controlling the ineducable sluggards who visited his wilderness paradise.

"But there's nobody here except us!" I protested.

He grinned off into the trees and said, "You just wait," and he mounted a solemn thesis against the women who came into his park anticipating showers, flush toilets, blow-driers, electrical outlets, and the like. Again he folded his thickish features into a grin and said, "They might as well stay home."

What I found freakish about him was not so much the reptilian mannerisms, the gazing and grinning that had so gotten to George, as his almost sociopathic fundamentalism, his rule-mongering, the fact that he was so fiercely literal—in a way intended not to inform or enlighten but to frustrate and thwart. When I asked, "Is there much hunting up here in the fall?" he said, "I dunno; I'm not here in the fall. I quit on Labour Day."

"I mean in the area."

"I don't live in the area."

"Oh, where do you live?"

"Ten mile south of here."

"I meant hunting in the Catskills generally."

"Lots of it."

"What do they hunt?"

"Deer, bear."

"Many bears up here?"

"None—I don't allow any garbage left around here. Carry in, carry out."

"I mean in the area."

"Like I told ya—I don't live in the area."

FOUR OR FIVE MILES east of Tannersville, at Haines Falls, I came to what appeared to be a luxurious old resort, built low, California-style, its separate buildings spread among immense lawns and gardens, the whole of it stretching back up into the mountains. "The Peace Village," said a sign at the road.

Curious, I wandered in past the office along a path that led to the largest of the buildings, as well as toward a lone male figure who was gardening in the heat.

"Hi!" he called as I approached, and within seconds he had introduced himself as Derek Gilmore and was describing to me the work of the Brahma Kumaris World Spiritual Organization. The outfit has its headquarters in Rajasthan, India, plus a hundred or more "learning centres" worldwide, including half a dozen in the New York City area, one right on Fifth Avenue. As I would eventually read in the literature, all of these aim at "fostering positive human values by focusing on the unlimited potential of the mind through the practice of Raja Yoga meditation."

The local three-hundred-acre site had once been a rollicking high-end hotel—the Rivoli or Ravioli or something—and had been bought several years ago and converted.

Derek was from Fife, Scotland—an ex-alcoholic, ex-doper who lived free for now at the Peace Village in exchange for six or seven hours of daily labour.

"I like the idea of the place," I told him and asked (more skeptically than I had wished to sound) where the money came from to operate it.

"Wealthy donors," he confided. "But everyone is welcome here. Nobody ever asks for money."

He invited me into the four-hundred-seat dining room—high-vaulted, dark, empty—where he plugged in an electric kettle.

"American tea is weak," he said matter-of-factly and informed me that the head cook at the Peace Village was from Nova Scotia and imported Red Rose tea from Canada because it has "a bit of a kick."

And so we drank Red Rose tea. And got a bit of a kick. And ate biscuits so kickless they were a kind of meditation unto themselves. I told Derek about my walk. And he told me how, by the ancient philosophy of the East, when a man had fathered a family and was into middle age, his earthly mission became the singular pursuit of enlight-enment, a process typically undertaken by *walking*—sometimes for years, alone, across thousands of kilometres of wilderness and trail.

"C'mon," he said eventually, "I'll introduce you to another Canadian."

As we left the building, we passed a low-flying yellow-and-red flag emblazoned with the words *Supreme Father*. Again hearing myself sound more skeptical than I might have liked, I said, "Who exactly *is* the supreme father?" (Beyond the rhetoric of liberation and balance, was there some supreme *human* figure, some psycho-spiritual CEO, to whom everyone bowed and brought kicky tea and arrowroot biscuits?)

"It's the god Shiva," Derek said calmly. "Light and enlightenment."

This show-stopping answer was still resonating as we entered a room in the sleeping quarters where a youngish man named Kessel Callender, originally from Guyana but more recently from Montreal and Toronto, was doing minor renovations. When I was introduced to him as a guy walking from Lake Superior to New York, he asked immediately about my diet. I offered a faintly self-admonishing acknowledgment that I was eating a lot of protein and that I wasn't a vegetarian as I assumed he and Derek were. Understandably, I stopped short of mentioning that I was stuffing back four-wiener hotdogs at every opportunity and as much as a kilo of red meat a day. Kessel was generous in suggesting that it wasn't just the content of a meal that nourished or impaired the senses and soul but the "loving and peace-ful spirit" in which the meal was prepared and eaten.

It was all a slightly humiliating reminder of George's and my recur-rent grousing over the acquisition and preparation of our food. At least we ate harmoniously. As for beer, it was a non-starter at the Peace Village, the assumption seeming to be that even modest consumption of alcohol is a hindrance to clarity of perception and incompatible with equanimity of spirit. Inasmuch as almost *everything* in the culture is incompatible with equanimity of spirit—politics, television, employ-ment, unemployment—I suspected some deductive slippage here and thought that if George were on hand (with his irreducible belief that in vino exists *veritas*), he might mount a listenable case to the contrary.

As I prepared to get back to the road, I mentioned that, in the days to come I intended to increase the likes of garbanzo and mung beans as a source of protein in my diet—and to the degree I ended up stick-ing to this agenda, might have named thumbtacks and coarse-screened gravel as well.

Derek walked me a hundred metres east along the highway before wishing me *"Slangavah!"* which he said is an old Scottish send-off meaning cheers. He gave me a gentle Peace Village handshake and told me that my visit had been good for him and that he wished me—what else?—peace. I thanked him for the tea and hospitality, and told him that the visit had been good for me, too (the truth being that I'd have been happy to spend a day or two in the village if the urge to keep moving had not been so strong and if I'd thought George would be able to stomach such purity of appetite and spirit).

DURING FOUR WITHERING HOURS that afternoon, I walked nearly thirty kilometres downhill—sometimes at such a relentless angle of descent that after ten or twelve kilometres I began to get intense pains in my Achilles tendons and heels. Even the tops of my toes, driven persistently into the ends of my shoes, began to chafe.

The reason for this exaggerated descent was that, unlike the inland flanks of the Catskills, which rise gradually through the Appalachian foothills, the east flank falls as steep as a castle wall into the Hudson River Valley.

In places on the switchbacks where the road was narrow, well-shadowed rock cuts dropped straight onto the pavement, leaving no room for shoulders, let alone walkers. Elsewhere, dense stands of forest crowded the roadside or leaned out over it, impenetrable to the sun. For the cars, it was business as usual, the sportier models whining through their gearboxes, as close as possible to full throttle. For me, it meant there were spots where I had to time my dashes from one patch of shoulder to the next so as to avoid being felled by wheeled shrapnel.

As always there was roadkill, including a pathetic baby raccoon, no blood, apparently asleep, with its tiny hands folded by its chest. And an exquisite little box turtle, as neat as a toy, with delicate yellow rick-rack around its blackish green shell. And a bat, of all things, the first I had seen on the road, its wings outstretched near the centre line, leaving me to wonder how a bat, with its sonar and speed, could be struck by a car.

At a spot perhaps ten kilometres east of Haines Falls, the mountain fell away below me into a precipitous rocky chasm about a hundred metres across. There were cars parked nearby, and in the sun-laced depths below, twenty or more young men and women—of college age, judging by the stickers on the cars—were partying naked, shrieking and laughing and taking occasional plunges in the stream. I watched for two or three minutes, suppressing a quiet ache to be down there—on the rocks, in the water, in the skin of a younger, freer (less driven or repressed?) version of myself. Then I continued my own steep plunge into the valley. I have had the inspirational advantage of growing up, first, on the Ottawa River and then on the St. Lawrence. I love those rivers and have drawn lifelong sustenance from them. But I am fascinated by all rivers, and having wanted for years to see the Hudson, I was juiced by the thought that at some point before sunset, I would.

At Palenville, the town sign proclaimed, "Proud home of America's first artists' colony." But when I stopped at the public library on the ground floor of a graciously defunct hotel, not one of the six people inside, including the librarian (who had lived in the town all her life), could offer even a clue as to where or what the colony might be. I said to the librarian, without prejudice, that I thought this put some strain on the sign's claim of town pride in the historic first. "Oh, no," she said sniffing, "we really are an extremely proud town." And then, "It's just that we don't take our history from public signs."

"Apparently we don't even read public signs!" hooted a middle-aged patron at no one in particular. And with that the librarian was off into the recesses of the library. And I was off down the road.

As it turned out, my first sight of the Hudson did not come until the next morning. I had run out of energy several kilometres west of the river, had phoned George, and met him at dusk by a U-pick strawberry farm on the fertile agricultural plain west of Malden.

We spent the night in the van, at a roadside clearing near West
Saugerties, a village made famous during the late 1960s when the rock
group The Band lived there in a big pink house, swiped groceries from
the local store, and recorded their reputation-making album *Music
from the Big Pink.*

At about midnight, squirmy from the heat, George and I abandoned the van and took a walk under a hazy half-moon. I felt bad
about ragging on him that morning and told him so, and we came as
close as we ever came to any sort of verbal reconciliation over our
various contretemps.

The truth was that I was exhausted in the heat and knew well that
I had been pushing myself too hard. George, too, admitted exhaustion, mostly inner, and that night expressed his first real trepidation
about getting close to New York City. He told me he had no notion of
what might still be there for him, and he wondered aloud if, at his age,
he'd be able to stand what he called "the crush, the relentlessness, the
poverty—and all this terrorist shit."

I reminded him that we had either dodged or outlasted all our earlier
apprehensions and that so far things had only gotten better. Certainly,
the U.S. had been a good deal friendlier than we anticipated.

"New York isn't the U.S.," he said quietly.

One of his greatest concerns was the cost of everything—the
legacy of a lifetime of having to shave pennies and, more specifically, of being forced from the Bronx, unable to go to a part of New
York where life might have been more livable. George had been
reading the New York newspapers and asked me now if I knew what
a one-bedroom apartment cost in the city. I told him we didn't need a
one-bedroom apartment, that we had a good hotel in the centre of
Manhattan for as long as we wanted it.

"Free," I added. And to cheer him up, I conjectured our accommodation as a three- or four-room suite on the thirtieth floor, with king-
sized beds, a whirlpool bath, and a fridge full of European beer. "And
a big view of Central Park."

In reality, after sixty days on the road, such lodging seemed less like a literal destination than some fanciful allegorical cartoon. As perhaps it would turn out to be. Privately, I had no idea whether our accommodation at the Warwick would be the presidential suite I had described or a couple of cots by the furnace or loading dock. Actually, the Warwick didn't even know George was coming—I had never told them I had an accomplice. Of course I didn't dare tell George this. Instead, I assured him (with what would eventually prove to be impeccable accuracy) that I didn't think Ray Slavin was going to let us down.

IN THE MORNING, out of curiosity—and in need of a breather—we drove the twenty or so kilometres over to the town of Woodstock, namesake of the legendary 1969 rock festival, to see if we could find Yasger's Farm, the cornfield where the festival had taken place.

Like Cooperstown, Woodstock is a repository of nostalgia, in this case not for "straight" or Major League America, but for sixties counterculture, rock and folk music, the alternative version of Life, Liberty and the Pursuit of Happiness (during the sixties and seventies, the area was home to musicians such as Tim Hardin, Richard Manuel, Rick Danko, Paul Butterfield, Eric Anderson, Van Morrison, Robbie Robertson, Garth Hudson, and Levon Helm).

While the town has perhaps lost its cultural edge, there are still sixties die-hards around, middle-aged vegetarians and yoga devotees, at least some of whom, we learned, saw the Jimi Hendrix Experience take the stage at dawn to close the rock festival of the century on that sunny summer morning nearly thirty-five years ago.

One of them, a florid middle-aged man in a tie-dyed pink T-shirt and cut-off blue jeans—a man whose watery blue eyes hinted at epic excesses of the past—was sitting on the lawn of Lutheran Christ Church playing tentatively on an acoustic guitar as I poked along the main street, having left George contemplating the Age of Aquarius in a nearby coffee shop. The guy was clearly a survivor of that gilded age, and I asked rather sheepishly if he could tell me where the big concert had taken place.

During the last years of her dotage, my Grandma Scholey invariably said in response to any snippet of information uttered within earshot, "Funny, they never told me about it." Which expressed precisely my thoughts as Richard Prans explained patiently that Woodstock the concert hadn't actually taken place in Woodstock but near the town of Bethel some eighty kilometres away. As if to allay my embarrassment at not having had a clue, he cracked a spectral smile and said, "Most people don't know that."

The truth is I *had* known about Bethel (sort of), but had always assumed it was more or less the same place as Woodstock.

"Woodstock was *supposed* to be in Woodstock," Richard said. "But the town backed down. Didn't want the crowds."

Richard, who like Edmund Wilson is a native of Red Bank, New Jersey, had been nineteen at the time and on his way to California, driving a mouldering Triumph sports car with a friend, when he got word that a rock festival was shaping up back in New York State. He said, "We turned around in St. Louis."

The car's innards quit in West Virginia, forcing Richard and his friend to take the bus from there.

Richard described the three-day festival as the best time of his life—with the best energy and the best music. He recalled, in particular, the British band The Who, performing their rock opera, *Tommy,* and how as they played through the wee hours of Sunday morning, darkness gave way to dawn, and the sun, "this magnificent neon pink ball," rose behind the stage. "It was unbelievably beautiful. I mean all this was happening in a cornfield! It was 1969! There was no computerization! It was all just gorgeous and simple!"

What fascinated me about Richard was his simultaneous embodiment of both the highest ideals of the Woodstock generation (he was gentle, democratic, and protective in his regard for the planet) and the era's gaudiest and most dangerous excesses. During the late 1970s, he moved to Woodstock, met a number of the town's prominent musicians, and became a driver for Richard Manuel of The Band, who had lost his licence because of drug and alcohol offences. In 1985, he attended Manuel's funeral, after the keyboardist, in heroin-addicted penury, hanged himself in a Florida motel room. "By that time," Richard said, "I myself was doing everything up to and including smack." He popped Valium to relax, speed to keep going. He drank a half-gallon of vodka a day. His weight rose to four hundred pounds. "With the speed, it was as if you couldn't get enough calories."

In 1994, after a perilous six weeks in detox, Richard returned to Woodstock, knowing that to revert to heroin would kill him. He barely reached town when he ran into Rick Danko, the bass player for The Band, who had just bought what Richard described as a "great big bag of smack ... I absolutely craved heroin, was just crying for it. So we went right to his apartment and smoked it, and split a gallon of vodka and a bunch of speed."

After another stay in detox, Richard gave up drinking and drugs. Gave up smoking. Stopped guzzling coffee. Lost two hundred pounds. When he returned to Woodstock, he got a job caring for horses. He said, "I guess I have a bit of a sensitivity toward animals."

Notably, he stopped eating them.

He took up meditation. And organic gardening. He learned guitar and is today, as he put it, "building up the courage to go public."

When Richard had talked more or less non-stop for an hour, he said, "You probably want to hear about the musicians who lived here."

I told him I was happy to hear his story.

"It's amazing I'm around to tell it," he said, and George, who had joined us and was sitting on the grass, agreed (too heartily, I thought) that it was.

As we were about to leave, Richard grabbed my hand and shook it. However, when I asked for his address, he glared at me as if I had busted into his bedroom with a bazooka.

"What for?" he demanded.

I told him I wanted to mention him in the book I intended to write. "I thought I might contact you. But if it makes you nervous, don't worry about it."

After a silence, he said, "I guess it'd be okay." And in a tiny cryptic script, he wrote out his address, including no fewer than three phone numbers.

Richard said he had friends who had fled to Canada during the Vietnam War. "I would have gone up there myself, except I wasn't drafted because of my vision. They didn't want guys like me bombing for America."

George asked about the prospects for his music, and he patted his guitar and said, "I wish I could play this thing a little more confidently. I spent a lot of years blowing dope with people who could."

As we drove out to Highway 9W, on which I had been walking, we hit a wild thunderstorm, and had to pull over and wait—windows up, glass fogged, vent fan pushing hundred-degree air onto us through the dashboard.

George fanned himself with his hat and told me how, during his last months in the Bronx, he would go down to the New York Public Library to read, to write, to escape life's pressures—how amid all the books, he felt comforted and yet invalidated, in that he was sure his own writing would never be part of the grand continuum that surrounded him.

His thoughts turned to the next few days and how, as he put it, we were "running out of space" and "weren't going to find too many more places to pitch a tent."

Our plan all along had been to leave the van at the home of a friend of mine, a sports and music writer named Stu Hackel, in Dobbs Ferry, about forty-five kilometres north of the city. But George, whose plan was to take the train in from there, began now to apply a quiet pressure about the way I myself should go into New York City. He no longer wanted me to walk the final forty-five or fifty kilometres into

Manhattan. Said it was too dangerous, too complicated, the logistics too absurd. He said, "You have no idea what it's going to be like fighting your way through the traffic and expressways."

I snatched the map off the dashboard, opened it in front of us, and said, "After tomorrow, I'm on a straight run into the city. Right here. Number 9 Highway. East bank of the Hudson. Straight down Broadway to Times Square."

George questioned the respect that "a black crack addict" in the Bronx was likely to have for "an old honky hiker" in Ray-Ban sunglasses and a Swiss Army watch. I believe he harboured a genuine concern for my well-being. But he was also concerned that if I got lost or mugged, or if we got separated for a night without the phones, he'd be on his own at the worst possible time for him.

I suggested that we could both walk, and to brighten him up, got him reminiscing about his old haunts in New York. Together we would visit the Strand Used Book Store, the public library, and the Metropolitan Museum of Art, where George had passed countless hours as an art student. He would take me to Washington Square. And Greenwich Village. And across the Brooklyn Bridge. And to his old East Side bars. And of course to Harlem and to the Upper East Side, where he had lived on Ninety-second Street. And into the wilds of the South Bronx.

Meanwhile, the rain let up, and the sun reappeared, burning off the mist as we drove through the forests and fields toward the river.

10

The American Rhine

While the Mississippi and St. Lawrence are often perceived to be America's defining navigable rivers, the Hudson, too, is a signature, a "highway" that for five thousand years was part of an interior aboriginal trade route that included the Great Lakes and St. Lawrence and any number of bendy fast-flowing rivers to the west. The English explorer Henry Hudson was so impressed by the river, by its possibilities, that when he sailed into it in 1609, he was convinced he could follow it to the Pacific. Presumably, humble Henry named the river himself, although it must also have had a Native name that was (and perhaps still is) more descriptive of its breadth and disposition. What struck me most about the Hudson during my first exhilarating look at it was its relentlessness, its volume, its broad fetch—the "strong brown god" in it, as T.S. Eliot might have put it. Its banks are more pastoral than I would have foreseen so close to New York City—this despite my awareness that the river had inspired, lent its name to, an entire movement of nineteenth-century landscape painters. I had imagined industrial docks, manufacturing and fuel-loading sites. But the banks are willows, orchards, fields, low stone cliffs stretching as far north and south as I could see.

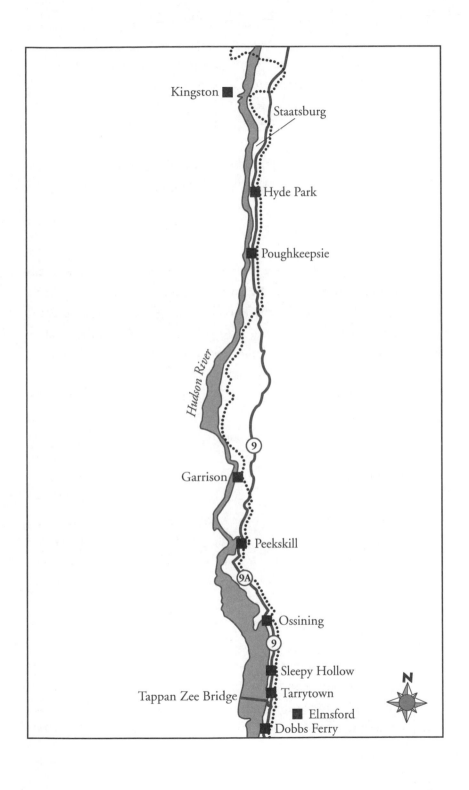

Kingston

Staatsburg

Hyde Park

Poughkeepsie

Hudson River

9

Garrison

Peekskill

9A

Ossining

9

Sleepy Hollow

Tappan Zee Bridge

Tarrytown

Elmsford

Dobbs Ferry

N

Like many of the bridges on the Hudson, the magnificent suspension bridge that crosses the river at Kingston was built by Mohawk Indians from Montreal and Cornwall, who learned their steel rigging during the early twentieth century on bridges around Montreal and on the burgeoning skyscrapers of Manhattan. I went to high school in Cornwall with a number of kids from the Cornwall Island Reserve whose fathers and grandfathers were Manhattan steel riggers and who themselves went on to work on New York bridges and towers, including the World Trade Center. It was often said of them that their extraordinary capability to walk girders three hundred metres or more above the street came from having no fear of heights. But it is more plausible to believe, as I heard it explained recently, that while the fear exists—fear being a basic human protective device—there is in the Mohawk makeup a capacity for risk-taking, a nerve, that enables them to suppress fear and as a result to work on unsecured beams, at times quite literally above the clouds.

As it turned out, two of the bridge's four lanes were closed because of construction, creating an intense concentration of cars in the two open lanes. In the absence of a sidewalk, I moved with step-by-step caution up the approach ramp, at one point "tightrope" walking along the thigh-high concrete barrier that marked the temporary edge of the road.

As we had arranged, George was waiting in the van at a little siding near the toll booths. I jumped in and as we passed the attendant, I shouted that I wanted to walk across the bridge—would it be okay?

"No walking on the bridge!" she hollered. "It's against the law! You have to keep moving!"

"I will keep moving!" I yelled, to which she replied that with the construction there was no room to walk anyway.

As we started up the incline, however, it became apparent that there was plenty of room. And about fifty metres past the booth, I asked George to stop, holding up dozens of vehicles behind, while I got out and hoisted myself onto a metre-wide steel beam almost two metres above grade and lumpy with rivets. And on this gritty girder—having to crouch at times to avoid being blown by the wind into traffic, or onto steel lattice work, or into the water below—I crossed the Hudson River.

In all, it took me twenty minutes, the traffic streaming by me on the left, the river appearing in dizzying silver glimpses perhaps thirty metres beneath me to my right.

At pretty much the top of the bridge, I stood for a minute, holding tight to a three-inch-thick suspension cable, looking back to the west at the voluptuous contours of the Catskills and north to where a two-hundred-metre freighter, a self-loader, executed a languorous tail slide around a bend on its way upriver.

A couple of bridge narcs in uniform, one of them female, were waiting for me as I came gradually down to the toll shack on the east bank. Central casting couldn't have invented them more convincingly, with their aviator shades, big bellies, and crossed arms. I could see the van parked several hundred metres up the highway and longed to be there. Meanwhile, anticipating an occasion, I pasted on my most ingratiating smile and, in an attempt to short-circuit their disapproval, bid them a cheery good afternoon while still twenty metres away. And from that point, I just kept walking, right up to them and right on past, still on the girder, as they blathered away about legality and responsibility and the cops—and how lucky I was that I wasn't killed by the traffic or didn't end up in the river, and that if I ever tried such a thing again, I'd be ..., at which point my ploy kicked in, so that by the time I was five metres past them and they realized I wasn't stop-ping, they had fallen as silent as if a switch had been turned off.

Where the road widened, I jumped off my girder onto the paved shoulder, and five minutes later reached the van and arranged with George to meet me at nine o'clock at Staatsburg, perhaps thirty kilo-metres to the south.

However, it wasn't until a couple of hours had passed, and I was nearly at Reincliff, that I was able to get close enough to the river again to be aware of its tides and of the smell of the sea.

We pitched the tent at Mills-Norrie State Park, a glorious old estate near Staatsburg where, during the evening, I walked a couple of kilometres along a riverside trail to where a mud-flat as black and shiny as rubber stretched for hundreds of metres down shore. Beyond it, vast patches of lily pads bobbed on the incoming tide, and beyond those, dozens of ten- or twelve-pound carp floated belly-up on the opaque and oily surface of the river.

During the next couple of days, I would get an impression of the Hudson as a kind of American Rhine, a legendary working waterway, both functional and shapely, except that the mountains here are the Appalachians not the Alps, and the castles alongshore are not so strictly the domain of old aristocracy as of theology, education, the military, industry, and culture: Mount St. Alphonsus, West Point, General Foods, GM, Vassar, Sing Sing, the Museum of the Hudson. And, of course, also of American "aristocracy"—the Astors, Rockefellers, Roosevelts, Millses, and Vanderbilts.

MY WALK SOUTH the following morning brought me to the town of Hyde Park, where Franklin and Eleanor Roosevelt's estate and the presidential library—yellow sandstone fortresses with the architectural gravity of the Middle Ages—have been converted into public museums. FDR's silhouetted profile, complete with specs and cigarette holder, appears on yellow banners throughout town, and as I walked beneath them, intermittently within sight of the river, I recalled the story of how when Eleanor returned from a visit to her doctor one day, FDR reputedly asked, "Did he have anything to say about that big fat ass of yours?"—to which she answered, "No, dear, he didn't mention you." But Roosevelt is certainly well mentioned in Hyde Park—on building and street names, and on businesses such as the FDR Cinema, the FDR Pizza Revue, FDR Tire Town, and the FDR Dog and Cat Grooming Salon.

Just up the road, at the highest point of the Hudson's shoreline, sits the two-hundred-acre estate of Frederick Vanderbilt, a grandson of the railway tycoon, who in 1898 bought the land, pruned and gentrified it, and erected the garish Renaissance-style mansion—in effect, a morbid beaux arts crypt—that is now public property and a protectorate of the National Parks Board.

Earlier that morning, I had, on a whim, mentioned to George that we should drop in to see the Vanderbilt mansion, that it would perhaps be instructive, might be just the thing to burnish up his socioeconomic prejudices. But he wouldn't hear of it—even the idea was an abomination.

In his absence, however, I paid my seven bucks and, amid craning pensioners in soft-brimmed hats and sensible shoes, went in for a look around.

And was rewarded. In fact, was barely through the front door when I found myself in a capacious room, a kind of salon, with a thirty-foot painted mural across the ceiling. The story is that Frederick had been the most morally responsible of the four young Vanderbilts—humane in business, faithful in marriage, conservative in politics and art. So it came as a surprise in 1962 when the National Parks Commission, which had recently taken ownership of the estate, found under layers of paint this ceiling mural depicting a party of naked young women, one riding a golden chariot, the rest dancing provocatively around a stooped old man whose head rests despairingly in his cupped hands. The painting is thought to have been done by the American artist Edward Simmons, and the old man is said to bear an uncanny resemblance to Frederick Vanderbilt himself, who clearly commissioned the work. The painting was instructive, perhaps even prescriptive, to a middle-aged traveller whose thoughts occasionally turned to the well-visited themes at hand.

The commentary of the guide, meanwhile, was awful—sounded less like a biographical or historical perspective than a kind of liturgy on the faith and just desserts of one who abjured decadence and self-interest in favour of the deepest moral and social commitment.

And who still went to hell—at least if the painting is any indication. Farther south on the Hudson, at Sleepy Hollow, John D.

Rockefeller built his estate, Kykuit, in 1896, specifically to outdo the grandeur of the Astor estate upriver. Hell came to John D. one night in the autumn of 1914, when members of the International Union of Workers marched north out of New York City, armed with clubs, knives, and stones, and attacked Kykuit, protesting their low wages, their abysmal opportunities for improvement, their long hours, and their dangerous and unhealthy working conditions. Until that time, Rockefeller had prided himself on his closeness to the working people of his empire, had enjoyed handing out dimes to the children of Tarrytown as a reminder of what glories were possible for them, and had refused to build a fence around Kykuit because it would separate him from those he loved—and presumably who loved him.

The construction of a high stone wall around the place began immediately.

Several days after seeing Kykuit and its wall, I would, with enhanced interest, come across Rockefeller's socio-political credo inscribed in stone in front of the family monument, Rockefeller Center and Plaza, on Fifth Avenue in Manhattan—every word of it a reminder, as Margaret Laurence once put it, that "people say anything."

Most people, of course, don't get to immortalize the "anything" they say on massive granite slabs in the centre of one of the greatest cities in the world. Unfortunately, Rockefeller was not most people—so there they are, his pronouncements on "law and man," on "power and responsibility," on "the dignity of labor," including his notions "that the world owes every man an opportunity to make a living" (no mention of making "a life"), "that thrift is essential to well-ordered living ... that truth and justice are fundamental to an enduring social order ... that Love is the greatest thing in the world, that it alone. ..." etc., etc.

Where "truth" is concerned, it is perhaps worth noting that when the great Mexican artist Diego Rivera was hired by Rockefeller to paint a mural depicting the state of world affairs for Rockefeller Center, Rivera thought it would be "truthful" to include images of Lenin and

Trotsky, whose revolutionary zeal was at the time spreading across half the planet. However, he was fired from the project for even considering such heresy. Beyond communism, the great unmentionables of the Rockefeller credo seem to have been sex and death—creation and transfiguration—themes that, according to Al Purdy, matter most, inasmuch as they "encompass all others," even though they do not make even cameo appearances at Kykuit or in the granite slabs on Fifth Avenue.

THE ROUTE SOUTH of Hyde Park was far less chaotic and obstructed than I had anticipated. Because old Highway 9—in effect Broadway Avenue—had been built amid the rock banks and bowers of the Hudson, and it had never been possible to widen it, commuters today tend to take the bigger north-south highways and freeways to and from New York City. Highway 9 is in many places still just two lanes wide. Where its shoulders were too narrow for my comfort, however, or I sensed a more sheltered or scenic route closer to the river, I would detour down to the banks—or get as close as I could without venturing onto the multiple railway tracks that are a constant along this stretch of the Hudson. Trains blasted by me, sometimes as frequently as every five minutes, carrying a perpetual run of people and goods into and out of Manhattan.

What was especially impressive, despite the trains and traffic, was that, even as I got within sixty or seventy kilometres of the city—well into Westchester County—the west bank of the Hudson remained rural, wild, spectacular. The view from Peekskill, for example, takes in Bear Mountain, a peak as high as the Catskills, while the terrain farther south is hills, forest, and rock palisades that when viewed from the east shore, seem to drop directly into the water.

The route along my own side of the river cut across fields, by rock cuts, and through extensive tracts of old hardwoods, generally the former estates of Manhattan industrialists built during American capitalism's unfettered *belle époque*. It is an irony that would have mystified Marx and Mao, but the existence today of these expanses of publicly accessible riverside forest is attributable entirely to the fact that the land was once the domain of very *un*accessible pirate tycoons, whose purpose in building was to get as far as possible from the public. Times changed, of course, and after World War II, it became fashionable among the scions of the very rich to give land back to the people. Had the land originally been distributed more democratically, it would today be chopped up into postage stamps and be treeless, private, and unavailable. So capitalism, which has not always had at heart the best interests of the less privileged, has in this case, like the socialist ideal, worked gloriously to their advantage—and to everyone's.

My walk south from Hyde Park ended for the day at the town of Garrison, where for half an hour I sat on a grassy embankment above the railway tracks, staring across the river at the great windowed coffin that is the West Point Military Academy. I was to meet George at the railway station there, and when he came along at about 7:00 P.M. and I asked if he wanted to walk down to the boating docks to get a better look at the military school, he let me know indisputably that he had no more interest in West Point than he had had in the estate of Frederick Vanderbilt. Or in another Hyde Park institution, the American Culinary Institute, a vast brick fortress run by General Foods and surrounded by parking for a thousand cars. I had walked past the place, and told George about it because I had read it was the world's biggest boot camp for chefs and that it incorporated training restaurants in which customers willing to take a flyer on the soups and sauces of rookie cooks could eat at cut-rate prices. Farther south in Poughkeepsie, however, where I stopped for coffee at a Dunkin Donuts, a woman told me her daughter worked there and that it was also a research facility, devoted to longer shelf life, more genuine artificial flavours, more natural unnatural textures, and so on.

In large part, I understood George's disenchantment with the greed and relentlessness of North American industry and with the politics of the U.S. military. And yet the history of the area and its buildings fascinated me, particularly a place such as West Point, built in the early 1800s close to where George Washington had kept his headquarters on the Hudson during the Revolutionary War. As I tramped along Highway 9 the following day, I passed a sign marking the place where the Continental troops had strung a chain from one side of the river to the other, just beneath the surface, to prevent British ships from sailing north into the area where Washington had his encampment. When I read this, I walked to a clearing where I could better see the river and stood gazing across to the far shore, attempting to imagine what kind of an engineering feat it must have been to suspend perhaps fifty tons of thick iron chain across a kilometre and a half of water, anchoring it in such a way that it would be positioned to catch a ship's keel or rudder whether at high or low tide. At the same time I found myself speculating on what had happened to the original inhabitants of the territory as the British and Continental troops fought it out over possession of the land. Had they been chased into the Catskills or Berkshires? Worse? As the French historian de Tocqueville reported during his investigation of America at about that time, "I saw the Natives, and they were begging."

Undoubtedly the most personal feature of my walk along this stretch was my stop on the morning of the twenty-seventh at the city of Peekskill, where the Hudson takes a tortuous loop before emptying into its broad lower basin. As a child, I had held Peekskill in reverential regard as the home of my mother's beloved cousin, Bessie, whom my mother visited on occasion and whom she spoke about often and with great affection. I met Bessie just once, when she visited us in Deep River, in northeastern Ontario, in perhaps 1957. She was suave and motherly and, because she lived in New York with her mysterious husband, Bert Utter, had about her a kind of moxie and glamour that in my child's mind was a function of skyscrapers and art galleries and show business.

Bessie was a hero, moreover, because when my mother visited her in Peekskill in, I think, 1959, she helped locate for me a pair of much

desired red chino pants of a sort popular with the New York hipsters
of that era.

Because my mother spoke of Peekskill and New York City more or
less interchangeably, my image of the former was understandably one
of tall buildings and great department stores. Even though I eventually knew better, I was perhaps vulnerable to letdown, and on walking
into Peekskill that morning, I experienced not so much a sense of
disappointment as a kind of echo of lost innocence in that the place
is a banal agglomeration of undistinguished architecture, the outskirts
of which are the usual assortment of warehouses, fast-food joints,
and malls.

Downriver at Ossining, I took an unscheduled stroll along the east
side of the vile old leviathan that is Sing Sing Prison. "The big house,"
as it has always been called, is an immense, dispiriting place that
extends right out into the Hudson on a vast concrete-and-stone jetty
designed to make escapes more difficult when the place was built
nearly two hundred years ago. In those days, the prisoners were transported upriver by boat from New York City—hence the famous phrase
to be "sent up the river." The prison's practices were, well into the
mid-twentieth century, particularly brutal and inhuman, because its
inmates, having operated in New York, were assumed, themselves, to
be brutal and inhuman. Whatever they were, I felt about them a
morbid curiosity, the thousands who had sizzled in the institution's
electric chair (apparently invented by Edison specifically for Sing
Sing), or been subjected to vicious punishments, such as being hand-
cuffed awkwardly to a cell wall or having their heads held under water
or being put in lightless solitary confinement.

One of the things that fascinated me most about Sing Sing was that
across the street from its bleak east wall, behind a dusty chain-link
fence, a colony of decrepit mobile homes had grown up, each with a
little television aerial or satellite dish, on ground that supported no
trees, no gardens, no grass. A few children's toys were strewn across the
gravel amid rusted cars, although nobody was out in the heat.

A weary-looking young black woman came along carrying a grocery bag.

"Excuse me," I said to her. "Do you know these streets?"

"Why?"

"I was wondering about this little settlement."

Without stopping or even looking at me, she said, "It's where people stay if they wanta be close to someone on the inside."

I stopped on the pavement and stared in at the frightful little shantytown—a kind of unofficial sub-prison for those who could not, or believed they could not, do without husbands or boyfriends or fathers, or believed those on the other side of the wall could not do without them.

The prison is advertised by the town as something of a heritage attraction—in fact, it appears front and centre on Ossining's promotional brochure. But clearly the guards haven't got the message, because when I stopped to examine one of the corner guard towers, a voice boomed out of a loudspeaker telling me to keep moving *now* because "this isn't a tourist attraction."

For a better view over the parapets, I walked uphill to where the local fire station looks out over the interior of the prison and across the Hudson beyond. For a few minutes, I sat there beside a gentle, hairless old man, and we talked about the prison, whose name, he said, is derived from the Sing Sing Indian tribe, which once inhabited the area. He had grown up in Ossining and said that in the old days, whenever there was an execution in the prison, the electric chair drew so much current that the lights would flicker in the nearby houses, which then and now stand right next to the prison gates. "From up here," he said, "you'd hear the prisoners rattling their bars when the condemned guy was about to get the juice, and then you'd get that flickering of the lights, and a while later you'd see a hearse or a truck pull up to the big door over there on the south side."

GEORGE AND I RENDEZVOUSED late in the afternoon at Kykuit, the
aforementioned Rockefeller estate at Sleepy Hollow. By coincidence,
in nearby Tarrytown, we met a striking bottle-blond nurse, Linda
Sarkitz, who was sitting on a bar stool at the Hudson River Inn, a kilometre or so north of the mighty Tappan Zee Bridge, which we could
see melting into the haze to the south. When we mentioned Kykuit to
her, she was quick to inform us, *mirabile dictu,* that for a decade or
more during the 1980s and '90s she had lived at the place, where her
ex-husband was the head groundskeeper, a job that carried with it a
small cottage on the premises. To this day, she told us, John D.'s
mansion is the home of his grandson Gerald, a man Linda characterized in such unflattering, penny-pinching terms that to record them
would risk a libel action. He was a man, she said, who demanded sixty
hours' labour a week from her ex, in exchange for sub-living wages
plus the cottage and the privilege of proximity to the wealthy. *Plus ça
change …*

The temperature was a dewy 101°F, and we had gone into the bar
primarily because we were hot and dehydrated. But George also
wanted to ask the locals about the identity of a square kilometre or so
of old concrete, a monumentally impressive slab, covered with trun-
cated pillars, stretching along the riverbank just north of the bar. The
ruin as a whole looked like one of those immaculately drafted Salvador
Dali wastelands—clearly, a spectacular industrial edifice had once
stood on the site. No sooner had we mentioned it in the inn than
Linda rallied the bartender, who scurried like a tour guide host to find
a book commemorating the historic General Motors automotive plant
that had stood next door for half a century. The book showed photos
of the factory at a time when it was turning out hundreds of sedans
a day, and Tarrytown was a player in the industry of the valley, not a
mere bedroom community for the affluent career slaves of New York
City. The plant, Linda said, was shut down during the 1980s because
it was putting so much gunk into the air and into the Hudson that
even those officials who had all along ignored or defended its depre-

dations grew alarmed and, despite the loss of thousands of jobs, were obliged to tell GM to take a hike. "They were the worst polluter on the Hudson," said an elderly man who, like Linda's father, had worked at the plant.

I told them I'd seen a lot of dead fish upriver, and the old man said, "Around here, we didn't have *any* fish for twenty years. And it'll be a long time before you can eat the ones we have now. Friend of mine once saw a gull fall right out of the air, dead, above the plant."

Linda scoffed at such stories, calling them "a dime a dozen," and we discussed how ironic it was that the Rockefellers, who had founded Standard Oil, had in Kykuit left two hundred acres of magnificent parkland to the public, after years of intrinsic collusion with an industry that had left *hundreds* of acres around Kykuit either dead under concrete or dead under toxic contamination. "Even at Kykuit," Linda said, "they put so much weed-killer on the lawns that the place'll be as contaminated as the car plant some day."

At one point, the bearded bartender leaned across to George and me and said, "Fifty years from now, Korean tourists will be coming up this river in a sightseeing boat, and some threadbare American guide, working for tips, will be telling them, 'Here is where they made their cars in the days when the U.S. was great.'"

What surprised me more than his comment was that it went unchallenged, even by the other Americans within earshot.

The bartender was an ex-marine, a combat vet, who was scornful of the attitude that the United States was hypocritical in entering Afghanistan when it hadn't gone into any of dozens of other countries whose governments were as bad or worse. "What do people expect?" he said. "Of *course* we go where our interests are greatest!" He believed the American military should be in Afghanistan, but voiced the view that even if it wanted to and had the moral foundation, the United States no longer had the "knock-out power" or the "international intelligence" to be a proper policeman to the world or to take on what he called "real opponents." He said, "I did ten months in Vietnam, and short of dropping the Big One, we threw everything we had at them, and it wasn't enough."

The Big One itself entered the conversation, and George pointed out that for all the President's talk about other countries posing a nuclear threat, the U.S. was still the only country ever to have used atomic weapons. "And it'll probably be the first to use them again," intoned the bartender.

During a lull, I asked if anybody knew what the name *Tappan Zee* meant and got quick consensus on *Zee*, which is the Dutch word for "sea." While the Tappan Zee Bridge is of relatively recent vintage, the local river basin has been known for several hundred years by the Tappan Zee name.

Linda, who had put back four or five glasses of white wine and was getting quite animated, took the opportunity to hold forth on the historic presence of the Dutch in the area, going back to Henry Hudson, who in 1609 had been an agent not of the English, his countrymen, who had more or less blackballed him as an explorer, but of the Dutch East India Company, and had thereby claimed the territory for the Netherlands. Which is the reason, of course, that Dutch names pepper the map as far north as Albany, beginning with Harlem and the Bronx (New York City was once New Amsterdam), and moving up through Peekskill, Fishkill, Plattekil, Catskill—on up to Rotterdam and present-day Amsterdam, west of Albany.

As GEORGE AND I LEFT the Hudson River Inn, I decided that, despite the heat, I would take ninety minutes and walk down to Dobbs Ferry where we would be leaving the car at Stu Hackel's the next day.

By the time George met me there at dusk, a thunderstorm was blowing in across the river, and in no time we were driving through rain as blinding as a car wash. We had spent the previous night cramped in the van at a roadside clearing north of Peekskill. But tonight we needed beds, as well as space, in which we could sort our belongings and pare down drastically for the trip into Manhattan. The trick would be to find a motel in rain that was now coming down so hard it was sitting four or five centimetres deep in the streets.

Linda had suggested a motel in Elmsford, a few kilometres north-east of Dobbs Ferry. And after waiting briefly in a parking lot for the rain to let up, that is where we went, still barely able to see the road signs or the tail-lights of the car ahead.

The place, as it turned out, was an old brick two-decker, shadowy and whorish, built on facing sides of what was perhaps a fifty-car parking lot. But it had a few vacancies and, at U.S. $100 a night, was as reasonable as anything else we were going to get this close to New York City.

The receptionists, two bulky young Asian men, sat as joyless as hemorrhoids behind bullet-proof glass and did their business with me across a stainless-steel tray with little sliding doors. Rooms were rented by the night or by the hour, and a sign over the check-in window said, "Minimum Stay Two Hours." However, judging by the comings and goings through the wee hours, few guests stayed longer than the ninety minutes or so it took them to wheeze through the positions, smoke the cigarette, and hit the can prior to their muddled reunion with the world beyond the air conditioner.

In the room, George lay on the bed, looking out through the bars on the window, and said quite cheerfully, "If you think this is bad, wait till tomorrow," and he reiterated his belief that I should just skip the last miles through the Bronx and Harlem, and take the train into Manhattan.

He was, I admit, not the only one who had advised me to alter my plans. Linda, for example, had suggested I cross the river into New Jersey and go in via the Washington Bridge. The bartender told me that while the city was three times safer than it had been in the sixties and seventies, he still didn't drive through parts of the Bronx and Harlem. "Carry a machete," he said, laughing.

My own point of view, I had told them, was that I'd walked through lightning storms, snowstorms, and a heavy bout of bronchial flu, past bears, pit bulls, and veering transports; had done 2,100 kilometres more or less on faith and a sense of adventure; and that at this stage it was of minor consequence to walk through a few derelict neighbour- hoods where no one had anything against me. Certainly, I had no intention of finishing my walk in the relative comfort of a train car.

"I respect your attitude," the bartender had told me.

It was true, too, of course, that more than ever I was now addicted to what I was doing—both to the bodily exhilaration and to the rawness of the daily experience.

Meanwhile the rain poured down, and at about 11:00 P.M., George went out, as he said, "for a walk"—which was generally his euphemism for searching out a bar where he could relax and have a beer.

I had walked forty-four kilometres that day and, now in George's absence, took my shoes off and began cleaning up my feet. By this point, I was missing four toenails, and from my descent out of the Catskills had blisters on the tops of each toe. I took out my nail scis- sors and a tiny retractable knife that hung on my key chain and began paring at the old calluses and skin that had been torn raggedy and, if not treated, would by tomorrow begin bunching uncomfortably in my sock. As always, I felt reassured that the skin underneath was bright and clean and unbroken. My shoes had absorbed their weight in mois- ture during the heat of the day and smelled like a tire fire. I pulled out the padded insoles, scrubbed them with motel soap, and when they were rinsed, propped them in the draft of the air conditioner. I washed several pairs of socks and began carefully to sort what I would need in Manhattan, including a white Columbia-brand T-shirt that I had carried unopened in its plastic packaging so as to better present myself upon arrival at the Warwick Hotel. And my notebook. And extra socks. And flip-flops. And a pair of blue jeans. George would carry it all in the little lumbar pack that, as yet, I had not found a consistent use for.

Physically, I was a skeleton. For a couple of glorious weeks in central Ontario, I had hit what for my age, I suspect, was peak condition. But gradually the heat had gotten to me, the cumulative exhaustion and dehydration. And the sun—I had had too much of it. The itchy little lines of scabs on my nose and ears had not responded to Penaten cream, the only skin medication I had. What's more, one of my calves was, even now, cramping unmercifully, as it tended to do on days when I had lost more moisture than I had been able to replace.

GEORGE RETURNED to the motel at about 1:00 A.M. and made a last attempt to dissuade me from walking the rest of the way. "Look," I said glibly, "if I'm destined to croak tomorrow, it'll make a good ending to the story. But you'll have to write it. In the meantime, there's no argument. I'm walking. From here. From Dobbs Ferry."

I went into the bathroom, took out a razor, and soaped my face. As I finished shaving, George called sonorously, "Charlie, I have something to tell you!"

I did not like the tone of his voice, and for a second stood motionless, the razor cocked inches from my chin. What could it be? That he had decided not to go into New York? That he had talked to those at home and had some catastrophic news?

As I emerged from the bathroom, he looked at me wearily and said, "I just wanted you to know that this trip has saved my life."

My heart did a kind of stutter step, and after a relieved pause I told him that it was great to hear him say such a thing. If it was true, and I had no doubt he meant it, it created a kind of ultimate rationale for what we had done. That my own life had been more or less redeemed by the endeavour was something I had not yet fully considered. But I was beginning slowly to realize that it had.

George and I talked in the darkness, against the sound of traffic whizzing along the main road. He said that more than anything it was the gift of time and distance that he had valued, and that had ultimately been so restorative. He said he believed our pace had "taken the fury out of things." We speculated on what it would mean to return to the rhythms we had left behind. Would there be lingering benefits, or did the benefits of such an endeavour reside largely in the doing? "At least," I said, "we'll know what the benefits are," and I mentioned the novelist Jim Harrison's notion that to get out there on the road in middle age restores the lost possibility for surprise.

There was a longish pause before George, unable to let the thought go, said, "I think you're in for a surprise tomorrow."

I slept fitfully, and awoke at about 4:00 A.M., thinking about my children and about the remoteness of this seedy Westchester motel. It occurred to me rather poignantly that the fact I had made it to New York was of no real interest to anyone other than myself—and that that in itself was perhaps a lesson worth walking for.

I awoke again at about 7:30, battling low-level anxiety that I knew would not disappear until I was out on the streets. For breakfast, I had to content myself with a take-out coffee and three or four custardy pastries bought at a bakery in Elmsford.

At about 9:00, George and I drove over to Dobbs Ferry to Stu and Sue Hackel's place, a comfortable old house on a verdant street, perhaps a kilometre from the Hudson.

"You realize," said Stu as we sat drinking coffee in his backyard, "that very few New Yorkers would do what you're going to do today."

But Stu is a writer, with a sense of story and curiosity, and was quickly into the spirit of things, with a map out, helping me finesse my route.

In the meantime, George had softened and was into the deliberation over routes and rendezvous spots. He and I agreed finally to meet at 3:00 P.M. where the Broadway Bridge crosses the Harlem River, linking the south Bronx to the north end of Manhattan. From there, George would walk the last twenty kilometres with me. For the most part, I would stick to Highway 9/Broadway Avenue, except for the first eight or ten kilometres.

Together, George and I walked down to the Hudson, whose widest point is here at Dobbs Ferry. George was carrying his knapsack, and before we parted, I gave him the belt-style lumbar pack that contained

all I was taking, including a crumpled scribbler that held every note
I had made since Sault Ste. Marie. As always, the commuter trains
were screaming by, and the smell of the salt water wafted up across
the tracks.

On the high bank above the train platform, within sight of the river,
we shook hands and wished one another well. "See ya in Manhattan,"
I said, and turned and walked south into Hastings and Yonkers at
my usual pace of about 110 metres a minute.

11

Manhattan at Last

I had not walked far when I experienced a sense of familiarity, of having come full circle, inasmuch as the dark rock palisades along the far bank of the Hudson bear an uncanny likeness to the diabase cliffs north of Lake Superior.

Several kilometres south into Yonkers, on Warburton Avenue and within sight of the river, I passed the big bronze statue of Henry Hudson that stands in a treed park on the grounds of the Hudson River Museum. I had no argument with the sculpture itself or its subject. However, the inscription was a slavering anthem to Hudson's having "discovered" the river, the gist being that the darker-skinned occupants of its shores had for seventy or eighty generations travelled it, traded on it, fished it, drunk it, bathed in it, celebrated it—all somehow *without* actually discovering it. I do not like to hear myself going on about such things—and I recognize that I am at best token-istic in my Native advocacy. But it is all so obvious, and there are so many small chapters in the grand lie that could be rewritten with the equivalent of a few strokes of the pen. And yet those in a position to pick up the pen don't do it. In New York City alone, the tacit devalua-tion of Native culture and history is glaring—as evidenced, say, in the

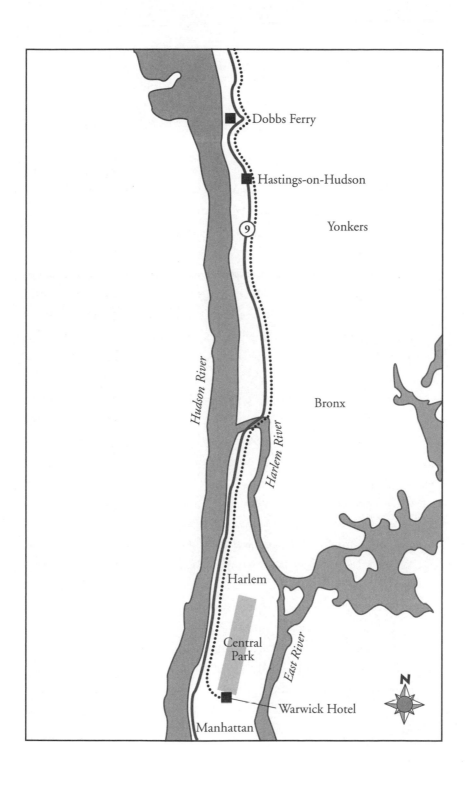

Dobbs Ferry

Hastings-on-Hudson

Yonkers

⑨

Hudson River

Harlem River

Bronx

Harlem

Central
Park

East River

Warwick Hotel

Manhattan

N

towering statue of Christopher Columbus at Broadway and Central Park West, with its attendant homilies to Columbus's "discovery" of America. Or in the Smithsonian-run Museum of the American Indian, which is located in, of all places, the Financial District of Lower Manhattan—in the old New York Customs House, no less, as if some malevolent decision-maker had placed it there for maximum irony. (I will say for the museum that when I visited it a few days later, it had on display a terrific collection of photos depicting the history of Canadian Mohawks as steel riggers in Manhattan.)

The northwest corner of Yonkers is an array of gracious and graciously derelict frame houses spread out along the river and train tracks. But the farther I walked south, the rougher it got until Warburton Avenue became, for a stretch, an unreconstructed ghetto of run-down apartment houses, of stores and businesses with heavily barred windows, and of dusty vacant lots strewn with bottles, old bricks, scraps of wrecked buildings, and cars. On one dissolute block, a hundred metres of chain-link fence had been flattened out onto the sidewalk. Behind it, a gang of nine- or ten-year-old boys was attempting to fan a smouldering mattress into a bonfire with the help of what appeared to be fragments of an old sofa. "Got any gas?" One of them shouted at me.

"You guys be careful!" I called back, secretly flattered that this kid from the 'hood had bothered even to notice me or to think of me as someone who might abet what was clearly bad action.

Occasional knots of young people made innocuous comments as I passed. The teenaged boys were for the most part dressed in absurdly loose pants, the crotches of which hung, in some cases, below their knees—this in contrast to the girls, whose pants, almost without exception, were absurdly tight, worn with lacy little bras or tube tops. The simple truth was that nobody I met seemed to want any more of me than I wanted of them. I spoke to anyone who made eye contact, and almost always they returned my greetings with offhand courtesy and curiosity.

By 11:00 A.M., the heat was intense, but I felt buoyant. My sense of inner well-being had become so pervasive during the past few weeks that when the thought surfaced somewhere south of Hastings that this was the last true day of my walk, it came freighted with urgency, with wanting to hold on. And as I tramped south through Yonkers, I resolved, more than ever, to make the most of the hours—to try to be a part of everything and everyone I encountered. The endorphins were running high, and however irrationally, I felt a quiet sense of invulnerability, as if juiced and protected by my innocence and goodwill. It could crash, and I knew it, which in a sense made it all the sweeter.

Pretty much everything from Dobbs Ferry south is solid city—not suburbs, city. The Hudson has, over the millennia, cut a fairly deep valley, the high banks of which run right down into New York, sometimes as far as a kilometre inland from the river. At a point in the centre of Yonkers, I walked east up the steep slope of Ashburton Avenue to Broadway, which, unlike dreary Warburton, was teeming with people, mostly Hispanics and African-Americans, a few whites and Chinese, and as always in this corner of the continent, a sprinkling of beggars and drunks.

I had already stopped twice to buy Gatorade, but was still parched, and stopped now at a McDonald's and guzzled a litre-sized orange juice. To use the washroom, I had to summon the security guard, who arrived packing not just the biffy key but a loaded pistol with enough fire power to blow the Hamburglar into New Jersey.

A few blocks farther south, I stopped to admire the window of an Oriental seafood store, and was drawn inside, where a couple of solemn young women were breaking up crab legs and moulding the shredded meat into golf-ball-sized spheres. These they dipped in batter and tossed into boiling oil. At thirty cents per, I indulged and bought ten, doused them in ginger sauce, and continued down Broadway gluttonously pleased with my purchase.

Where Broadway forked, I temporarily lost my bearings and asked a young Hasidic Jew for directions. "Way is it ya wanna get to?" he said in a Yonkers accent far thicker than I had anticipated from one so formally dressed and (undoubtedly) schooled. I told him I wanted to follow Broadway into Manhattan, and he said, "Whatza matta with the train?"

Stu had referred to Yonkers as "the town time forgot," and sure enough it seemed locked in another decade with its endless small storefronts, its absence of franchises, its narrow streets, and walk-up apartment blocks.

While I knew well by now that the meaning of what I was doing lay more in the steps than in the destination, destinations, too, define the arc and sensibility of a journey. Pilgrims have understood this for centuries; arrival counts. And I understood it intuitively as I crossed 262nd Street, settled in alongside Van Cortlandt Park, and experienced a deep, child-like satisfaction at having reached the Bronx and being at last in New York City.

As any child might, I wanted to tell somebody, to share my pleasure, to let them know I had made it. Or simply to call it out to the hundreds of people on the street. But always the observer, the recorder, I settled for compressing the thrill into private fuel and, with a revitalized step, pressed on toward Manhattan.

It perhaps goes without saying that the Bronx these days is pretty much solidly Hispanic and African-American, one of the relatively few exceptions being a scattering of elderly Jews, holdovers from the days when the Jews owned the territory, when there were more of them in the Bronx than in the entire state of Israel. I spent time in Israel during the early 1970s and met lots of old New Yorkers, many of whom had emigrated from the Bronx to Tel Aviv or Jerusalem during the 1950s and '60s. So I felt a kinship with them, and when I heard a couple of swarthy old men speaking Yiddish, I stopped for a minute to talk. One told me he had been to Israel twice, but otherwise had lived in the same Bronx apartment for fifty-one years. "Esther!" he said to his wife, who was standing ten or twelve metres away kibitzing with a friend, "thiz guy walked down from Kyanada." She limped over, looked at me through thick glasses, and said, "I yewsta walk all the way to Riv-a-dale Pok and back. But that was fordy-sum yeaz ago."

Just south of Van Cortlandt Park, the elevated railway cuts in atop Broadway, enclosing it in a shadowy gridwork, a kind of cage, that runs overhead for miles down into Harlem. Abruptly the openness of the park and its surroundings gives way to a kind of barrio of dense older housing, grocery stores, fruit stands, video and porn shops, grubby little bottle shops and delis, all interspersed with mysterious recesses and doorways, where in the heat of the day men and women sat in semi-darkness, some cooled by electric fans, apparently selling palmistry or tarot readings, or perhaps drugs or nothing. The streets, even this far north, are so congested with traffic that at the inter-sections it would have been easier and perhaps safer simply to climb onto the cars and use their roofs and hoods as stepping stones than to pick my way precariously through the bumpers, fenders, and horns. It is a part of the city where there are no trees or grass—just thousands of people, half of them kids and teenagers who, perhaps because the school year had just ended, had been galvanized into a Saturday cele-bration, high summer festivity. The barrage of voices, music, and traffic sounds was interrupted from time to time by volleys of rogue firecrackers, seeming to come from the railway overhead or the alleys or even rooftops. Up the side streets, fully dressed kids—some of the youngest fully naked—were running in and out of the spray from open fire hydrants.

Amid the crowd, in the heat, I felt like a slippery little fish swim-ming happily downstream, unnoticed, unimpeded, purposeful, both absorbing and reflecting the light around me. If there were sharks in the water, as predicted, I was unaware of them—or perhaps I saw them merely as other sunfish like myself. My only need, it seemed, was to keep walking and keep my eyes and ears open. And to keep drinking. As I got farther into the Bronx, I was stopping every twenty blocks or so to buy fruit juice or bottled water—the latter a reminder, in the clouds of exhaust, that one day we may well be sold bottled air, and will recall nostalgically the days when we could breathe through our noses for free.

Even on this intensely busy and overbuilt stretch of Broadway, nature does not shy away from cameo appearances. At one point, a grey squirrel squirted along the sidewalk within a metre of my feet, and a flock of healthy-looking sparrows alighted briefly around a hydrant. At the corner of 238th Street, a yellow butterfly came fluttering along above the traffic. Pigeons live in the grillwork of the elevated railway, and presumably at least a modest population of rats lives somewhere among the garbage piles and the detritus of the alleyways and basements. Beyond these, I was surprised regularly by extraordinary little rock outcrops, like visitors from another age, some of them two or three metres high, cut to accommodate the sidewalk or some barren parkette or bus shelter.

I counted off the blocks, 250th, 240th, 235th, and came at last to the old Broadway Bridge at the Harlem River, where I was to meet George. But during a tour of the sidewalks and boulevards—in and out among the stanchions and stairways of the overhead "subway" lines—I was unable to locate him. Impatient for a better look at this last of hundreds of rivers intersecting my path, I walked onto the bridge and stood staring into a dirty spur of industrial water, the banks of which have been reinforced with steel piles and concrete or have merged with the brickwork of old factories and disintegrating docks from the days when the Harlem River clearly meant more to north Manhattan and the south Bronx than it means today.

Beneath my elation at being where I was, I felt a contented exhaustion, and after a minute, I turned, walked back, and sat on a patch of clay, leaning against a light pole in front of a massive housing complex, without another Caucasian in sight. I had told George to give me five hours to reach the river, and pretty much to the minute, at three o'clock, he sloped off the bridge, having walked over from Marble Heights, where he had gotten off the train.

"You made it," he said smiling.

"*We* made it," I said. But rather than indulge in self-congratulation, we walked back out onto the bridge and marched briskly on south into Manhattan.

"Have you got my stuff?" I said nonchalantly when we had gone perhaps a block. He still had it, but gave me a moment's pause in describing how he had come close to leaving it on the floor of what he called "an Irish bar" in Dobbs Ferry, where he had gone for a draught or two before boarding the train.

Whereas the streets of the Bronx had been festive, Harlem was a flat-out party, an impromptu rave that had drawn throngs of Hispanics into the streets, old and young, sweating and laughing, scolding and razzing one another, milling around the food and fruit stalls, or the squawk boxes, parading muscles and flesh and clothes, as rap music boomed down the blocks, the volume swelling and receding, mixed with car horns, squealing tires, and the screams of children. As in the Bronx, there were open fire hydrants and an ongoing rattle of fireworks—and a sense that, even here, perhaps *especially* here, in what was once one of the most despairing and violent ghettoes in America, life was possible, life was livable, or dare it be said, life was good. While none of it had anything directly to do with George and me, the effect on us was that of an exuberant welcome to the city.

It was not until we had come down as far as 115th Street that for a little variety and shade we cut west over to the Hudson and continued south along the boundary of Riverside Park.

"Ya know," said George as we sat sprawled on a bench beneath giant hardwoods opposite Riverside Church, "if bin Laden had taken the walk we just took before he brought down the towers, I can't help thinking he would have had a different perspective on America."

The convoluted equation connecting contemporary Harlem to New York's Financial District (what *we* had seen, as opposed to what bin Laden saw from the remote mountains of Afghanistan) seemed best understood as a residual of the power and wealth that 250 years ago brought slaves to America—people whose social (if not literal) descendants now lived fifteen kilometres north of the Wall Street heirs of that early nexus of power.

Not wanting to gloat, but nonetheless wanting to make the point, I told George that at no time during the day had I experienced even the faintest hint of threat or intimidation.

"Things have changed," he said curtly, explaining that in 1970 the safety of a white guy walking through Harlem wouldn't have been "worth stink." In the days to come, George would attribute the change to what he perceived as a draining of anger and embitterment out of the black community—an evolving sense of self-worth and confidence, the roots of which lay in the riots and violence that during the early seventies had driven him out of New York. The corroborative evidence was all there—fewer murders and violent crimes, cleaner subways and streets, fewer drugs, better law enforcement. Half a dozen times over the next few days we would hear how the recently retired mayor, Rudolph Giuliani, a tough former federal prosecutor, had brought a new sense of order to the city. "The thing is," George said to me a few nights later as we walked in the Bronx, "he couldn't have done it in the sixties. There wasn't the money. It was all going into Vietnam. ... Think of it: they closed down the West Side Highway rather than repair it! You couldn't drive on it for potholes and crumbling concrete. It wasn't until the late seventies, early eighties, that Washington came to the rescue and bailed the city out."

What generally went unsaid was that the resurgence of the city—its late-twentieth-century prosperity and allure (and perhaps its brightness as a target for terrorism)—had been catalyzed by the regeneration of Lower Manhattan, which had itself been catalyzed by the building of the very towers whose destruction had again brought the city to its fiscal knees.

In the overwhelming heat, George was by now desperate for a beer. As always at this time of day, having walked perhaps forty-five kilometres, I was gutted and wanted nothing so much as a base, a bed, a bathtub, a little privacy. As a result, I couldn't stand the thought of sitting in a bar, even for fifteen minutes, and persuaded George that we should try to get to the hotel before it got too late. "Why don't you just buy some beer," I said, "and bring it to the hotel in your pack?"

Mercifully, a refreshing west breeze was slipping up off the Hudson as we walked down Upper Broadway in the twilight, past buskers and movie houses, designer clothing and lingerie stores, gourmet food shops, and restaurants. The cars screaming past us had been mysteriously transformed from the rusted Pontiacs of Harlem to pristine Audis and Mercedes—and, of course, into a tidal flow of taxis surging up and down Broadway for as far as you could see. What had been an exclusively dark-skinned crowd was now largely white and well-dressed and included, I thought, an inordinate number of sultry and solemn young women in sleeveless black dresses, black shoes, black eyeshadow, holding black clutch bags and, apparently, black outlooks (axe murderesses in training?), accompanied by equally funereal young men in summer-weight crow-coloured suits.

At Columbus Circle we turned east along the south boundary of Central Park, where in the shadows of the grand old hotels—the Park Lane, the Essex House, the Regency—men wearing greasy T-shirts and carrying plastic bags of their belongings were already staking out their benches for the night. As we would learn from a musician who had spent a year camped in Central Park, the competition for spots is fierce, and a homeless person who has over a period of weeks laid claim to a bench or nook will (with the help of compatriots who know the residency code) beat up or even stab—or, in extreme cases, murder—anyone who attempts to take it away from him.

At the top of Sixth Avenue, I did what I had been planning to do for weeks, walked back into the shadows of Central Park with the Columbia T-shirt that I had carried unopened from Thunder Bay and unfolded it, surprised to discover that it was long-sleeved. But the evening had cooled to the point where I could wear it comfortably—and feeling a little more presentable in fresh white, I emerged onto

Central Park South, from where George and I walked down Sixth to the corner of Fifty-fourth Street and the Warwick Hotel.

While the Warwick is not as prominent as the office towers to the south—or the biggest of the new hotels—it is nonetheless a gracious old skyscraper, thirty-five storeys high and shaped by the sort of setbacks, balconies, and stonework that have pretty much been abandoned in contemporary hotel design. At the front doors, I advised George that he should probably hang back a little while I got us checked in. He looked at me puzzled, and I admitted sheepishly that I had never told the hotel I was bringing anyone with me. "If you have to sleep in the park," I said, "I'll sleep there with you."

At the desk, I was greeted by a young Oriental woman, and I began to explain who I was. But before I could finish even a sentence, she smiled broadly and said, "I know who you are. Ray told us to expect you." She thrust out her hand and said, "We're really pleased that you're staying at the Warwick. Congratulations on your walk."

In all, the welcome was as warm and gratifying as any we had received—and George too was immediately an esteemed guest of the hotel.

Two young men, clearly prepped for the occasion, pressed in on the desk with a volley of questions about distance and pace and time on the road. One of them eventually showed us to our accommodation on the fifth floor, mentioning casually as we approached the door that Elvis had used the suite during his earliest visits to New York.

"Elvis Presley?" I said, recognizing immediately the stupidity of my inquiry.

"Yes, that Elvis," he smiled.

Except for a brief stay in the Drake in Chicago, the Elvis suite was by a considerable margin the most sumptuous hotel quarters I had ever occupied. After weeks in a threadbare tent or in the back of a van, it seemed an all but unaccountable luxury. For several minutes after we arrived, George wandered around in it, shaking his head, repeating, "I dunno. I just dunno." The suite's undiscounted price, I could not help noticing on the door, was a zippy U.S. $650 a night, about a thousand Canadian. There was a vestibule, a dining room, a living room; a bedroom with an armoire, dressers, and television; and of course, a pair of king-sized beds. And half a dozen deep-set windows. And twelve-foot ceilings. And floor-to-ceiling drapes with tassled valances that looked as if they had been stolen out of a rococo funeral parlour. And a surfeit of hardwood and upholstered furniture—a total of nineteen places to sit (not including the toilets). A bowl of fresh fruit sat on the French dining table, along with a tray of French bottled water and a box of French chocolate truffles.

The view across Sixth Avenue took in the Midtown Hilton, a big lifeless box of a place, and the Citibank Plaza, where night after night we saw the same willowy prostitute ghosting in and out of the shadows, clothed in a flowing black dress. We eventually grew curious about her and began to speculate on her routines. Then one night as I was headed out for souvlaki at about 2:00 A.M., the elevator door opened, and there she was, smelling of dense floral perfume, older than I had imagined, with a gentle bony face, like anybody's mother or sister, except that her make-up was as thick as drywall, and her eyes were spectral and uncertain. I said hello to her as I got on, she returned the greeting, and we stood there like posts until we emerged into the lobby, and she stepped briskly out the side door of the hotel.

The view east on Fifty-fourth Street included the neon sign of the Ziegfeld Follies—appropriately enough, in that William Randolph Hearst is said to have built the Warwick in 1927 for his girlfriend, the actress Marion Davies, whom he had met during her years as a show-girl at the Follies, and for her friends in show business, some of whom also danced with Ziegfeld. Over the decades, we were told, hundreds of show people and athletes had stayed at the hotel, including Marilyn and DiMaggio and Nureyev. Cary Grant lived for years on the twenty-seventh floor. The Beatles stayed here on their early trips to New York.

Having relaxed for a few minutes, we went out and bought food in an all-night grocery store on Sixth Avenue, and sat in Central Park,

George with a beer, I with my customary restorative of Gatorade. We ate a barbecued chicken down to the ribs and watched the horse carriages load up their fares and clip-clop off along Central Park South before angling up into the park.

"It's a long way from Pancake Bay," George said quietly as we re-entered the hotel suite. But in many ways he adapted to the new digs more quickly and thoroughly than I did, spreading his books and beer cans and clothing—and tobacco and tabloids—across virtually every flat surface in the suite. As for myself, I felt a proprietary pleasure at having delivered our little road show into unaccustomed pampering and luxury. And yet a part of me shared George's skittishness. "Well," I said to him as I dumped myself into a brocaded and well-padded easy chair, "nobody deserves it more than we do." But it didn't sound very convincing. In fact, even as I spoke, I was reminded of Hamlet's famous dictum that if "each man got what he deserved," none of us would escape whipping.

My ambivalence was, of course, not merely about a luxury hotel (which, by anybody's standards, was an unambivalent blessing) or about this most turbulent city at this unsettled time in its history. It was about a developing turmoil within—about the completion of an endeavour that had restored and sustained me, that I had become addicted to, and did not want to end. If it had taken gumption to get started back in the spring blizzards along the north shore of Lake Superior, it was going to take every bit as much to stop.

It was not until later that night, as I lay sleepless, that I felt the full starkness of the fact that the journey, if not the adventure, was over, that I was no longer even a traveller in the old sense, but a tourist in a grand hotel.

It did not take me long to realize that I would have to commit quickly to some sort of psychological methadone program, a way of returning in stages to less obsessive and addictive activity. What it meant in practice, I concluded, was that for as long as I could, I would have to keep walking.

And that is what I did—with as much energy, initially, as I had put into any kilometre of walking since leaving Thunder Bay.

AT PERHAPS ELEVEN the next morning, George and I kicked out along Fifty-fifth Street, where he intended to show me his old workplace, the Kennedy Gallery. But given thirty years of change, it hardly surprised us that it had been erased by skyscrapers, reduced to a figment of George's memory and imagination.

At the public library, on Fifth Avenue at Forty-second Street, we pored over the Berg Collection, a vast archive of manuscripts, letters, and artifacts salvaged from the bric-a-brac and papers of some of the most prominent English-language writers of the past couple of centuries. The library had recently spent $12 million to acquire Jack Kerouac's papers and mementoes—a terrible and poignant irony, I thought, in that barely thirty years ago, Kerouac had died in penury, all but begging for a few dollars from anybody he could persuade to pay him for a magazine article, television appearance, or poem, all increasingly difficult to sell in the accelerated drunkenness and illness that eventually killed him in Florida at the age of forty-six. Nevertheless, it fascinated me to see the invented table games of his childhood, the photos and manuscripts, some of them handwritten, and the thick roll of teletype paper that, legendarily, had become the manuscript of *On the Road*. Among other things, Kerouac's harmonicas, reading glasses, and jackknife were on display in a glass case—the merest flotsam of a life, and yet powerful for me in that during my teenage years, it had been Kerouac more than anyone who had given me an inkling of the romance and satisfactions of writing, the sense that perhaps I, too, could travel and have adventures and tell the stories.

In the reading rooms on the third floor, I did what I suspect all writers do in the New York Public Library, and checked for my own books in the computerized catalogue. I was happy to find three or four of them in the permanent collection and giddy to discover in the circulating collection an unaccountable eighty-one copies of my book *The Circus at the Edge of the Earth*. As well, I found a copy of George's *Finding Mom at Eaton's* in the permanent collection. But when I told him, he refused to believe me. So I led him to one of the dozens of catalogue computers, punched in the coordinates, and brought it up on the screen.

For the next hour or so, he was atop the world and explained to me as we walked down Fifth Avenue that in finding the book there, some shadow, some alienation, had been cleared up. He had, in fact, written parts of the manuscript in those very reading rooms, at a time in his life when his world was disintegrating and it seemed impossible to him that anything he wrote would ever make the grade. And now his work, too, was there among that of the gladiators.

We agreed to meet during the dinner hour at Washington Square down in Greenwich Village, and while George went in search of a celebratory beer, I took a stroll over to Grand Central Station, then farther east to the Chrysler Building, that most memorable and fanciful of skyscrapers, as brilliant and delicate as an icicle above the skyline. As a child it had intrigued me, and still does, that the building's gargoyles, perhaps fifty storeys up, are vastly enlarged replicas of Chrysler hood ornaments from the 1920s.

I had had some surprises during nine weeks of walking, but none of them quite equalled the sensational effect of striding down Fifth Avenue in the hundred-degree heat of the late afternoon and realizing at Madison Square Park not only that the avenue ahead had been cleared of traffic—the barricades and cops were all in place—but that I was about to be joined by a fast-moving parade angling into Fifth Avenue on foot from, I think, Broadway. Within moments a street-wide ambush of women appeared out of the cross-street to my right carrying a twenty-foot banner emblazoned with the words "10th Annual New York City Dyke March."

The result of this unexpected confluence of paths was that I made my first foray into Lower Manhattan in a dozen years accompanied by some five thousand celebrating lesbians, perhaps a quarter of whom were wearing nothing from the waist up. Fortunately, I had been practising, and knew what to do in the presence of five thousand walking women. Basically, to shut up and walk with them.

I located George amid the crowd in Washington Square, where the parade had devolved into a tub-thumping political rally. Together we walked up to Twelfth Street to the Strand Used Book Store, the self-anointed "largest used book store in the world." There, for two hours I was, I suspect, as happy as a human being can be in a crowded, dusty, and hellishly hot labyrinth of books. Blessedly, there were electric fans situated here and there throughout the store—fans that had the curious effect of steering people's literary tastes into areas of the inventory where they stood the best chance of avoiding heat stroke.

MY NOTES, during those first few days in New York City, were a crazy quilt of scribblings on, among other things, the fiery little fruit seller on Central Park West who, when I bought cherries at $2.50 per (midget) bag and was picking them two or three at a time from his bin, screamed at me hysterically that there was to be "No selection, sir, *please!*" Did I think *he* wanted all the rotten ones?

And on the way in which street beggars in Lower and Midtown Manhattan stake out positions near garbage containers in the public plazas and parks so that over the lunch hour they can be first to the bread crusts and french fries when a sated secretary or bank clerk deposits the remains of a lunch.

And on the inveterate walking practices of Manhattanites who are said to take two-thirds of their journeys on foot—as well they might in a city where the cost of monthly parking would fetch a decent two-bedroom apartment in most small cities in North America.

And on the Gay Pride Parade, an outrageous celebration of non-conformity that took place on June 30, forming up in the streets around the Warwick, which for several hours milled with thousands of participants from universities, churches, social service agencies, political constituencies, immigrant societies, health care agencies, athletic teams, affirmative action and support groups, social clubs, arts clubs, dance and theatre companies—and of course, bars and nightclubs and gyms. It was Vassar, Cornell, Yale; was the Riverside Church, the Metropolitan Community Church, and the Brooklyn Belly Dancers Association with its bright orange banner and even brighter orange prayer: "May all people everywhere be happy and free!" To this end, they had become walkers, egalitarians; and irrespective of one's views or orientation, the scene called forth a deeply democratic sense of the validity of all lives, not just those sanctioned by money, politics, or history.

DETERMINED NOT TO SLOW DOWN, I spent most of that afternoon walking the Upper West Side and, in the mid-evening, walked way up into Harlem, attempting, I suppose, to reconstitute a measure of the happiness I had felt coming into the city.

I ate dinner on Malcolm X Avenue, in a big old-style diner, owned and run by enthusiastic Cubans, none of whom spoke a word of English. A couple of muscular NYPD officers, whose arms filled their shirtsleeves like carved logs, occupied one of perhaps thirty Formica tables, arranged in rows around a big horseshoe-shaped counter where I sat eating jerk chicken and saffron rice. The cops bantered in Spanish with the waitresses, until a static-edged voice erupted out of their two-way radio to report a robbery in progress, and the two of them were on their feet and on the run out the door, one shouting back over his shoulder that they'd be back for their food, to keep it hot.

As a random core sample of the state of the police department, it was a far cry from media and movie portrayals of New York cops as indolent cynics more likely than not to turn a deaf ear to a reported robbery so as not to interfere with their meal or socializing or siesta. The heroic image of the Giuliani-era white knights is surpassed these days only by that of the New York City firemen. One of the most prevalent bus shelter ads at the time of my visit was for the NYFD, which had placed big back-lit "Heroes Wanted!" signs all over New York, aimed at filling the vacancies left by the fatalities of 9/11.

I WALKED IN Greenwich Village and Hell's Kitchen, and along the Hudson River docks—and at some point each day, well up into Central Park, "ground as overused," wrote Edward Hoagland, "as the banks of the Ganges." But being a newcomer, I strolled with idle fascination among the wedding parties, nannies, and Rollerbladers; the middle-aged nerds with their remote-controlled boats and biplanes; the sunbathers, whose oiled hides, it seemed, were a kind of bodily coefficient of photovoltaic cells, storing the sun's radiance for the months to come. And the voiceless little enclaves of the homeless.

One of the more rewarding aspects of these weltering halcyon days was George's immense satisfaction at returning to the streets he had, until recently, believed he would not see again. Despite his recent trepidations about the city, he was as happy as I had seen him in years, visiting bars, art galleries, clubs, contacting old friends in the fine-art field.

On July 1, at perhaps nine in the evening, George and I walked way up Second Avenue into the Upper East Side. Everywhere, it seemed, the apartments and low-rises he had known had been torn down and replaced by towers. And as we approached Ninety-second Street, where George, Winnie, and David had had their first decent digs in New York, he expressed a certainty that the old five-storey walk-up would not be there. But amid blocks of reconstruction, as if by some miracle, it was standing. And so were the little corner store, the old trees, and a few of the old bars. We stood outside in the shadows as George reminisced about the neighbourhood, recalling decades-old gossip as if it had sifted through the ceiling cracks that morning. Eventually, a young woman came along, eyed us skeptically, opened the locked door of the building, and went in. And a few seconds later—most intriguingly and satisfyingly for George—the lights came on in his old apartment.

For George, as I have mentioned, the great unanswerable remained the notion that he might, with fortitude, have been able to stick it out in New York. And on this night he was picking up a decidedly pinkish glow in the rear-view mirror. On the other hand, he had spent the previous evening at Broadway and Sixty-first, where he stopped to listen to an aging black street musician, a "disco" violinist. It was not until George had listened for nearly an hour, increasingly impressed by the old man's inventiveness and dexterity, that he approached him and discovered he was the once-renowned jazz performer John Blair, a man who had played with Miles Davis, John Coltrane, and Sonny Rollins—who, by the mid-1980s, however, was keeping house in Central Park and now busked for quarters, accompanying amplified disco tunes, which he told George were "what people wanted to hear."

As fascinated as George was to have met Blair, he was distressed to see an icon of his past brought low. He was convinced, he said, that if he had attempted to stay, he, too, would have ended up "on the street playing for coins."

If he needed confirmation of where his life had arguably been headed, he got it the following night, when we walked up into the second of his old neighbourhoods in the southwest Bronx. We had gone up early, so that we could take in a Yankees game, which I had the temerity to imagine would give us a chance to relax. But it was anything but relaxing. The game was played at such a distance from where we were sitting in the upper deck along the right field foul line that without the help of the giant video screen in centre field or the corroboration of the scoreboard, it was impossible to tell which player was which—or even to see the ball most of the time. So there wasn't a hint of the fabled Zen of watching the subtlety of baseball unfold. What's more, the place was filthy, at least the upper deck, which was unswept and sticky underfoot.

And it was expensive. Before he even got in, George was obliged to check his backpack for five dollars. On a night of nearly a hundred degrees, I twice spent almost six dollars for a container of pop. And

four dollars for a program. And five for a beer for George. And nine
for a pair of mediocre hot dogs. With a modicum of imagination, you
could hear a great clatter of coins funnelling endlessly down through
the innards of the stadium into the Yankee dugout, where the
combined annual payroll is $180 million.

Midway through the seventh inning, before the traditional "stretch,"
the PA announcer asked everyone to rise, to remove their hats, and
observe a silence "for the fallen of September 11 and for those on
foreign soil defending America's freedom." The "silence"—observed by
about half the people around us, while the others chatted away—ended
after four or five seconds when the voice of the late Bessie Smith
erupted out of the loudspeakers at perhaps 130 decibels, singing "God
Bless America." Which had, itself, barely cleared the centre-field fence
when a ripping version of "Take Me Out to the Ballgame" came
pouring out of the same speakers.

I am not typically squeamish about aggressive behaviour on the part
of sports fans, but eventually I grew weary of the half-dozen or so fans
in our section who screamed repeated obscenities, not so much at the
opposing team, the feckless Cleveland Indians, as at the *idea* of an
opposing team, so that their tirade lacked the wit and specificity that
might have begun to redeem it. What beauty there was for me lay in
gazing over the outfield wall to where the setting sun cast an orangey
pink glow on the tenements and towers of the south Bronx—and in
the vast shapely parabola of the stadium.

The Bronx after dark seemed a good deal more sinister than it had on
the afternoon of our arrival, and as we walked up the Grand Concourse
away from the stadium into the shadowy warren of streets and alleys that
was George's old neighbourhood, we were several times startled by cars
shrieking around corners on the edge of control—or by thrown bottles,
or in one case what was clearly a gunshot.

The Bronx, like Harlem, is a prolific gallery of spray-painted graf-
fiti and murals, and after we had visited George's building and were
walking back south, we came to a brick wall onto which a street artist

had air-brushed a five-metre-high likeness of a young Hispanic ballplayer in a Yankees uniform. The surrounding imagery consisted of local buildings, a ball diamond, a giant rose, and perhaps thirty words of script, which I knew from my elementary Spanish was a tribute containing the words *heart*, *God*, and *love*.

As we stood examining this striking piece of folk art, a man of perhaps thirty bounded out of a basement doorway and was instantly beside us. "I saw you from the window," he said in breathlessly inflected English. "You're interested. My name is Hugo. The guy in the picture was my friend. His name was Mon."

Hugo explained to us at galloping speed that Mon, a local hero on the ball field, had been "shot dead—a jealousy thing," that the painting was the neighbourhood's memorial to him, and that despite occasional murders and street fights, the area was gradually being transformed for the better. George told him he had lived up the street thirty years ago, and Hugo described how in the years after George's departure, the neighbourhood had deteriorated into dereliction and violence—and ultimately a series of fires that had left buildings reduced to shells. "It was drugs," he said. "Everybody was dealing. Kids were shooting heroin. They talk about Ground Zero. When I was a kid, *this* was Ground Zero."

According to Hugo, it was a contingent of neighbourhood parents, mostly mothers, who eventually decided that if they and their children were going to survive, the dealers and crack houses had to go. The change of attitude had been a forerunner of better policing, harsher drug sentences, and through city and state funding, the rebuilding of the street.

Behind us on another wall, the same artist who had painted the ballplayer had worked up a kind of *fin du monde* nightmare in which crack cocaine was portrayed as a bloodthirsty blue spectre rising out of a manhole to grab a terrified kid by the ankles. "That's how it was," said Hugo, and he grinned into my face from perhaps a foot away. "Now guys like you can come up here in the middle of the night and not get your throats slit."

THE COMMENT WAS STILL RATTLING around in my skull when, a day later, George and I summoned the will to pay a visit to the other, the official, Ground Zero. Even then, the visit was not so much part of a plan as an inevitable gravitational urge toward the great earthen hole and the tattered and dusty memorials that stretched like Mexican shrines along Church and Vesey Streets. We had come out of the Museum of the American Indian by Battery Park, and as we walked up through the Financial District, I said, "Maybe we should have a look while we're down here." And without further communication we cut over to Church Street and, as one might approach an open grave, stepped gingerly toward the edge of the precipice. Access was restricted, except on Liberty Street, where a long line of tourists, gawkers like ourselves, were inching along, peering through chain link above the hoardings that surrounded the immense subterranean excavation.

My reaction was initially one of astonishment at the magnitude of it all, the volume of space that had been left, below ground and above. But astonishment was quickly supplanted by a dismayed curiosity at what I had heard called "the tourism of terrorism," people firing away with cameras as if at any other tourist attraction, whole families arranging themselves for videos and still shots, mugging and laughing and posing.

I would like to think I had something conclusive or insightful to say about the experience—but in the face of it a kind of suspension sets in, an absence of perspective, and I was left, as I'm sure many are, making lame attempts to imagine the morning itself, to visualize, say, the planes coming in along the Hudson or the parades of escapees streaming through the smoke and debris—was left, in effect, with television images, repeating like video loops or a song heard one too many times.

For me, the most compelling sights were the empty and damaged buildings left standing on the periphery. Several of them had been sheathed like Christo sculptures in sky-high white or black bags, custom-cut to their dimensions, the effect being that of monstrous tombstones. What most captured my attention, though, were the thirty-metre-wide scorch marks on the cladding, where, clearly, heat intense enough to transform steel and glass had erupted onto them, from as much as two hundred metres away. George, who had not wanted to come at all, stood by the hoardings, fascinated, sketching the scene into his notebook.

Our response to it all was to walk for miles along the waterfront, through Battery Park to where we boarded the ferry and rode more or less in silence across the harbour to Staten Island. On the return journey, a sturdy African-American woman of perhaps forty told us that when the first plane hit the tower on the morning of September 11, she had watched from the same ferry we were now riding, and that for the first time in her twenty years of taking that ferry daily to work, it had turned in the middle of Upper New York Bay and churned back to Staten Island.

Another witness, Robert McKeon, the night porter at the Warwick, told me that when the first tower crumbled, he had been on the table in his chiropractor's office on the East Side, and that a mass scream had erupted from the waiting room where people were watching on television. "We all went running outside," he said. "I told them, 'It's still standing! It's there in the smoke! I can see it!' I thought I could still see it in the smoke."

From the ferry terminal, we walked north along the East River and stopped at Pier 17, within sight of a half-dozen moored tall ships, where I sat on a bench and phoned home to tell Matt and the girls I would see them in a week. I was moved by the sound of their voices, and Eden was curious to know if I had "seen 9/11," whether they'd gotten "all the people out yet," and whether I was safe.

As darkness settled and the lights came on, we walked out across the Brooklyn Bridge, which when it was built in 1885 had been the biggest on earth and is still perhaps the most beautiful, with its brick towers, gothic arches, and spirographic cables. One of the beauties of the bridge is that it was made for walkers as much as for vehicles (in its early years, horse carriages), so that to this day a wide upper deck, entirely independent of car traffic, allows people to walk, bike, or Rollerblade freely between Brooklyn and Lower Manhattan.

At about 11:00 P.M., we walked up into Chinatown, where in the extreme heat the garbage piled waist-high in front of every little establishment was getting all the encouragement it needed to stink. On Mott Street, we found the only noodle joint open, a sterile little place clad in Arborite, where the food was excellent but where the middle-aged waiter took a dislike to us and refused to speak either while taking or delivering our order. The *coup de grâce* was his reaching up and switching the house television to one of those reality medical shows featuring, on this night, abdominal surgery with close-ups of scalpel work and intestines.

THE NEXT MORNING, I sat in a coffee shop on Fifty-seventh Street, with my notebook open, attempting to condense a paragraph or two on the meaning of being where I was and of my weeks on the road. But the more I tried, the more frustrated I felt at trying to reduce it to a few paragraphs.

To complicate matters, I had in part lost my taste for explanation, was more aware perhaps than ever that the over-examined life is not worth living either. Which is not to say there were no decipherable lessons—but only that their meaning was not as neat as it might have seemed in the projections of April, when I had not taken a step.

One thing I did know and could articulate about the lessons was that in some part they had been *un*lessons. It is one of my longstanding themes, and I think a reliable one, that inner progress is at times less about accumulating than about letting go and clearing out assumptions. The road had given me a chance to let go—not only of what was comfortable and assumed but of a life that had passed.

Early on the morning of July 3, in heat that by nine o'clock was already oppressive (the radio was reporting a pavement-level temperature of 105°F in Midtown Manhattan), I walked over to Third Avenue to the CBC studios to do an hour-long radio interview with Cathy Alix for a program called *Ontario Today*. I had gotten satisfaction out of my brief Wednesday chats with my friends at CBC in Thunder Bay—which, while intended for a local audience, had in fact been going across Canada (and I would eventually learn as far as Australia) in syndication. But it felt good to do the longer interview, which, in effect, forced me again to attempt to put words to the messages of the trip.

I told Cathy (perhaps risking a pomposity) that I believed endeavours such as mine permitted the imagination to go to work—to "produce" in a world where production is typically measured in economic terms and where imagination and its shrinking coterie of practitioners are increasingly marginalized or ignored.

As for history, it seemed to me a walker was not so much an interpreter of the past as its living residual (if you want to know what your ancestors knew of the world, go out and walk a few hundred kilometres of it). I said that in doing what I had done, I felt I had restored for myself a lost continuity—a union of decades, forests, and street grids—and that I had been both a stimulus for and a beneficiary of that restoration. Which is not so far-fetched a thought. No less a thinker than George Santayana said that we ourselves are the light between the endless constellations we inhabit—said that in connecting realities we invent new ones, as I had invented my days on the road.

THE NEXT DAY was the Fourth of July, and during the afternoon I walked alone down to Lower Manhattan. It surprised me that in the wake of America's biggest tragedy and on the birthday of Independence, most of the stores along Fifth Avenue were open and thriving: Saks, Burberry, the Gap, FAO Schwarz. Amid the endless outpouring of patriotism, and the anguish for the departed of September, one might have expected a few hours' respite. But New York is, after all, "the city that never sleeps" (at the forefront of a culture, as Thoreau might have put it, that never quite wakes up). One of the problems with patriotism, of course, is that taken too far it can be bad for business. And America (and increasingly its northern neighbour) has little tolerance for what is bad for business.

At the Battery Park seawall, I stood with perhaps a quarter of a million people and watched the fireworks above New Jersey and Staten Island. The security was dense. Throughout the afternoon, the cops had been stopping every car headed into Lower Manhattan. They walked dogs through the crowd, buzzed the harbour in helicopters and speedboats.

For all of it, the display in the end was ordinary. I had expected something splashier. What I did not realize was that I had missed Manhattan's main show, which took place a few miles upstream on the East River. But I didn't care. I was happy to amble back up Broadway— past the dapper old Woolworth Building, with its high golden top; and the Wall Street McDonald's, undoubtedly the only one anywhere with solid brass arches; and the New York Sun Building, with its (arguable) message that "the Sun Shines for All." Past the gas lamps around City Hall and the old New Amsterdam pasture, where according to the historic plaque, "hungry sheep" grazed through the seventeenth and eighteenth centuries—their role filled today by hungry indigents who graze the garbage containers for sandwich and pizza crusts.

Up in Madison Square Park, a dozen men and three or four women were asleep under the plane trees, some dressed in tank tops and shorts, others in layers of winter clothes. As always, where the homeless congregate, there were shopping carts piled, in some cases, two metres high with belongings. Misery, of course, is not limited to the poor. At the subway stop at Twenty-third Street, a middle-aged drunk in a business suit and paisley necktie was splayed out on the sidewalk, his face puffed and bleeding, as a woman in a little black dress and strappy shoes tended patiently to his needs.

Just up Broadway from Thirty-fourth, you get the first hint of the glow from Times Square, still eight blocks to the north. Slowly, inevitably, you are engulfed by the crowds and sounds and lights; neon as bright as the sun; hucksters and sketch artists; hookers and street musicians; the smells of burgers and popcorn and perfume; and of vomit and urine and the fragrance of horse manure that drifts over from the little NYPD office set right in the middle of Broadway.

I dodged through the traffic on Seventh Avenue, then continued on past the Ed Sullivan Theater, the offices of Random House Inc., and came eventually into the vicinity of the Warwick. But I wasn't yet ready to call it a night. So I walked on up into Central Park and sat for a while near the Pond, on a rock outcrop that reminded me of my boyhood summers on the Precambrian granite of northern Ontario.

AMONG THE MORE OBVIOUS REASONS that we left New York when we did was that, even with free accommodation, the city is an endless sinkhole for money—you can hardly take a breath without laying out a five-dollar bill. At $1.10 a minute on the hotel phone, the cost of getting and answering my emails had, alone, been close to $200. Also, having consumed nearly $4,000 in unapplied hotel charges, I was burdened by a growing sense of delinquency about our status as guests of the Warwick. The hotel had been generous beyond reckoning, and with the exception of paying for the phone lines, we had not dropped a nickel in the place.

But it was also the relentless pressure of the city that by the night of July 5 brought us to a realization that it was time to go.

That morning as I went out for coffee on Fifty-seventh Street, I turned to a voice below me on the sidewalk and discovered a healthy-looking young man sitting beneath a makeshift cardboard awning with his black dog, surrounded by what I suppose was the extent of his belongings—a cushion, a plastic water cooler, a shopping cart full of clothes and bed covers.

"How about a dollar?" he said.

I gave him two, and in exchange for this philanthropic largesse, he told me in answer to my questions that just a year ago he had been employed in a downtown bank. He had been fired, he said, had gone briefly on social assistance but had had problems there, too, and had been tossed off the roll. One day, with the $2,000 rent on his apartment unpaid and nothing in the bank, he had simply walked away from his residence, leaving his books, his furniture, and his leased car (empty of gas) in the apartment garage. "Now we live here," he said sardonically, tousling the head of his Labrador retriever. "And there's a lot less pressure on us than where we lived before."

An hour later, as I came out of a deli on Park Avenue with an overpriced egg sandwich, I was accosted by a frail and desperate-looking Asian man who demanded that I give him my food. I looked at him, not quite comprehending what he had said, and felt suddenly suspended in the balance, subjected to a fatal test of values. Being a good Canadian and a creature of compromise, I said, "Why don't I split it with you?"

"Because I'm hungry!" he cried—a response so irrefutable that to have ignored it would have been an instant ticket to hell, bought with considerably more resolve than I had to spend at that moment. So I simply handed over the sandwich, wrapping it respectfully, I thought, in the napkin that went with it. As if to remind me that respect was not the issue here, he promptly threw the napkin at my feet and marched off without a word.

As a child, I was intrigued by the promise of the television detective series that there were "eight million stories in the Naked City." And yet the stories the program dramatized were invariably tidy and tractable compared to most of those you glimpse along the sidewalk.

That evening, as I settled to my dinner in a nondescript little restaurant on Forty-seventh Street, a dishevelled old man humped into sight on the sidewalk, wearing a pile of hats and carrying a broom pole on which he had stacked half a dozen rolls of toilet paper. He was carrying a kind of sandwich board that listed perhaps fifty of humanity's more glaring moral trespasses and was staggering under the weight of a ten-foot-long cross built of six-inch timbers, a ghastly contrivance on which an actual crucifixion might have been carried out. On the old man's face, there was a look of Goya-like torment that, cartoonish as it all seems, had the effect on me of a kick in the teeth.

Late that night as I walked up Lexington Avenue toward the hotel, I came upon an elderly black clarinetist playing his heart out—subtle, abstract tunes echoing up the street to no audience at all.

I got back to the hotel resolved to tell George that I had had enough and was ready to go. But I didn't have to. When I entered the suite he was slumped on the chesterfield, looking like a pug fighter who had gone one or two rounds too many. He glanced up at me and said, "I've gotta get outta here," adding that the freedoms and stimulations of the first few days back were dissolving rapidly.

"Well, let's go then," I said. And we agreed that we would head out the following day.

DESPERATE THE NEXT MORNING for a last walk in the city and wanting to get some souvenirs for the kids, I booted it down Sixth Avenue in the rain, and angled east along Broadway. I scrambled through Macy's, feeling rushed and incapable, picking up, then reject-ing, this item and that. I had not eaten breakfast, and in the sub-terranean food halls, I could not resist buying a chunk of baked salmon at the gourmet seafood counter. I must have looked hungry—or perhaps just pathetic—because when the young female clerk had weighed and priced the fillet and had handed it to me, she said quietly, "Sir, give me back your plate, and I'll put some sauce on it." With the plate in her hand, she took a glance over her shoulder, cut a chunk of salmon perhaps twice the size of what she had already given me, and slipped it aboard.

As I ate, I recalled an essay by the New York writer David Sedaris about a stint he had done as an employee of Macy's—in particular his revelation that somewhere in the recesses of the store there were cells, lock-ups, where the dozen or so people who are caught ripping Macy's off in an average day are imprisoned until the police show up.

With my rogue salmon undigested in my stomach, I had a freak presentiment of being held there myself, and beat it out onto Thirty-fourth Street where, on the side of the immense Victoria's Secret store (Victoria's secret being somewhat less subtle than my own), I came eyeball-to-ankle with the six-storey-high likeness of a leggy model wearing a black bra and garter belt and not much else.

With the exception perhaps of a Jersey tomato or cucumber, it is impossible to find a souvenir of Manhattan that is made in even the same time zone. Eventually, in one of the many souvenir shops that crowd Fifth Avenue north of Thirty-fourth Street, I cached my cynicism and bought hats and T-shirts and ceramic banks, all made somewhere on the far side of the planet, and a made-in-China mouse pad showing the Twin Towers erect and whole and glowing like fuses in the afternoon sun.

None of it was even remotely satisfactory. However, as I walked past a street vendor a few blocks farther north, my attention was galvanized by a smallish poster of the tightrope walker Philippe Petit. I knew the story of the day in 1974 when, at the close of business hours, he and a pair of assistants had somehow concealed themselves in the basement of the north tower of the World Trade Center and, in the middle of the night, had climbed the stairs to the roof and strung a cable from one tower to the other. The poster showed Petit dancing on the wire as the sun came up—walking, as it were, on air.

It was the ideal image on which to quit New York, and having forked over ten dollars for it, I beat it up the steps into the public library, up to the reading rooms, where I sat staring into the magnificent arches and chandeliers. As I so often did during those last days of my walk, I got thinking about the sadness and uncertainty back home, and lapsed gradually into a kind of reverie of landscapes and rivers—and of longings. To be whole, to be constructive, to outmanoeuvre despair. Or outwalk it. Which as much as half a dozen other motivations, I suspected, was what ten weeks of walking had been about.

By the time I got back outside, the rain had stopped. In the heat and humidity, the air seemed devoid of oxygen.

When I got to the hotel, George was out. A note said he had gone to buy Melody a gift.

For the time that remained, I sacked out on the bed and, as I had done so often in the roadside forests or fields, fell quickly asleep.

My dream was perhaps predictable. I was walking. Toward a New York–like city that I could see ahead of me surrounded by water. Except that rather than a highway, my path forward was a narrow strip of soil, a kind of floating peninsula across the waves. And as I walked, it was crumbling silently into the water behind.

An hour later, George and I taxied over to Grand Central and boarded a northbound train for Dobbs Ferry. At Stu and Sue Hackel's, a neighbourhood barbecue was in progress, a belated celebration of the Fourth of July. We shared in the party, and when it was over, Stu urged us to stay the night. It was a generous offer, but we had been seventy days on the road, and at that point I wanted to drive. Almost as much as I wanted to keep walking. So, rather than prolong our stay, we said our goodbyes at about midnight, got into the van, and headed north up the Hudson toward home.

Acknowledgments

T wo groups of people richly deserve my thanks—those whose kindness, insight, or generosity helped me prepare for or complete my journey, and those who helped and encouraged me during the long months of writing. Unfortunately, many of those who advanced my physical journey—by giving directions, information, a drink, or even just a bit of company or conversation—did so without an exchange of names and must be thanked anonymously.

For their valued help in my preparations, many thanks to my former neighbours Gerry and Lila Siddall, my old friend Harvey Botting, and more recent friends Bob Edwards and Bruce Hyer; to Dennis McPherson of the Native Studies Department at Lakehead University, Steve Scollie at the Skihaus in Thunder Bay, Jeff Timmins and John and Liz Roffey of the Canadian arm of Columbia Clothing, Greg Maude of the Ontario Provincial Parks system, Heather Armstrong of Rogers Communications, Marilyn McIntosh of Tourism Thunder Bay, James Little of *Explore* magazine, Corinne Zadik of New York City Tourism, and the folks at Carbon Computers in Toronto.

For their help along the road, my thanks to Kal Nikkila, Lloyd and Willa Jones, Shaun Parent and the gang at the Mad Moose, Dorothy and Pete Colby, Stephanie and Mike Jones, Lynn McLeod and Steve Roedde, Jackie and John Field, Carol McLaughlin and Dan Diamond, Adele and Kevin Parkinson, Luke Webster, Cameron Lory, and Sue and Stu Hackel. And to my friends at CBC Radio, who followed my journey so faithfully: Susan Wade, Cathy Alla, Gerald Graham, Lisa Laeko, Mike Bryan, Carol Amadeo, Barry Wheaton, and Ron Desmoulais.

Since the writing of a book is such a diffuse and protracted endeavour, it is almost impossible to name everyone who made a difference. Among those I can name, I owe sincere gratitude to my young housemates on Madeline Street in Thunder Bay: Nicki Crawley, Erica Jenkins, Kristin Brooks, Walter Mainville, and Miranda Currie—and to my friends and landlords Maija and Jari Sarkka. I owe profound thanks, too, to Doug Livingstone, Julie Benc, Jack Haggarty, Marjie Betiol, Ellafern Poindexter, Roz Maki, Jake MacDonald, and Robert Lannon. And to my ground support at Penguin Group (Canada)—first, Diane Turbide and Debby de Groot, for their continued belief in my efforts, and in recent weeks, my copy editor, Sandra Tooze, for her most patient and painstaking work on my manuscript.

Sincere thanks are also due my editor on the project, John Pearce, who with goodwill and great expertise guided the manuscript's transition into a book. And my agent, Jackie Kaiser, at Westwood Creative Artists for her wise professional advice and her personal encouragement throughout.

Lastly, and most deeply, my thanks to George Morrissette, without whom there would have been no walk or book—and to my family, especially my sisters, Susan and Ann, and my children, Matthew, Georgia, and Eden, who as always were, and are, the light at the end of the road.